TAF VALLEY LIVES

An account, with 200 photographs, of the life and times of working class families in a rural Welsh valley through the twentieth century.

... where time stood still for longer

Denley Owen

The right of Denley Owen to be identified as the author of this work has been asserted by him in accordance with the Copyright, Designs and Patents Act, 1988

Copyright ©2015 Denley Owen

ISBN 978-0-9932299-6-1

All rights reserved. No part of this publication may be reproduced, stored in retrieval system or transmitted in any form or by any means electronic, mechanical, photocopying, recording or otherwise, without the prior permission of the publisher, except in the case of brief quotations embodied in critical articles and reviews.

Published in the United Kingdom in 2015 by

Cambria Books, Wales, United Kingdom

I
bawb â diddordeb
yn
'y llwybrau gynt lle bu'r gân'

To
all with an interest
in
'the paths where once there was singing'

ac ar gyfer
Owain a Steffan; Cai, Llyr, Iestyn
a Beca Hedd.

Contents

FOREWORD 1
ACKNOWLEDGEMENTS 3
MAP 4
INTRODUCTION 5
FAMILY TREE 8

Part I   c 1900 – 1938: CHILDREN, CHORES AND CHAPELS 9
   1.1 Born to toil 9
   1.2 Suffering in silence 10
   1.3 Chapel Activities 12
   1.4 School and discipline 14
   1.5 Farm Bailiff 14
   1.6 A child goes labouring 16
   1.7 Farm workers and coal miners 18
   1.8 Unfit homes and tuberculosis 22
   1.9 Change on the horizon 28

Part II   1938 – 1948: BLAENWAUN COTTAGE AND CANERW - war, toil and chapel 69
   2.1 1938 – 1944 69
   2.1.1 Hazards and confinement 69
   2.1.2 A year on the farm 74
   2.1.3 Mishtir 80
   2.1.4 That telegram 84
   2.2 1944 – 1948 88
   2.2.1 Motorbikes, buses and cars 88
   2.2.2 Labour landslide 91

2.2.3 Chapel events	92
2.2.4 Pony express	96
2.2.5 Homework the priority	100
2.2.6 Recreation	103

Part III 1948 – 1958: CEFN – toil, chapel and 'isgol Whitlan' 131
  3.1 1948 – early 1950s 131
    3.1.1 Hazards and freedom 131
    3.1.2 The house of Cefn 136
    3.1.3 Pigs, cows, fish and rabbits 138
    3.1.4 The 11+ and a new world 144
    3.1.5 Heywood's odd-jobs, newspapers and boxing 147
  3.2 Early 1950s – 1958 151
    3.2.1 Rugby and soccer 151
    3.2.2 The 1950s General Elections 152
    3.2.3 Studies and sport change everything 153
    3.2.4 'Rupture' repair 159
    3.2.5 Running and winning with Davies Maths 162

Part IV 1958 – 1996: GLANRHYD – farming, travelling and arthritis 193
  4.1 End of 'remoteness' 193
  4.2 Time takes its toll 202

Part V 1996 – 2001: MINAFON – end of the road 223

A GRANDSON REMEMBERS 225

TIMELINE 229

FOREWORD

In his first book, Dr Denley Owen introduced us to the life of the upper social class as he described the life and interests of W.R.H.Powell, the liberal and enlightened squire of Maesgwynne, Llanboidy.

This book, ***TAF VALLEY LIVES***, is totally different. It deals with a later period, much of which the author remembers personally which enables him to give a more intimate description of life in this beautiful valley during the twentieth century. It introduces the reader to the lives of the working class, usually referred to in Welsh by the endearing term 'Y Werin'. Denley has chosen to give a detailed description of the lives and experiences of four generations of his own family, particularly those of his parents, thus reflecting the lives of the Taf Valley families in general.

The book is divided into five parts and a brief look through the contents list will attract readers of all ages. The older generation will reflectively recall the activities and pastimes in which they were similarly involved, including life during World War 11 and the great changes and advancement which took place when it was all over. Those of middle age will be reminded of those changes, realise how they benefited from them and when comparing the different periods, will appreciate the sacrifices made by their parents. The younger generation will be fascinated by the description of the conditions, customs and pastimes of their ancestors and compare them with the stories related by their own grandparents. Some may even be inspired to do some further research themselves. The whole work is enriched by a large selection of well-chosen photographs.

The revolutionary changes in education, the opportunities offered by the improvement in transport facilities and the evolution in work prospects during the second half of the century is impressively conveyed as Denley recalls the academic and athletic success enjoyed by himself and his brother. For two boys from the Taf Valley, used to competing in village sports, to be suddenly introduced to the latest methods advocated by international coaches must have been truly inspiring and as a former staff colleague of Hubert Davies at the Grammar School, I can vouch for the effectiveness of his training sessions!

This book presents a wealth of information and if it was not for its publication, much social history could sadly be lost within a generation or two. We are therefore greatly indebted to Denley for his invaluable work; he deserves the admiration of both the historian and the interested general reader alike.

Haydn Lewis.

ACKNOWLEDGEMENTS

I am hugely indebted to my wife Lon for her patience and unfailing support for this project.

I am grateful to my brother Bryan for his memories and photographs and for useful suggestions.

I wish to thank Thomas Lloyd, O.B.E., D.L., F.S.A., Wales Herald of Arms Extraordinary and Miss Muriel Bowen Evans, M.A., of the Carmarthenshire Antiquarian Society for their interest and encouragement to publish this book.

Taf Valley historian Haydn Lewis B.A., National President of the Hywel Dda Society and former Deputy Head of Whitland Grammar School, kindly agreed to write the Foreword for which I am most grateful.

Among those whose kindness and cooperation helped make the book possible are:

Glynwen Bishop, Mair Davies, Dr. Meurig Davies, Suzanne Davies, David Edwards, Dafydd Jones Evans, Mary Evans, Meirwen Evans, Merle Evans, Gerwyn Eynon, James Griffiths, Wyn Howells, Brian Isaac, Rhydian Isaac, Gwynedd James, M.B.E., Janet James, Wil and Tegwen James, David John, Nan Jones, Eurfyl Lewis, Alan and Joanne Owen, Richard Owen, Trefor Owen, Clodwyn Phillips, Delyth Phillips, Roy Reynolds, Hywel and Fanw Thomas, Marina Thomas, Yvonne Vaughan, Brian Williams, Mostyn and Dil Williams.

The publisher and staff at Llyfrau Cambria Books could not have been more helpful during the production process for which I am especially thankful.

Finally I should point out that inaccuracies in the book are all my own.

Denley Owen

Cover Design : Logopro and Design Elements.

Background to the front cover is an oil painting *Gwal y Filiast* by Lon Owen.

MAP

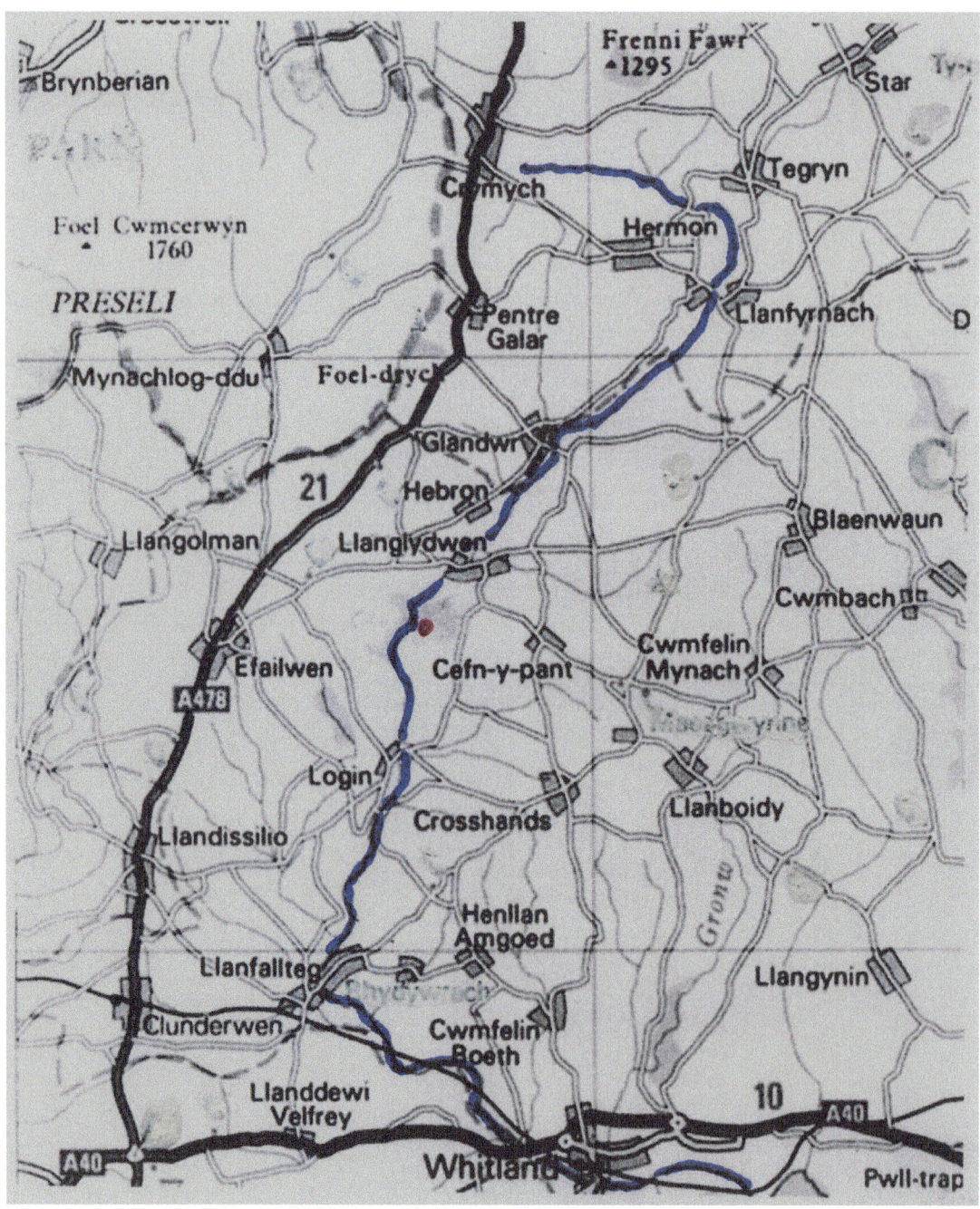

INTRODUCTION

The River Taf flows from the Preseli Hills near Crymych past the villages of Glogue, Llanfyrnach, Rhydowen, Llanglydwen, Login and has travelled 12 miles when it reaches Llanfallteg beyond which the landscape flattens and the river meanders around Whitland and St Clears to enter the sea by Dylan Thomas' Boathouse in Laugharne. In 1873 a branch railway from Whitland, winding its way close to the river, reached Crymych; twelve years later it reached its final destination of Cardigan and the Cardi Bach was born. In 1926 Herbert M. Vaughan in *The South Wales Squires* described the Taf Valley as 'a most remote and little-explored region of west Wales. … In this valley mansions are scarce; the Church is very weak; Dissent is embittered and all-powerful.'[1] To describe a valley served by a railway as 'remote' might sound surprising but the railway did help create a largely self-sufficient community whose inhabitants might well have felt remote from the outside world.

The railway was laid to serve the Llanfyrnach lead mine and the Glogue slate quarry but the expected economic benefits did not materialize and the mine closed in 1890 and the quarry in 1926. On the other hand the farming community benefited from the convenience of moving livestock by rail from marts at Cardigan and Crymych and from having milk-churns collected from the stations and delivered to factories at Cardigan and Whitland. Rabbits, in plentiful supply in the wooded valley, were sent by rail to the industrial areas of south Wales and the midlands of England.

However the railway's greatest effect on the Taf Valley resulted from its stations acting as growth-centres for businesses which lead to a largely self-sufficient community stretching from Llanfallteg to Crymych. For example, Llanglydwen before the railway was simply a crossing-point for the river Taf where there was a public house (Penybont Inn) and two cottages (Taf and Tigen). After the railway arrived all the needs of the community not locally produced were brought in by rail; businesses mushroomed and soon there was a village shop, a flour mill, a saw mill and carpenters shop, an agricultural store, a woollen mill, a butter factory, a smithy, a boot maker, two coal yards and a village hall.[2] Similar development to a greater or lesser degree occurred at the other villages between Crymych and Whitland and the railway provided a more direct line of communication along the valley than did the roads. By the early twentieth century the greater Taf Valley community of around 4,000 inhabitants was a vibrant one and entertained itself with gusto through chapel organised activities of cymanfaoedd canu (singing festivals), cymanfaoedd ysgolion Sul (Sunday schools festivals), eisteddfodau, penny-readings, concerts and dramas together with village-committee-organised events such as agricultural shows, carnivals and sports-meetings. Few inhabitants voluntarily ventured outside the comfortable confines of the close-knit community during the first half of the twentieth century and in that sense it was cut-off from the outside world of towns such as Carmarthen with its cinemas and dance hall and the valley may well have merited H.M. Vaughan's 'remote' label. A lady compelled to visit a relative in the Carmarthenshire mining village of Tumble expressed on a post-card her feelings while away from the Taf Valley: 'Although I am in Tumble my heart is still in Wales'.

The claim that Dissent was 'embittered' was probably an exaggeration rooted in the conflicts of the previous century but that it was 'all-powerful' was undoubtedly true as evidenced by the two-to-one ratio of chapels to churches and by the experience of families described in this book.

For over four generations most of my ancestors – both maternal and paternal – lived and laboured in the Taf Valley and my parents, born in 1917, laboured and died there as did the overwhelming majority of their working class contemporaries. I was of the generation first offered the eleven-plus hurdle in the late 1940s which, if cleared, opened a way out of labouring but also out of the Taf Valley. In the early 1950s a wide-spread switch to road transport took place; buses and cars mobilised the community and the valley's remoteness faded away as did many local shops and enterprises; lorries took business from trains and in 1964 Beeching's axe finally killed-off the Cardi Bach. Chapel influence declined as did the use of the Welsh language as the new-found mobility led its speakers out of the valley and non-Welsh speakers moved in.

In this book an account is given of the life and times of working-class families in the Taf Valley – with particular emphasis on my parents – and how those lives were affected by social and economic changes during the course of the twentieth century. My sources for the first half century were recollections by my brother and myself of the verbal accounts given us by our parents (Heywood and Lil) and other family members together with Lil's notebooks in which she described some of her childhood experiences and recorded various events and incidents throughout her life. The notebooks contained family trees for her side as well as Heywood's side of the family. In addition her collection of letters, cards, newspaper cuttings and photographs were priceless primary information. The chapels' annual reports provided a yearly check on people's where-abouts and were especially useful up to the 1950s when virtually every person in the Taf Valley belonged to one chapel or another. Much of the account from the mid 1940s onwards was based on my brother's and myself's own experiences. From 1972 to 1992 Lil's diaries provided a comprehensive record of life in Glanrhyd during a period of rapid socio-economic changes which rid the valley of its 'remote' tag and freed its people from Dissent's 'all-powerful' hold.

A few days after Heywood's funeral his grandson, Richard, recorded some of his memories of childhood holidays at Glanrhyd a quarter of a century earlier. Many of the farm practices described had succumbed to mechanisation and modernisation but Richard's experiences were unforgettable to him and while his assertion that calves never forget may be disputed it is certainly true for us humans that past experiences make us what we are.

Denley Owen

[1] Herbert M. Vaughan, The South Wales Squires, Methuen, 1926

[2] D. Hywel Davies, The Carmarthenshire Antiquary, Vol. XXXIV, 1998

THE AUTHOR

Born in *Y Ty Rownd* in the Taf Valley, Denley Owen attended Penygaer County Primary School, Whitland Grammar School and the University College of Swansea. He was employed by the Atomic Energy Authority before joining Llandovery College. In retirement he has followed his interest in family and local history and is the author of *Powell Maesgwynne*. He and his wife Lon have two children and six grandchildren.

FAMILY TREE

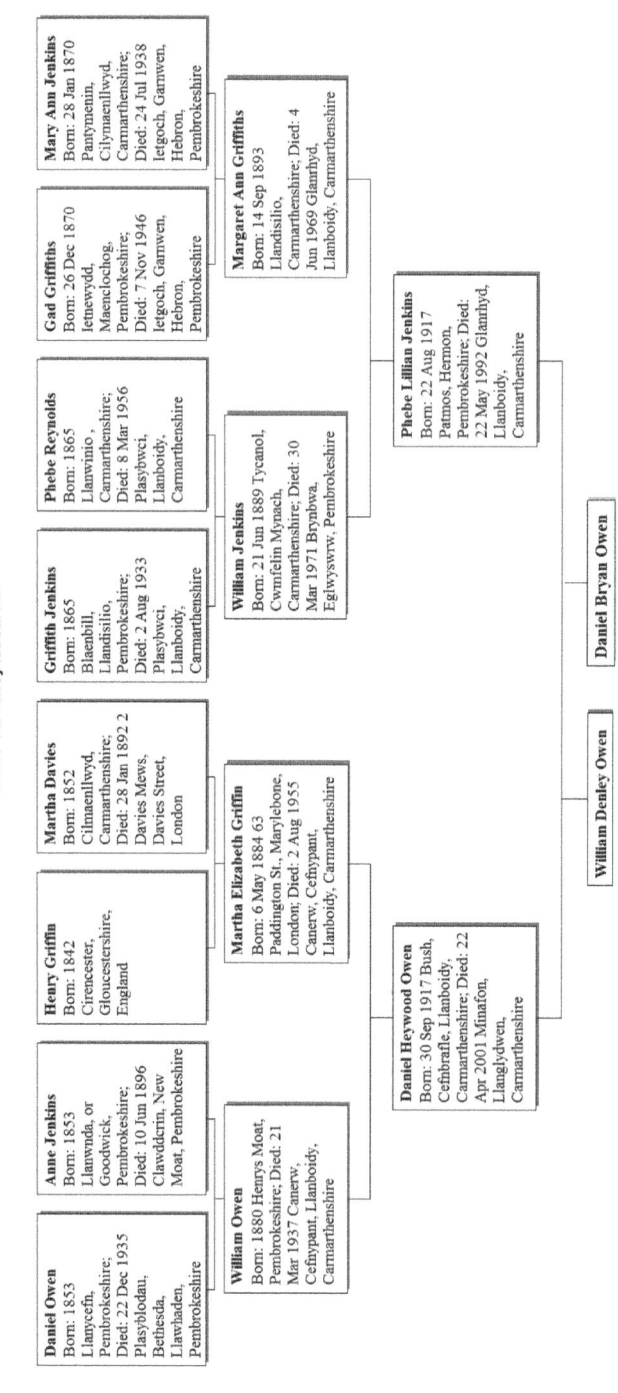

Part I
c 1900 – 1938: CHILDREN, CHORES AND CHAPELS

1.1 Born to toil

My grand-father, William Owen, was born in 1880 in Yetrhiw, Henry's Moat, Pembrokeshire. His father, Daniel, was a farm labourer who lived to the ripe old age of 82 years. His mother, Anne, gave birth to eleven children over a period of twenty years before dying on the birth of her last-born. William was destined to be a farm labourer and after a stint on a local farm White Hook, Bletherstone he made his way in 1909, probably as a result of attending hiring fairs (*ffeiri cytuno*) at Maenclochog and at Crymych to the Taf Valley. After a year or so at Glandwr Isaf Farm, Llanglydwen, Carmarthenshire he moved to be a ploughman at Frowen (Lewis) in Llanboidy Parish at which time he transferred his Independent Chapel membership from Glandwr to Cefnypant. Already a member at Cefnypant was the dairy maid at Frowen (Lewis), Martha Elizabeth Griffin (1884-1955). She had moved to Frowen in 1908 from Fronganol, Llanboidy having previously served at Blaenwaun Farm, Llanwinio, at Hafod y Pwll, Eglwysfair a Churig and at Lan, Cilmaenllwyd after her school-leaving job of a children's nurse at Cefn, Login.

Martha Elizabeth Griffin was born in London. Her mother Martha (nee Davies) had been, in the early 1870's, a maid in the service of her grandparents at Cross Inn, Efailwen, Llandisilio where she might well have met coachman Henry Griffin in the course of his duties ferrying his master between his home at Pentypark, Clarbeston Road and his parents' abode in Cardigan. Henry, born in Cirencester, had moved to west Wales in the 1860s to be a helper in the stables at Stackpole Court, Pembrokeshire - home of the landowning Cawdor family. Henry and Martha married in Narberth in 1875 and moved to London where, by 1881, they lived in Marylebone District. Henry had reverted to stable-helper and Martha was a cook. Their daughters Martha Elizabeth and Emily Alice were born in 1884 and 1886 respectively. Tragedy struck the family in 1892 with the death of the mother, Martha, from tuberculosis. Unable to cope Henry summoned-up the courage to put his young daughters on a train at Paddington Station with labels around their necks indicating their destination as Narberth Road Station (Clunderwen today) in Pembrokeshire. Henry was never heard of again. The sisters were met at Clunderwen by their grandparents William and Elizabeth Davies who took them into their care and registered them as pupils at Ffynonwen School, Cilymaenllwyd in March 1892. Four years later 14-year-old Martha left her family's care and began her career in service as a children's nurse at Cefn, Login.

A clue to the character of William and of Martha is that they were subscribers to a book published in 1909. This was a biography of the Reverend O.R.Owen who had been a popular minister at Glandwr and Cefnypant Independent Chapels for 31 years before leaving for Liverpool in 1904 where, after only four years, he died suddenly. The fact that they subscribed shows the high esteem in which they held the much loved minister and he was probably the major influence in ensuring the couple's life long commitment to the cause at Cefnypant Chapel.

1.2 Suffering in silence

In 1912, the servants at Frowen, William Owen and Martha Elizabeth Griffin married and settled in the small-holding of Bush near Cefnbrafle, Llanboidy where they had three or four cows from whose milk and its products they drew their physical and financial sustenance. To supplement their meagre income William laboured at nearby Cilgynydd Farm and, sometimes was taken on by the the council as a stone cutter to help provide raw material to maintain the area's roads. There was a council storage area (*cwtsh cerrig*) near Bush where the council kept a supply of large stones and boulders. My uncle Spencer (James Spencer, b 1916, third child of William and Martha Owen), remembered half a dozen men including his father sitting in the *cwtsh cerrig* with aprons of leather or perhaps sacking and using hammers to chip away at the boulders to produce the fine stones used as surface dressing on the roads. William was probably taken on by the council when extra hands were required. Their first child, a daughter, was born in 1913 and apart from 1914 and 1919, a child was born every year up to and including 1921 after which there was a four year gap before another two children arrived in 1925 and 1926. William and Martha had a total of nine children and their fourth, my father Daniel Heywood, was made to carry a name suggested by his uncle, James Owen (1893 – 1953) who was at the time serving with the Somerset Light Infantry in the so-called Great War of 1914 – 1918 and had been involved in a battle with some connection with the name Heywood. My father recalled that times were hard but that he and his brothers and sisters were always clean and well dressed. That says much for his mother's industry and care because the family's financial circumstances must have been difficult to say the least. Heywood put it more starkly: 'We did not have two pennies to rub together', a statement which reflects the rural poverty experienced in the 1920s when 'starvation wages' were often less than outdoor relief benefits. Yet the family's donations to Cefnypant Chapel were very generous at 12s. (60p) a year from 1914 to 1918 which was 50% above the average donation. And they found it possible to raise their contribution to £1 a year for 1919 and 1920. Although few others matched the Bush family's 67% hike, most made significant increases in 1919 which probably indicated the determination of Cefnypant members to hang on to their highly regarded minister, the Reverend P.E.Price who was, undoubtedly, a target for other pastorates seeking to appoint a minister. It is likely that chapel officers appealed to members to increase their donations so as to negate any outside financial inducements offered to Reverend Price which might tempt him to leave Cefnypant … never mind that many members were on subsistence levels themselves. In fact farm labourers were the 'have-nots' of rural society – a society whose community life was based on the chapel and the Christian teaching of 'love thy neighbour'. Yet the chapels and ministers failed to involve themselves in the everyday life of their underprivileged members in their hour of need. One exception was the Reverend E.T.Owen, Llangeler, the son of a farm labourer, who declared in 1924 that socialism meant putting Christian principles into practice and he criticized fellow Nonconformist ministers for their reticence.[3] A year previously in the General Election he had increased the Labour vote in the Carmarthen constituency by 1,200 to beat the Tory into second place.[4] However the Reverend Owen was a lone voice and the chapels and ministers were, overwhelmingly, dominated by middle class values and their written and unwritten rules of behaviour had the effect of forcing rural poverty to be 'suffered in silence'.[5] Even the harrowing experience of losing 35,000 Welshmen killed in the First World War which is generally accepted to have delivered a serious blow to chapel-influence in society had but a minimal effect in the Taf Valley and other areas of rural Wales. The loss of life continued after the war as a result of the deadly 'Spanish' 'flu which took the lives of over 10,000 mainly young people in Wales during 1918-1919 including at least three members of Cefnypant Chapel: farm servants Rachel Thomas and Jane Twigg of Abertigen and Catherine Davies of Cware.

It is worth mentioning that in 1918, David Lloyd George from Llanystumdwy, north Wales was then at the height of his powers as Prime Minister and victorious war leader. But he had been a hero to the ordinary people since before the war when as Chancellor of the Exchequer in the Liberal government led by Herbert Asquith he introduced his social reforms that ushered in the beginnings of the Welfare State. Lloyd George, who had been inspired by schemes he had seen on a visit to Germany, introduced the old-age-pension in 1908 - perhaps the most compassionate and desperately needed of the measures. After the war the Ministry of Health was established in 1919 to bring together the medical and public health functions of central government, and to co-ordinate and supervise local health services in England and Wales. It made improvements in areas such as housing, public health, food and medicines, and also offered advice to voluntary hospitals where most of the medical training took place at that time. In 1920 the unemployed were given a statutory right to Benefit and the Old Age Pension was doubled. (The right to free medical treatment for everyone came about by the founding of the National Health Service on 5 July 1948).

3. David A. Pretty, *The Rural Revolt that Failed 1889-1950*, UWP, 1989, p.172.

4. Ibid., p.170. 5. Ibid., p. 161.

1.3 Chapel Activities

In the early decades of the twentieth century, life for most people was a combination of hard work and chapel activities. The temptation of the pubs was there of course, but entering public houses was vigorously condemned from the pulpits and to many a preacher the pub provided a ready made example of the devil's work. For six days a week most men laboured all day on farms as did most single women as maids. Most married couples had large families and looked forward to the children leaving school at 14 years-of-age to become additional sources of household income. (School leaving age was raised to 14 in 1918; it had been 12 since 1899). A break from the drudgery was possible only on a Sunday when most of the population would converge on their chapel for hour-long meetings at 10.00am, 2.00pm and 6.00pm. The Sunday School would be held either in the morning or in the afternoon; the other two slots would have a preacher delivering a sermon or on the occasional absence of a preacher a prayer meeting would be held with the deacons taking a lead role. Some members looked forward to prayer meetings because many a person on his knees would carry on an entertaining chat with his God. Heywood recalled one of these chatty prayers by a young Englishman who had settled in the Welsh speaking community and had acquired the language. A committed Christian he was always ready to share his thoughts loud and clear with his God and with the congregation: *'Ti mor glyfar.... Ti'n gwbod popeth ... Ti'n clywed popeth .... Ti'n gweld popeth... yn y dydd ac yn y nos .... Ti fel gath'* ! (You are so clever ... You know everything... You hear everything ... You see everything ... in the day and also in the night ... You are like a cat!)

On some week-nights there would be more meetings in the chapel vestry such as young people's meeting (*cwrdd y bobl ifanc*), Band of Hope and rehearsals for the *Gymanfa Ganu* (Singing Festival) and the *Gymanfa Ysgolion* (Sunday Schools Festival). Members would also organize Penny Readings in the Chapel and would invite concert parties and drama companies to perform at Llanglydwen or Llanboidy village halls.

The annual Chapel Report would be studied closely by members ... not so much to check the accuracy of the figures but to see how much so and so had contributed in donations! Anyone who was not a member of a chapel would be a bit of an outsider and anyone who deviated from accepted behaviour patterns particularly for example, regarding getting a girl into trouble would feel completely ostracised. Escape to America or Canada would often be seen as the way out. Therefore, it is no wonder that belonging to a chapel and maintaining their donations at the highest possible level was a priority for the overwhelming majority of people, at least in rural Wales, in those days.

The Owen children's regular attendance at Sunday School, from the age of five or so, was helped by their Sunday School teacher, John Samson, headteacher of Henllan Primary School, calling at Bush every Sunday and giving the children a lift in his *trap a poni*! The trap was of a round construction and on rainy days, a very large umbrella was opened to keep them dry! John Samson served as a Sunday School teacher at Cefnypant from 1920 to 1929 and is best remembered for his effort during the late 1920s to get the children to learn, memorize and recite the 176 verses of Psalm 119 (*Y Salm Fowr*)! The Psalm's verses are divided into 22 groups of eight and John Samson's method was to get the children to learn eight verses every week. Although it would have been possible to complete the learning process in 22 weeks it appears that the final test took place after the children had been allowed about a year to memorise the 176 verses. The Owen children, whose father had been Sunday School Superintendent (*Arolygwr yr Ysgol Sul*) for 1924, had to learn a few verses every evening after school and were not allowed out of the house until the set verses had been mastered. John Samson promised a Bible to every child who succeeded in this mammoth exercise of learning. It turned out that seven Bibles were presented and five went to the Owen children! I remember listening to Heywood reciting *Y Salm Fowr* ... once learned, never forgotten.

The Sunday School children were also taught to sing the Sol-Ffa. John Davies, Parcyrhos was the children's conductor and he would unroll the modulator sheet, hang it on the wall and put the children through their paces. John Davies did not have the same success as John Samson did with the Owen children. In 1929 under the auspices of the Sunday School, Heywood collected £1-3s-8d (£1.18) for the London Missionary Society for which he was presented with a book entitled *On the Banks of the Grand Canal* by Myfanwy Bryant B.A. The collector was largely monolingual at the time; he was yet to master the English language through reading *The Welshman, Carmarthen Journal, Narberth News, Western Telegraph* and any other newspaper he could lay his hands on. In 1930 members of Cefnypant Chapel elected William Owen as one of four new deacons to join the four already in office.

1.4 School and discipline

The Owen children attended Penygaer School, Login, to where they walked about one and a quarter mile along a tarmac road from Bush. Later from Canerw they walked about the same distance but now across fields, through a wood and along a narrow road to reach the school. Two of his school friends were George (Llewelyn) Sguborwen and Ted (Reynolds) Cwm and they were often up to no good ... once they let the wind out of the tubes of the School Inspector's bicycle wheels! Needless to say a severe caning was the standard punishment for such misdemeanour. Heywood recalled headmaster Rhydderch Evans' furious temper when upset by some mischief from the class: he would tighten the knot in his tie, shrinking it to a pimple, shout 'By Gum!' and then he would throw his cane, smashing it against the wall ! Sometimes the cane would snap and he would send a couple of senior pupils out to cut another from the plentiful supply in the surrounding hedges ! Those actions it seems were standard procedure and must have been quite effective in releasing the headmaster's pent up anger since the only real damage was to the cane. As in schools, discipline was often physically enforced in the home and William Owen was not averse to using the cane but Martha was always at hand ready to step in to restore peace. On Saturday afternoons the elder Canerw children together with others such as the Reynolds children of nearby Cwm walked nearly three miles to Calfaria Chapel, Login to attend Band of Hope meetings. Outside the vestry, after the meeting, a few Login boys were in the habit of challenging their Cefnypant counterparts to a fight. After avoiding trouble for several Saturdays one of the Cefnypant group, Jim Cwm, surprised the loud mouthed challenger with a right hook which sent him flying - no more was heard about a fight! When their school days were over some of the Owen family walked to attend evening classes at Penygaer School run by the Headmaster in the 1920s and 1930s.

1.5 Farm Bailiff

In 1925 William Owen secured the job of bailiff of the 100 acre Canerw Farm and the Owen family moved there when the owner, Daniel Martin Thomas, left to take over Rhydygath Farm, a few miles away in Llanfyrnach Parish. Martin Thomas' parents belonged to two of the major farming families in Llanfyrnach Parish, Thomas of Bwlchsais and Nicholas of Graig and he benefited – property wise - from the fact that many of his uncles and aunts were unmarried. He was the son of a minister of religion and had intended following in his father's footsteps but the First World War changed his mind although he remained a generous contributor to chapel funds. Martin Thomas visited Canerw quite often and brought three or four labourers with him to assist with farm work. Hay-making was very labour intensive in those days with men and women using pitch forks (*picwarche*) to shake the hay and spread it over the field to dry. When the hay was deemed ready to harvest it would be raked into rows and the rows converted into mounds of hay (*mwdwle*) ready to be pitch forked on to the *gambo* (wain or dray). When rain interrupted field-work he would usher the workers into a *storws* (storehouse above the stables) where he entertained them with a sermon. Another time while waiting for the hay to dry Martin Thomas called the labourers together for a game of 'pitch and toss' before returning to work.

The main duty of William Owen as farm bailiff was to look after a flock of sheep and some store cattle together with managing activities at the Canerw Clay Pits. There was a rich seam of clay in a field comparatively easily accessed from the farm lane. The clay was in much demand for use in making culm or *peli*. People would come from far and wide with their horse and cart and they would be charged for the clay by the cart load. More often than not a few blocks of clay would have to be unloaded from carts before the horses were able to pull their loads up the short sharp incline from the pits. The rules did not allow these blocks to be re-loaded!

The boys Spencer, Heywood and Garfield were involved early in helping their father with his duties. Spencer recalled that he and his brothers, before going off to school, were detailed to go out, in turn, to the fields to look over and count the sheep. He remembered reporting 'all present and correct' one morning. However the next morning Heywood returned from his inspection saying that one sheep was suffering terribly from maggots (*cynrhon*). William Owen immediately wanted to know why Spencer had missed seeing this problem the previous morning and Spencer knew then that farming was not for him ! 'Heywood was very sharp and saw things immediately'. Spencer became a carpenter.

In the late 1920s Martin Thomas gave up farming Canerw and rented it to William and Martha Owen who immediately went about changing it to a dairy farm. Dairy farming received a boost in 1933 with the establishment of the Milk Marketing Board which provided a secure market and relatively stable prices in the face of international competition. The coming of the motor lorry at this time overcame the problems of milk collection from farms not well served by railway stations. One result of farms being contracted to the M.M.B. was that fewer farmers' wives and daughters produced and sold their own butter and by the end of the 1930s this practice had largely died out.

In those days the mode of travelling was usually on foot or on horse back or in horse-drawn vehicles. Heywood recalled travelling by *poni a bodi fach* (pony and small cart) with his parents and brothers and sisters a distance of about 10 miles to visit the only grandparent that he ever knew, his grandfather Daniel Owen (1853-1935) at Plasyblodau, Bethesda, Pembrokeshire. And there he remembered seeing a short man with a white beard 'reaching to his knees'.

Canerw had been a centre of early Nonconformist religious meetings and it may have been the first house in Wales to be licensed for Nonconformist gatherings. There was a dark room (*ystafell dywyll*) at the foot of the stairs which had no windows and during periods of persecution in the seventeenth century people hid in this room. In 1688 Stephen Hughes known as *Apostol Sir Gaerfyrddin* (The Carmarthenshire Apostle) ordained a man by the name of Owen Davies to minister to dissenters at Canerw. Almost two centuries later in 1878 at the instigation of the Minister at Glandwr, Reverend O.R. Owen, a new chapel was built on land, near to Canerw, at Cefnypant which made redundant a smaller building erected in 1842 jointly by Glandwr and Henllan churches for the purpose of holding regular Sunday Schools and services. An interesting feature in the boundary wall separating the chapel grounds from the road is the stone platform enabling those arriving on horse-back or in a horse-drawn trap to dismount easily. The land for the new chapel was donated by W R H Powell M.P. (1819-1889) of Maesgwynne, Llanboidy. Speaking in 1878 on the occasion of laying the foundation stone (inscribed with the words 'Memorial Stone'), W R H Powell recalled his childhood memories of walking with his father from Maesgwynne Mansion across a few fields to see hundreds of people sitting in the open air at Canerw listening to famous preachers delivering their message.

Cefnypant Chapel enjoys a rural location a mile and a half from the river Taf and Llanglydwen Village which in those days had a railway station, a tavern Penybont Inn (*tafarn Y Bont*), smithy, carpenter's shop and Pretoria General Stores supplying human needs as well as animal feed. St Cledwyn's Church, like Cefnypant Chapel, is also about a mile outside the village and the nearest school at that time, Penygaer, was two miles from Llanglydwen. Another school, also two miles from the village, at Pantycaws Hamlet, was called Llanglydwen School. Penygaer School, Llanglydwen Village and Cefnypant Chapel form a triangle with Cefnypant one mile from both Llanglydwen and Penygaer which are two miles apart (distances being 'as the crow flies').

1.6 A child goes labouring

In 1931 on leaving Penygaer School, Heywood left home to be a junior farm servant (*gwas bach*) at Sarnau, Llanboidy with Eben Davies and his sister Mary Ann. A neighbouring holding was farmed by a particularly mischievous character and the occasion of Eben's marriage provided a heaven-sent opportunity for a prank. In those days, getting married was a very sensitive matter to some couples and they would do everything possible to keep the event a secret! A reason for secrecy was the tradition in rural areas of making it as difficult as possible for the groom to reach the chapel or the Registry Office for the ceremony. Doors and gates would be fixed and roads blocked by fallen trees. If the bride was expecting a child, the wedding was referred to as a shotgun wedding and guns would be fired as the groom left his home for the ceremony! But mischief-makers would let off a few shots in-any-case to upset the apple-cart! Eben was a very serious and sensitive character who had never been away from home but at the age of 46 had decided to get married. Heywood was sworn to secrecy as were the few others who had to be in the know. However on the big day as Eben left the house confident that he had out-witted potential trouble-makers he was startled out of his wits as two barrels of a shot gun were discharged! His neighbour had not been outwitted and it was he, from behind a nearby hedge, that gave Eben the fright of his life together with an implied message which took nine months to disprove! Heywood was blamed for the leak but was adamant that he was not responsible.

Although Heywood spent only 3 years at Sarnau he left a lasting impression on neighbouring farmer Tom Glanrhyd who, 25 years later, was to offer him the tenancy of Glanrhyd.

In those days farmers were not required to pay National Insurance for servants under the age of 16 years and it was the practice at Sarnau to release the servant at this age. His father had arranged a new work place for Heywood and in 1934 he moved to Frowen, Cefnypant, Llanboidy to be a servant with Joshua and Clarice Phillips. He followed his brother Spencer who left Frowen to become an apprentice carpenter with James Jenkins, Rhydowen. At Frowen Heywood acquired many skills from his experienced co-worker Dafi Reynolds. He learnt how to make a rope by splicing strands of chord; how to thatch hay ricks with reeds; how to trim hedges and how to put harness on horses (*gwisgo ceffyle*) for them to perform different tasks such as pulling a cart and a *gambo* and dragging a plough and a harrow.

The master, Joshua Phillips, owned a car – one of the first in the locality. The local shopkeeper also owned a car and he, on his maiden voyage, learnt that there was more to stopping a car than to stopping a horse; his first outing ended only when the car ran out of fuel.

When Heywood started at Frowen he slept in a stable loft (*llofft stabal*) and had to put up with rats running all over him and gnawing at his greased leather bootlaces. The mistress, Clarice, was not happy with this situation and she arranged for Heywood's elder brother Spencer, the carpenter, to enclose a corner of the attic for Heywood to sleep in comparative safety and peace from the rats. Heywood worked extremely hard ... all day at Frowen and late evenings at nearby Canerw. Not only was he a hard worker but he was also very obedient to the wishes of his boss. However, the following incident shows that there was a limit to what he was prepared to take. It was a rainy day but Joshua instructed Heywood to cart animal dung to the fields (*hala dom*). Heywood wrapped a sack (*llywanen*) over his shoulders and proceeded to load the cart using a fork (*fforch*) and then drove the horse and loaded cart up to the fields where he unloaded the dung in small heaps at regular intervals. The empty cart was taken back to the yard and the back-breaking loading was repeated and the full cart again driven to the field and unloaded as before. There was no let up of the rain but Heywood's hope of being allowed to leave this dreadful job for another day did not materialise. Late afternoon the rain eased and the boss Joshua appeared in the field and after pacing between the heaps of dung he approached Heywood and complained that the heaps were too close together. Heywood could not take any more and he threw the fork into the ground and suggested to the boss that he try doing the job himself! Heywood walked back to the farm fully expecting to be sacked for his action and he started packing his bag. The mistress Clarice got wind of what was happening and the kindly woman told Heywood to unpack his bag and to leave the matter to her. Nothing more was heard of the incident - a great relief to Heywood because he had by then realised he had over reacted although in the circumstances it was quite understandable.

The only respite from manual labour in those days was on a Sunday when it was customary for all to attend chapel two or three times. No wonder the chapels were full … it was a welcome break from their daily toil for labourers, servants and maids to follow the custom of the age. Attending chapel enabled workers to meet and to share tales and perhaps get up to some mischief before returning to another six days of grind until the following Sunday. The full chapels, I suspect, had little to do with a thirst for religion but rather reflected the need for men and women to have some 'recreational' time.

1.7 Farm workers and coal miners

In 1936 Heywood's future wife arrived at Frowen in the person of 19-year-old maid Phebe Lilian (Lil) Jenkins. They would be co-workers for a year until the death of William Owen required Heywood to take over responsibility for running Canerw Farm on behalf of his widowed mother. In 1935 as servant at Blaiddbwll Farm, Lil was a member at Glandwr Chapel and contributed a total of 13s.6d. to the cause. In 1936 she gave 4s. to Glandwr Chapel before leaving with a letter of recommendation (*ymadael trwy lythyr*) for Cefnypant Chapel where she contributed 2s.6d. for the remaining months of the year. Lil was the daughter of William Jenkins (1889-1971) and Margaret Ann (Griffiths)(1893-1969) both of whom had left school at 12 years of age to become farm workers. For a few years prior to their marriage in 1912 both had worked at Coynant Farm near Pantycaws. They were committed chapel-goers with William a Baptist and Margaret Ann an Independent. By the time Lil was born in 1917 William was a coal miner which work was better paid than labouring on a farm; in 1918 farm servants were fortunate to earn 30s. (£1.50) a week and worse was to follow as the post-war slump hit farming and wages were cut. On the other hand by 1925 a miner's minimum wage was up to 48s. (£2.40) a week which was enough to keep William working in a coal mine in Gorseinon, returning home to Carreg Grwca Cottage, Llanfyrnach Parish on the slopes of Foel Dyrch, Pentregalar every other weekend or so.[6] In the summer Foel Dyrch was covered in winberries (*llysie duon bach*) and these were avidly collected by the Jenkins children to supplement their diet. They attended Glandwr School by the River Taf in Llanfyrnach Parish for which the 1921 Census data reveal that 98 per cent of the population spoke Welsh and 55 percent spoke only Welsh. Such figures would have been typical of all west Wales parishes at that time apart from those in South Pembrokeshire.

William Jenkins was a miner for about ten years from 1917 which was time enough for his face to become marked with blue scars whose acquisition by miners is so well described by George Orwell in *The Road to Wigan Pier*: 'Every miner has blue scars on his nose and forehead, and will carry them to his death. The coal dust of which the air underground is full enters every cut, and then the skin grows over it and forms a blue stain like tattooing, which in fact it is. Some of the older men have their foreheads veined like Roquefort cheeses from this cause.' (In 1957 I actually visited the coal mine in Gorseinon where my grandfather probably worked. The coal-face was reached by crawling through a 3-foot-high tunnel for about 10 yards. I had an attack of claustrophobia on the outward and on the return crawl and only just managed to keep the attack under control. How people could work under such conditions is beyond my understanding.) Gorseinon was in the anthracite part of the south Wales coalfield and the demand for anthracite coal withstood the slump which hit the steam-coal producing areas of the Rhondda, Cynon and Rhymni valleys from the mid 1920s. In the summer of 1927 unemployment was 10% in the anthracite area of Ammanford but was 40% in the steam area of Ferndale. (There was a temporary surge in demand for Welsh steam-coal from 1922 to 1924 due to a strike by miners in the USA in 1922 and the disruption of coal production in Germany when France occupied the Ruhr in 1923/24. But the fleeting prosperity of the coal field as a whole was reflected in the unemployment figures: just 1.8% for Wales' miners in April 1924. But just over a year later the corresponding figure of 28.5% for August 1925 was a grim reflection of the horror of the crisis that had hit the main sector of the Welsh economy. A General Strike followed in 1926 and massive outmigration from Wales' industrial areas meant that the country's population in 1931 was less than it was in 1921. Despite this reduction in population, unemployment reached 42.8% at the height of the depression in August 1932.)

Contrary to the implication in its name, Pentregalar, is a collection of half a dozen or so houses rather than a village. But the area has an important place in the history of Welsh literature. Its most famous son was T E Nicholas (1879-1971), or *Niclas y Glais,* the Christian Minister, poet agitator for the working class and pacifist. After the first World War he trained as a Dentist and became a Communist although he continued to preach the Christian religion. An account of childhood in Pentregalar is given in *Estyn yr Haul.* Brief accounts of the lives of famous men born in Pentregalar can be read in *Gwyr Llen Sir Benfro yn yr Ugeinfed Ganrif.* In an earlier age, Pentregalar was put on the map by a remarkable man called Siams Dafi (1758-1844). He is commemorated at Pentregalar by a memorial stone, unveiled on 26th May 2007. An account of his life is given in a booklet *To Remember Siams Dafi* by T Mair Davies on behalf of 'The Siams Dafi Society'.

In moving away to find work in the coalfield William was following in the footsteps of his father Griffith Jenkins (1865-1933) who, a generation earlier, left his job of labourer/coachman with W.R.H. Powell, M.P. at Maesgwynne, Llanboidy around the time of Powell's death in 1889 to work in the mines of the Rhondda leaving his family at home in Cwmfelin Mynach. No doubt he had been attracted by the higher wages paid in the mines. By 1901 he had returned as coachman/groom to Squire Roch at Maesgwynne and was living with his wife and seven children at Plasybwci, Llanboidy.

My mother Lil's maternal grandfather, Gad Griffiths, was also a farm servant before becoming a small holder and labourer in Gilfach Quarry and later in Garnwen Quarry, Hebron after his marriage in 1891. He and his wife Mary Ann had seven children but the youngest succumbed to the dreaded illness of the age, tuberculosis, at the age of thirty. Mary Ann's father, Benjamin Jenkins, was the embodiment of many rural characters of the times: hard working labourer, father to a flock of children (nine in his case) and committed chapel-goer despite being excommunicated for a year for fathering his first born out of wedlock. Benjamin, an expert at breaking-in young horses, was elected deacon at Nebo Independent Chapel, Efailwen in 1899 where he was the precentor, an acclaimed Sunday School teacher, learned in the scriptures and knowledgeable in debate. His wife Ann was the daughter of Edward Davies (1798-1881), a leading figure in the local community during the mid-nineteenth century. In addition to farming 117 acres at Pantyrodyn Farm, Cilmaenllwyd, Edward practised the skills of a veterinary surgeon, performed the duties of registrar for marriages, was learned and had a large library. A strong supporter of the temperance movement he was a deacon at Nebo Chapel for 29 years. He sent some of his nine children including Mary Ann to a school in Narberth where they lodged and enrolled as members of Tabernacl Chapel during school terms.

My grandparents William and Margaret Ann Jenkins, committed Christians as they were, gave generously to the cause. From 1922 to 1928 they contributed on average £1 per annum shared between their respective chapels. In 1928 William Jenkins ended his stint as a coal miner and returned to the borderlands of Carmarthenshire and Pembrokeshire to become a tenant on the Dolwilym Estate of the Protheroes in 'the green glade deep in the valley bottom, on the banks of the River Taf, sheltered by steep wooded hillsides, a sylvan hermitage aptly christened "The Happy Valley" by the new mistress of Plas Dolwilym, Emma Jones Protheroe in 1813' to where the family moved from the Preseli Hills. They occupied a small holding consisting of a round house (*Y Ty Rownd*) usually referred to simply as 'Cottage' and a few fields sufficient to support about four cows. Margaret Ann made and sold butter and William laboured wherever work was to be found including a couple of weeks unpaid for Squire Protheroe in return for the right to plant a few rows of potatoes on Dolwilym land. Settled with his family, William was soon involving them in his passion for singing. His *pedwarawd* (quartet) and *wythawd* (octet) parties based on himself and son Vince as tenors, son Johny as bass and daughter Lil singing alto were soon collecting prizes at penny readings and eisteddfodau. People would travel from afar to hear their rendering of *O Mor Bêr* … (In the Sweet …).

Oes mae gwlad sydd yn harddach na'r haul,
Ni a'i gwelwn hi draw, draw yn glir,
Yno'n disgwyl ein gweld mae ein Tad,
Cawn fynd yno i orffwys cyn hir,

Ni gawn ganu caniadau rhai pur,
'Rol cyrhaeddyd y lan brydferth draw,
Bydd ein henaid heb drallod na chur,
Heb ofid, na hiraeth, na braw

Am y cynnal a'r cadw trwy'r daith,
Am oludoedd y cariad mewn Iawn,
Byth i'r Drindod mewn Undod heb drai,
Bydd y nefoedd o foliant yn llawn

Vince was secretary of the Sunday School at Cefnypant from 1936 to 1940 and was conductor of the the children's choir from 1941 until 1943 when he and his wife Elfair and son Geoffrey left the area. In 1940 Vince became a member of the famous concert party 'Bois y Frenni' from the Preseli Hills established by the Penygroes schoolmaster W.R.Evans. At the time Vince worked in Insurance and was known in the concert party as 'Vince Insiwrans'.

By the mid 1930s William had obtained employment with the County Council as a 'road man' responsible for the up-keep of a length of road. He earned about 46s. (£2.30) per week which may have been double the wage of many farm labourers[7]. The work involved keeping drainage ditches clear of debris so that surface water flowed freely off the road. Potholes had to be filled-in and spring and summer growth on verges and hedges had to be trashed and collected. William remained a 'road man' until retirement. Like many other 'road men' William took great pride in his work and his length of road was immaculately kept. He was invariably ahead of schedule with his maintenance but that was not necessarily to his advantage because there was always a lazy 'length man' not too far away who was well behind his schedule and William was then sent to help him out.

[6]. David A. Pretty, op. cit. p.174. [7]. Ibid., p. 193.

1.8 Unfit homes and tuberculosis

Outdoor life at out-of-the-way *Y Ty Rownd* in the 1930s was as pleasurable for the children as it was arduous for the parents. Cromlech Gwal y Filiast of pre-historic fame was situated directly above *Y Ty Rownd* but there was a dangerous steep drop into a quarry between the two. Lil and Vince were on one occasion playing near the cromlech when they decided to run home and Lil miscalculated her path and suddenly noticed the edge of the quarry looming! She deliberately ran into a tree and although seriously shaken-up she had probably saved her life by her instant action. A few hundred yards up-river was *Plas* Dolwilym (Mansion) headquarters of the Dolwilym Estate although the squire Captain David Garrick Protheroe (Captain Dai) and his sister Miss Protheroe lived in the nearby dowager house of Glyntaf. Captain Dai inherited the Dolwilym Estate on the death of his brother, Baldwin, in 1908 – the year of the fire that gutted Dolwilym Mansion. The family moved to Glyntaf and although the mansion was rebuilt it was never lived-in again. The squire treated his tenants very well but Miss Protheroe left no doubt as to how the lower class should treat her. On one occasion she complained to William Jenkins that Vince and Lil had walked past her in the woods that morning without saluting and wishing her 'good morning'. Thereafter, whenever 'Miss' came into sight my mother saluted and muttered repeatedly 'Good morning Miss' until the woman passed by and was out of sight. Fishing the river Taf was enjoyable recreation which occasionally provided a healthy meal and the railway and its trains served as a reasonably accurate clock. On being waved-down a train would slow for a passenger from *Y Ty Rownd* to hop-on to be taken to the outside world as far as Whitland or Cardigan. The children walked about two miles across fields and through woods to school at Pantycaws Hamlet where a Roman causeway once ran and is commemorated, in corrupted form, in the hamlet's name. A few years earlier in the age of the 'Welsh Not' a Pantycaws schoolmaster's entry in the school log-book revealed that he, as well as the pupils, was a Welsh speaker first and foremost: '… children sent home early because there was a big saw in the river'! [8] (the word for flood in Welsh is *llif* which is also the word for saw as in sawing wood)

William's comparatively high wage supplemented by income from the sale of home-made butter meant the family's financial situation at *Y Ty Rownd* was the best it had ever been. However the living accommodation provided in the Round House for parents and five children left much to be desired. Cottages in rural areas were described as damp, overcrowded, insanitary, dilapidated and unfit for occupation. Poor housing together with low wages led to a 25% reduction in farm workers in Carmarthenshire between 1931 and 1936 as they left the rural areas in search of better housing and jobs. Tuberculosis did in fact take its toll on three out of the five Jenkins children with two boys recovering after extensive treatment at sanatoriums but a daughter succumbed to the dreaded decline dying at sixteen years of age despite her mother's insistence that God would effect her recovery. Lil was a maid at Blaiddbwll, Llanfyrnach at the time, and she received a letter of condolence from her boss John Harries who was a patient at the County Hospital, Haverfordwest recovering from an attack by a bull which seriously injured his hand:

'Dear Lil, I was sorry to hear of the death of your dear sister Nancy and unable to attend the funeral yesterday. It is a great blow to you all to lose such a quiet and kind hearted girl at such an early age. I'm sure your parents feel it terribly. May their strength hold under this great strain. I have a good idea what it is by now of pain and to see others in it too. One fellow died here last night, seven have died since I'm here and one after going home – so is the 'Way of the World' – someone always under the hammer. Since I'm in here I'm trying to think that there is some one worse than myself. I've missed your letters very much which I was reading over and over, you can write again when you feel better. My hand will be a very very long time healing, it will never be right of course, may be that they'll have to cut it off yet. Please accept my sympathy all of you during these dark hours of your lives. John H.'

Lil's friend, Mattie, worked on a farm about six miles away and would, probably, not have been allowed time off to attend the funeral as is implicit in her letter of sympathy.

Treaskell Fach
St Clears.

My Dear Lil,

It was with deep regret that I learned of the passing away of your Dear Sister Nancy, so I express my deepest sympathy to you in your great sorrow, also to all at your home, I know it is a sad time with you all, as you know Dear Lil, that I know what it is to mourn after a loved one, so I do feel for you all deeply. When I lost Dear Mam I thought that I could never live without her, but somehow or other I had strength to bear all, Trusting that you will have the same, in this sad bereavment of yours. My only wish is that I could be at the funeral, but as it is impossible, I write you these few lines, I think of you all day and my heart mourns with you though I am far away.

May God bless you, and comfort you all, in your sad bereavement. This with great sorrow.

Your affectionate friend
Mattie xxx.

P.S.

I had written you a letter as usual, but I could not send it when I heard of your sorrow, until I had sent you a word of sympathy, so if you'll drop me a line to say that you are in Blaiddbwll, as I expect you are at home now, I will be very thankfull. Give my love to them all at your home as I am deeply touched by your great sorrow.

In Nancy's obituary in the *Welshman* she was described as of 'gentle and amiable disposition' and a 'faithful member of Cefnypant Congregational Chapel' where 'she took a keen interest in the Sunday School. Possessing a fine voice, she won many prizes at different competitive meetings'. The previous year she had 'won the first prize at the Urdd National

Eisteddfod at Carmarthen for a piece of needlework'. Among the floral tributes were 'Teulu Canerw' and 'In remembrance, Capt and Miss Protheroe'.

Vince spent months in sanatoriums in Talgarth, Breconshire and in Sealyham, Pembrokeshire and in a letter to his sister Lil in 1937 described his efforts to keep warm during a cold-spell: 'It is very cold now these days but as it happens I do not feel cold. I have got my red coat, three blankets and a rug on now and sister gave me a hot water bottle Wednesday.'

A generation earlier tuberculosis had wreaked havoc in the Davies family of Penbontbren Cottage, Cwmiles deep in the Taf Valley. James Davies was an uncle to Heywood's mother, Martha, and she had spent three or four years of her childhood with James and his wife Sarah and their young family. Five years after Martha left to go into service tuberculosis took its toll with James dying in 1902 followed within a year by three of his young children aged between five and nine years. Widowed Sarah was left with five children, three of whom went into service in the greater Taf Valley area, but Sarah moved with her two youngest boys, Stanley and James, from the rural Taf Valley to the industrial Gwendraeth Valley. If it was the hope of better paid jobs for her young sons that prompted Sarah's move it was a hope that was realised because two decades later Stanley and James visited their cousin Martha in Bush and left a lasting impression on Heywood's young mind because they came on a motorbike and therefore must have been well-off compared to his own impoverished family.

Considering the appalling state of rural housing David Pretty wrote 'Not surprisingly, the tuberculosis mortality rate in the Welsh rural counties exceeded that of England'. Carmarthenshire and Pembrokeshire plus five other Welsh counties occupied the top seven places in England and Wales. 'Such housing and sanitary conditions were a disgrace to the Welsh countryside and a slur on the inactive local authorities and rate-conscious class that controlled them'.[9] A classic example of the controlling class exercising their muscle to prevent a labourer's voice being heard on Carmarthenshire District Council occurred in a Taf Valley by-election in 1921. A local farm labourer and Agricultural Workers Union and Labour Party activist and member of the district wages committee, Edwin Davies, agreed to be nominated as candidate by the National Union of Agricultural Workers. The farmers of Llanglydwen Ward reacted with alarm and as reported in the *Cardigan and Tivy Side Advertiser* of 25 February 1921: ' A meeting of ratepayers at Pengawse Farm, Hebron decided to nominate Capt. D.G. Protheroe, Glyntaf as candidate for the seat rendered vacant by the death of Mr Thomas Davies J.P., Pretoria Stores, Llanglydwen. ... a keen contest is anticipated.' During his extensive and courageous canvas Edwin Davies was subjected to much abuse and sarcasm from the farming fraternity before losing the election by 72 votes to 38. The parish consisted mainly of small free-holders and one of them wrote that it was very re-assuring that the extreme ideas of George Lansbury's followers did not appeal to those 'level-headed crofters' and that Captain Protheroe, as the largest rate-payer in the parish, could be relied upon to look after the interests of the rate-payers. It might have been expected that the farmers of Llanglydwen Parish of all people would have had some sympathy for the plight of their labourers and servants; after-all their grandfathers, in a pickle eighty years earlier, had been backed by their labourers and servants when they initiated the Rebecca uprising at Efailwen.[10]

Edwin's activities on behalf of the working class continued and on Saturday 25 February 1922 he was one of three delegates from Llanglydwen – Simon Evans, Gorsfach and Tom Owen, Brynfedwen were the others - at a Labour Conference in Carmarthen when a Divisional Labour Party in West Carmarthenshire was established. The Reverend E.Teilo Owen, Saron, Llangeler was elected president and addressed the meeting in Welsh. The Reverend Owen twice contested the Carmarthenshire parliamentary seat for Labour during 1924 and took around 30% of the vote on both occasions thus laying the foundation for Labour to take the seat from the Liberals in 1929 with Daniel Hopkin's victory.

Capten Dai continued to use Dolwilym Mansion on special occasions such as Rent Day (*Dydd y Rhent*) when tenants were received and entertained there. Lil recalled three big days (*diwrnode mowr*) in the calendar associated with the gentry (*gwyr mowr*) of Dolwilym/Glyntaf around 1930.

One was the 'meet' of the Carmarthenshire Hunt (*mît y cwn hela*) at Glyntaf. The children were allowed a day off school. Activities began with sandwiches, cakes and drinks brought out from the kitchens by the maids and shared out among the gathered throng. After this enjoyable preliminary the Huntsman would blow his horn and the hounds would move off followed by red coated riders and a fleet of followers on foot making for vantage points where they hoped to see a chase and perhaps a kill. Others would make for Penybont Inn (*Bont*). But which ever way they spent the day it was a tired workforce that made their way home to tackle the evening milking on the day of the Hunt.

Another big day (*diwrnod mowr arall*) was Rent Day (*Dydd y Rhent*) when the tenants - about two dozen of them - attended at Dolwilym to pay their rents. They would come for the rent lunch (*cinio rhent*) and would enjoy plenty of food, drink and tobacco and afterwards the children of that part of the Taf Valley would enjoy what for most if not all of them was their best meal of the year. According to Lil, everyone looked forward to *Dydd y Rhent* ... obviously Captain Dai was pretty fair as landlords went.

The third big day concerned the Otter Hounds (officially the Pembrokeshire and Carmarthenshire Otter Hounds) of which Captain Dai was MOH from 1906 to 1934. The pack was kept somewhere near Carmarthen (*lan sha Gyfyrddin 'na*) but was followed by all the landed gentry, male and female, of the county including Captain Dai's sister of Glyntaf. Otter hunting took place twice a week during the summer when the rivers were low. The hunters dressed in blue with brown hats and all had an otter's paw as a badge on their hats.

Another big day – all-be-it an unofficial one - for the children of the Taf Valley (*Dyffryn Taf*) occurred on a particular Saturday during the summer holidays when Captain Dai took his Otter Pack and followers to hunt by invitation in another locality. In the absence of Captain Dai and his sister from Glyntaf for the whole day, two of their maid servants left at home would organize a picnic for the children at the site of Cromlech Gwal y Filiast known locally as *Carreg Llech* which was on a bank above *Y Tŷ Rownd* and about half way between Glyntaf and Dolwilym mansions. All sorts of goodies would be in plentiful supply and everyone looked forward to the Otter Pack's away-day tea party at *Carreg Llech* because, apart from Christmas day and the occasional birthday, there was nothing to compare with it in those days.

Another attraction at Dolwilym was the walled-garden which was looked after for Captain Dai by a full-time gardener, Evan Higgins (1872-1947), who lived with his wife Elizabeth (1861-1943) in Dolwilym Cottage, usually referred to as Tŷ Higgins, on the driveway to Dolwilym. Mrs Higgins did not enjoy good health … probably she suffered from arthritis … and Lil and other children used to help her around the cottage. Evan Higgins was very kind and was forever sharing out garden produce to the people living locally. The children particularly looked forward to visiting the Glass House when the grapes were ripe and the children were allowed to eat as many as they could manage!

[8] Aneurin Talfan Davies, Crwydro Sir Gâr, Llandybie, 1955, p. 259

[9] David A. Pretty, op. cit., p. 194.

[10] E. T. Lewis, *Efailwen to Whitland,* Lodwick, Carmarthen, 1976, vol. 2, p. 80.

1.9 Change on the horizon

On leaving school in 1931 my mother, Lil, having been presented with a Bible by her parents, followed the well-trodden path of countless previous generations of labourers' daughters: she went into service. She became a maid at Llanglydwen Smithy (*Yr Efail*), where the mistress was a keen jam-maker with blackberry jam her speciality. Picking blackberries was a seasonal activity for everyone in those days when fruit was gathered rather than bought. Lil remembered the time when the Blacksmith and his wife and their man servant and herself together with a neighbour went out to the fields to harvest the blackberries from the hedges. The party would have been in full view of anyone on the opposite side of the valley and it seems that George of Rosehill (*Siors Rhoshill*) was one such observer because he wrote a verse to commemorate the occasion:

Y boss, y gwas, y forwn
A'r misis hefyd hi
A'th allan un diwrnod
I bigo mwyar du
Cymdoges hefyd joinodd
I gal tam bach o sbort
Bydd ardal deg Llanglydwen
Byth mwy o jam yn "short".

Although the blackberry expedition was not recorded on film, Lil's initiative in buying a Box Camera after she started earning ensured that many events, places and people were photographed in the 1930s and many have survived. There are photographs of Cottage, haymaking and numerous family groups. I remember the Box Camera at Blaenwaun Cottage and a few photographs survive from that period as well. However I do not recall it being used extensively ... perhaps the cost of the film and its development by Will R Rose was affordable to an unmarried maid but not to a married mother of two. When Lil was at *Yr Efail*, her friend (and second cousin-once-removed) Nan, daughter of Dafi and Lissi Reynolds, Cwm was a maid at nearby Rosehill, home of the blackberry bard. Nan recalled that Lil's brother Vince had a motorbike and so did his pal Ellis Davies, Tigen, Llanglydwen (who was a second cousin to Heywood). After Sunday evening chapel, Nan and Lil would sometimes persuade the motorcyclists to take them for a motorbike ride around the country lanes of the area. In those days such frivolity was frowned upon and especially so if it took place on a Sunday. But it seems they avoided attracting the attention of anyone who might instigate censure measures against them.

Lil recorded some events for the years 1937 to 1942 in one of her numerous note books which were a great help in compiling this account since my memory does not reach back that far. For 1937 she wrote: 'Heywood's father passed away on 21 March 1937 at the age of 57 years. Heywood had to go home to help his mother finish bring up the children. He bought a cow and calf at Clynderwen mart for …' The sentence is incomplete and we shall never know the price he paid for the cow and calf. The landlord, Martin Thomas, was very keen to sell Canerw at this time but Martha Owen was not interested in buying the farm. Martin Thomas then offered Martha one thousand pounds to leave Canerw but again she refused and she was allowed to stay there as a tenant. Heywood was 20-years-old when he left Frowen to go home to Canerw to take over responsibility for the farm and, as entered in Lil's notebook…'his brother Gordon age 16 took his place at Frowen'.

It was still the age of the chapel in the Taf Valley and the labourers' and servants' breaks from daily chores were limited, more or less, to an annual chapel-organized trip to the seaside and to the customary down-tools on Sundays so as to attend chapel two or three times. However, some among the working class were looking for ways of increasing choice of employment opportunities for their children and to this end secondary education was seen as a crucially important enabler if only they could afford it. Lil's parents arranged for their youngest son Johnny to attend Whitland Grammar School by taking advantage of the convenient train service past the *Ty Rownd* to Whitland which was, obviously, affordable whereas lodging in Whitland was not. At the same time their income was, presumably, low enough for his school fees to be waived as was the case, at the time, for most working class children in Wales.[11] Johnny spent two years in the grammar school before leaving to have treatment for tuberculosis after which he became an apprentice cobbler.

William Jenkins' belief in the vital role of education in improving the prospects for working class children was implicit in his command to his daughter Lil when she left *Y Ty Rownd* in 1939 with her first-born – '*Watcha di bod y crwt hwn in ca'l isgol Whitland*' (Be very sure that this boy gets to Whitland [Grammar] School). (She never wavered from fulfilling his command).

William must have sensed that major changes were on the horizon which would widen the prospects of the working class. The expansion of the welfare state in the 1940s showed he was right but the downside was the Second World War which claimed so many innocent lives among them his and Margaret Ann's eldest son Clifford. At the same time, in the 1940s, increased mobility in the form of motor cycles, cars and especially bus services brought Taf Valley communities within easy reach of cinemas, dances and public houses in Carmarthen and other towns. Although such secular entertainment was frowned upon by a few chapel die-hards it was enjoyed by most. At the same time new opportunities for labourers' children to receive free secondary education opened eyes and widened horizons. These external experiences weakened the influence of chapel culture within the communities and initiated a decline in chapel membership. Secondary education and increased mobility also contributed to the decreased use of the Welsh language in everyday life in the Taf Valley as more Welsh speakers left the area to further their careers and non-Welsh speakers moved in to a community not equipped to absorb them.

However if Heywood and Lil at their wedding in 1938 could have known that time had already been called on their cloistered world in the Taf Valley they would have enjoyed their day even more in the knowledge that a way of life which seriously limited the opportunities available to their class was heading for extinction and in the not-too-distant future labourers' children, benefiting from free education and health care, would at last feel the playing field beneath their feet begin to level.

[11]. Gareth Elwyn Jones, *The Education of a Nation*, UWP, 1997.

Cromlech Gwal y Filiast near Llanglydwen, at the heart of Dyffryn Taf. The valley's anchor to ages past.

Llanglydwen

LLANFALLTEG

LOGIN CARDIGAN

Cwm Waunbwll, Hebron.

Glandwr

William and Martha Elizabeth (nee Griffin) Owen, author's grandparents: stalwarts at Cefnypant Independent Chapel.

Martha Griffin (nee Davies) and daughters, Martha Elizabeth and Emily Alice, in London c1890.

'Clean and well-dressed' Owen children of Bush, Cefnbrafle:
Alice and Martha Ann; Spencer, Garfield and Heywood; Gordon and Morfydd.

James Owen (Heywood's uncle) took time-off from World War I in early 1918 to marry Lizzie Mary Mainwaring.
They lived in Felinfoel, Llanelli.

Margaret Ann Griffiths (author's grandmother) and Martha Mathias, co-servants in 1911 at Coynant Farm, Pantycaws showing-off their Sunday-best.

William and Margaret Ann Jenkins (author's grandparents) with Clifford in 1912.

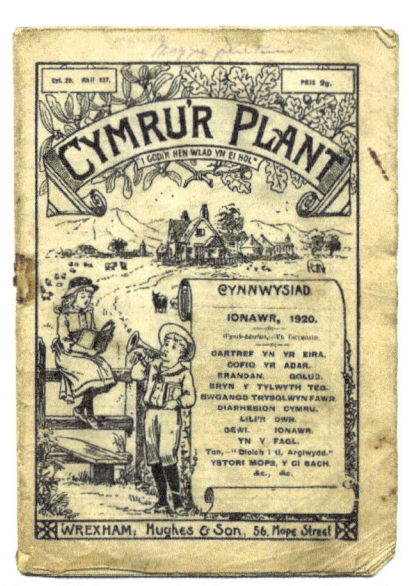

The Jenkins children got hold, occasionally, of a copy of O.M. Edwards' magazine.

Jenkins children of Carreg Grwca, Pentregalar: Vince, Lil, Nancy and Clifford.

Gad and Mary Ann Griffiths of white-washed Ietgoch, Garnwen, author's great-grandparents.

Benjamin and Ann Jenkins, Pantycaws, Efailwen, author's great-great-grandparents..

Phebe Jenkins, Plasybwci, Llanboidy – author's great-grandmother.

Griffith Jenkins, Plasybwci, Llanboidy (author's great-grandfather); his son Jack, Maesgwynne Lodge; Glyn John, Maesgwynne Farm Cottage; Ifan Lewis, Llwynteg, Llanboidy labouring at Maesgwynne in the 1920s.

Canerw in the 1940s. Prior to opening the Independent Chapel at Henllan Amgoed in 1697 Canerw had been a centre for religious gatherings and such meetings continued to be held there up to the 1820s.

Dolwilym Cottage (Y Ty Rownd)

Plan of Y Ty Rownd.

The River Taf is a few metres to the left of the railway

Johnny haymaking at Y Ty Rownd in 1935.

Outside the front-door of Y Ty Rownd in 1935: William and Margaret Ann Jenkins, Nancy and Johnny.

Tea-break during haymaking at Y Ty Rownd c1930

David and Elizabeth Williams, Abertaf/Minefield, Llanglydwen.
David was game-keeper/labourer at Dolwilym during early 1900s.

In front of Dolwilym Mansion c1905. Third from left is David Williams of Abertaf/Minefield, Llanglydwen, labourer at Dolwilym. The squire at the time was John Baldwin Bridges Schaw Protheroe who had a renowned pack of Beagles.

Cefnypant Independent Chapel built in 1878
on land donated by W.R.H. Powell, squire of Maesgwynne, Llanboidy.

A native of Mynydd Bach, Swansea, The Reverend Phillip E. Price was minister
at Cefnypant Independent Chapel (with Glandwr) from 1904 to 1946

Reverend Ifan Afan Jenkins served Moriah Independent Chapel from 1909 – 1931. Unusually in those days he travelled in the 'Bible Lands' and brought back a bottle full of water from the River Jordan, which he used over subsequent years to baptize Moriah's children..

William Jenkins, son Johnny and Edward Eynon in their Sunday-best enjoy a stroll on Tenby's south beach on the occasion of Cefnypant Chapel's Sunday School trip in 1937.

Joan, Dorothy, Rowina and ------ Davies, Butt Cottage, Llanglydwen, in Tenby with Cefnypant Chapel Sunday-School in 1937, take a break from sand-castle building to sample the lollypops .

Cefnypant Chapel members make the most of their trip to Tenby in 1937.

Left: Mattie Phillips, 'Behold', Glandwr about to don her swim-suit at Tenby in 1937.
Right: Nan Reynolds, Cwm, Cefnypant about to join Mattie.

John Samson, schoolmaster at Henllan Amgoed and Sunday School teacher at Cefnypant Independent Chapel. The Owen children enjoyed a ride in his trap to Sunday School. A large umbrella was opened over the trap on a rainy day.

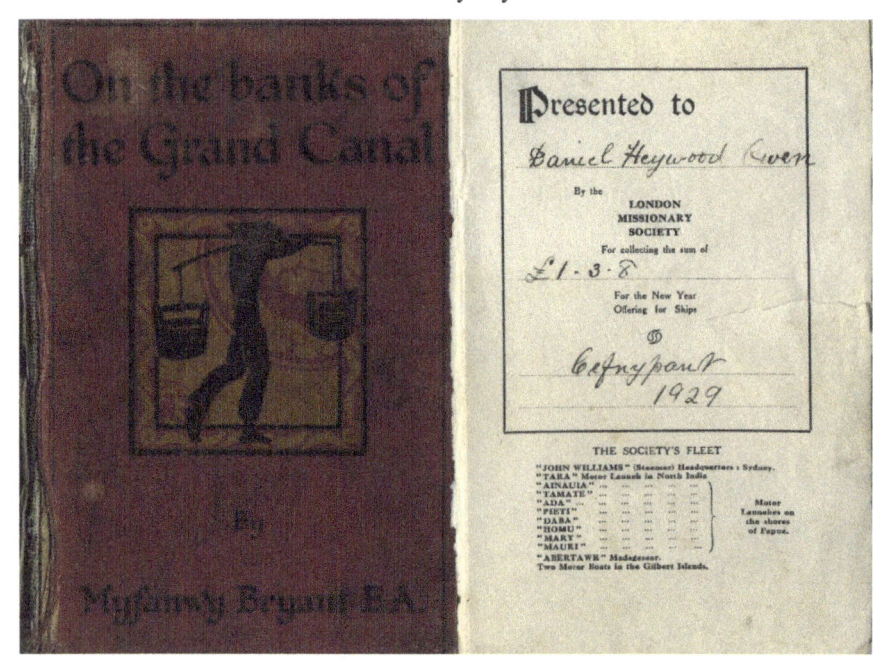

Heywood's prize from the Christian Missionary Society

Penygaer School 1924. L/R back row: Dai Davies, Parc-y-rhos; Tom Reynolds, Cwm; Cranmer Evans, Blaenffynnon; Wil Phillips, Trehir; Laurence Davies, Cilgynydd; Gwilym Llewellyn, Ysguborwen; Archie Phillips, Trevilla. Fourth row: Ms Davies, Waunglocsen (assistant teacher); Alice Owen, Bush; Martha Ann Owen, Bush; Doris Phillips, Trehir; Lizzie Ann Adams, Llain; Gwyneth Jones, Lanfach; Conie Thomas, Clundedwydd; May Davies, Parc-y-rhos; Mr W. Rhydderch Evans, Plascrwn (Head Master). Third row: Gwen Davies, Llainddel; Gwen Owen, Llwyngog; Mildred Evans, Rhos; Cida Evans, Blaenffynnon; Pheobe Rees, Lleinau; Getta Davies, Llainddel; Kate Davies, Cefn; Nan Reynolds, Cwm; Marged James, Penbontbren. Second row: Lyn Evans, Blaenffynnon; Cecil Davies, Parc-y-rhos; Megan Evans, Blaenffynnon; Sophia Bowen, Tynewydd; Dilys Davies, Llainddel; Min Davies, Cefn; Anna Thomas, Llwynon; Gertie Evans, Rhos; Bessie Reynolds, Cwm; George Reynolds, Cwm; Heywood Owen, Bush. Front row: Cliff Llewellyn, Ysguborwen; Dany Llewellyn, Ysguborwen; Sam Davies, Cefn; Gwyn Davies, Parc-y-rhos; Ifor Evans, Rhos; Garfield Owen, Bush; Ted Reynolds, Cwm; Spencer Owen, Bush; Lloyd Llewellyn, Ysguborwen; Jim Reynolds, Cwm.

Llanglydwen (Pantycaws) School c1904. Fifth from left, second row from top is Margaret Ann Griffiths, author's maternal grandmother.

A class in Llanglydwen (Pantycaws) School c1904.

1910

Back Row: *Miss Griffith; Ruth Devonald; Mary Jones; Mary Ellen; ? Moore; Mary Ann Bowen; ? Moore; Lizzie Roberts; Morfydd Jenkins.* Boys: *John Marsden Davies, Garnwen; John Gruffydd, Yetgoch; ? Morris; Dewi Davies; John Gruffydd, Trehowell; Ben Morris, Rhyddu, son of Amaziah; Tom Saer; T. J. Lewis; Ben Howells.*

Back Row: *John George – Master; Hannah Williams; Catherine Thomas; Phoebe Williams; ? (Rhydcoedbach); Maggie Jones; Getta Mathias; Martha Ann Davies; Sarah Jane (Pantemaen).* 2nd Row: *Annie Howell; Phoebe Mary Devonald; Jane Owen; Bronwen Davies; Frances Davies; Lizzie Griffiths; Martha Ann (Glynteg); Elizabeth Morris; Martha Mary George; Marged Ann Reynolds.* Boys Back: *Daniel (Clyngarw); Ben Rees; Tom Davies; Willie (Pantemaen).* Boys Front: *George Morris; Brython Davies; Johnny Stephens; Andrew Twigg; Danny Stephen; D. W. Evans; Tommy Reynolds; Alfred Reynolds; Elwyn Howells.*

Glandwr School 1910. John Gruffydd and Lizzie Griffiths were siblings of Margaret Ann Griffiths, author's maternal grandmother.

William Jenkins with two of his children, Vince and Lil (author's mother) at Y Ty Rownd in 1937.

Vince entertaining the girls after chapel service, late 1930s. L/R: Anna Thomas, Llwynon Shop and Post Office; Mary Catherine Blethyn, Cware; Lil Jenkins, Dolwilym Cottage; Meima Jenkins, Tower.

Clarice Phillips, the kindly mistress at Frowen Farm in the 1930s

Left: Lil, servant at Frowen Farm, on a visit to her parents at Dolwilym Cottage 1937
Right: Heywood, dressed for chapel, in 1937

Heywood with brother Elfed and nephew Ernie on his Royal Enfield in 1937 ready to be part of the new world of post World War II.

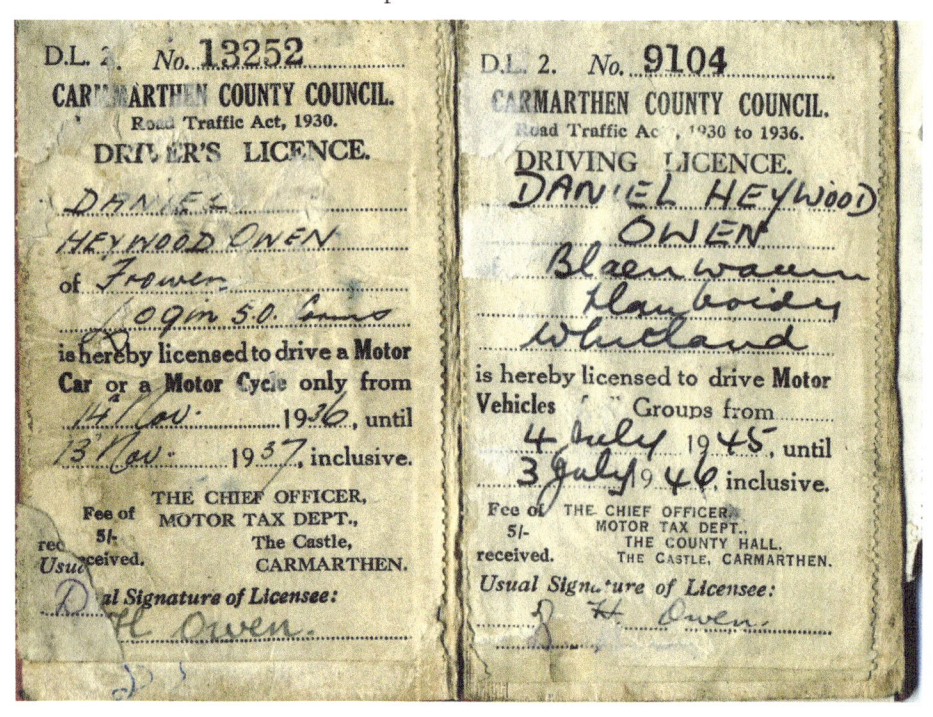

Two of Heywood's Driving Licenses.

'Hala Dom' Carting and spreading dung – the most physically demanding job on a farm.

Arnold John, Rhydyparc, Blaenwaun in the corn-field in 1933.

Haymaking near Login 1905

A thirst-quenching break from threshing.

Login Choir in 1932:

L/R front row: Jane Bowen, Pen-y-graig; Alice Thomas, Rhydymerydd; Olwen Jones, Ael-y-bryn; Bessie Lewis, Yet-fawr; Mag Jones, Isfryn; May Lewis, Yet-fawr; Primrose Thomas, Llysmyfyr; Mildred Evans, Rhos; Nan Davies, Waunglocsen; Gertie Evans, Rhos; Maudie Evans, Bryn-banc; Maggie ------, Maes-y-ffynnon; Eadel Thomas, March-gwyn; Kate Evans, Rhos; Maggie Llewellyn, Llandre. Second row: Mag Lewis, Yet-fawr; Mair Bush, Cefnbrafle; Sophia Bowen, Pen-y-gaer; Polly Llewellyn, Llandre; Iris Gravell, Ty'r Ysgol; Louvine and Ella Davies, Maes-yr-odyn; May Lewis, Maes-y-ffynnon. Third row: Hannah Evans, Ffynnon-wen; Bess Evans, Allt-y-felin; Rose Lewis, Ffosddu-fach; Martha Phillips, Sychpant; Let Jones, Bachsylw; Ann Phillips, Llain; Maggie Evans, Tynewydd; Rev. W.S. Thomas; John Davies, Felin-cwrt; May Lewis, Glanrhyd; Lilian Owen, Abertaf; Ann Llewellyn, Ffynnon-wen; Mer Jones, Bronwydd; Lizzie Llewellyn, Llandre; Alice John, Lan-teg; Mrs Gravell, Ty'r Ysgol. Fourth row: Mrs W.S. Thomas, Llysmyfyr; Mary Evans, Gwynlais; Mary Davies, Felin-cwrt; Mary Edwards, Llan; Mary Davies, Glascoed; Sophia Morris, Post; Phebe Morgan, Pumsaint; Polly Jones, Rhiw; Alice Jones, Sunnybank; Louisa Rowlands, Glan-yr-afon; Mary John, Crossing; Sarah Rees, Llain; Maggie Lewis, Siop; Lizzie Lewis, Penclippin; Sarah John, Llwynderw; Olive Davies, Rhyd-wen; Elizabeth Williams, Glyngarw; Tom Lewis, Arosfa; Parry Lewis, Siop. Fifth row: Willie Gibbon, Tredai; Martha Mathias, Ty Capel; Mary Jane Davies, Cwmbach; Polly Davies, Cefnbrafle; Lizzie John, Cefnbrafle; Martha Davies, Felin-cwrt; Annie Rees, Blaencwmau; Lizzie Mary Davies, Waunglocsen; Gertie Eynon, Waunffrwd; Lizzie Gibbon, Maes-y-ffrwd; Maggie Owen, Llwyn-glas; Marged Thomas, Y Fron; Rhys Thomas, Marchgwyn; Johnny Williams, Glyngarw; Jim Mathias, Cwm-bach. Sixth row: Tommy Morgan, Pumsaint; Dan Evans, Rhos; William Griffiths, Llety; Hamley John, Crossing; Harry Evans, Rhos; Huw Jones, Rhyd-wen; Danon Evans, Allt-y-felin; Vince Jones, Rhyd-wen; George Lewis, Arosfa; Will Lewis, Yet-fawr; Walter Owen, Abertaf; Jack Lewis, Glanrhyd; Cliff Williams, Maes-y-ffynnon; Daniel Gibbon, Maes-y-ffrwd; Walter Owen, Llwyn-glas. Seventh row: Mr Gravell, Ty'r Ysgol; Johnny Owens, Blaencwmau, Dado Owens, Blaencwmau; William John Eynon, Waunffrwd; Percy Thomas, Glyndedwydd; Wynford Griffiths, Gwenlais; Will Rowlands, Glan-yr-afon; Idwal Jones, Rhyd-wen; Handel Thomas, Rhiw; Willie Thomas, Y Fron; Cliff Lewis, Yet-fawr; Albert Evans, Tynewydd; Tom Lewis, Ffosddu-fach. Back row: Jackie Morgan, Pumsaint; James John Davies, Rhyd-wen; Jack Thomas, March-gwyn; Trevor Llewellyn, Llandre; Dai Phillips, Fron-haul; Ifor Jones, Ael-y-bryn; Danny Llewellyn, Ysgubor-wen; Danny Llewellyn, Llandre; Bert Noise, Llundain; Bila Evans, Post; Maurice Llewellyn, Llandre; Stanley Evans, Penclippin; Emlyn Thomas, Marchgwyn; Abel Llewellyn, Llandre.

Login Drama Group 1925

Nebo Drama Group performed 'Rhys Lewis' c1910. Catherine Morris, maid at Llwyn-yr-ebol Farm, (later Catherine John of Rhydyparc, Blaenwaun) is seated second from right.

Left: Phebe Morris, Clunbach, Llangolman (Rhydyparc, Blaenwaun in her old age).
Right: P.C. Caleb Morris, son of Phebe Morris. Brought up in Clunbach, Efailwen he left the area to find work and eventually joined the police-force and was based in Llangamarch

Phebe Morris at Rhydyparc with her daughter Catherine John c1930.

Left: Hannah Howells, Tynewydd; Catherine John and Miriam Morgan, Rhydvilla at Rhydyparc, Blaenwaun c1920.
Right: Stephen John, Bryn, Llangolman – expert horseman

Pat and Eppie John, Rhydyparc, Blaenwaun c1921

Margaret Evans (nee Jones), Wernlas, Login grandmother to the educationalist, poet, entertainer and founder of 'Bois y Frenni' concert party W.R. Evans

Sarah Davies, Penbontbren, Llanglydwen

John and Ann Evans, Penclungarw, Blaenwaun c1920. They celebrated their Diamond Wedding with a party at Penclungarw in 1936.

Pat and Eppie John, Rhydyparc, Blaenwaun in their baptism dresses ready for their total immersion at the hands of Reverend R. Parry Roberts, Mynachlogddu at Cwmfelin Mynach in 1932

Cyril Isaac, Iet-y-garn, Blaenwaun (later of Rhydyparc, Blaenwaun) c1936

In 1936 Cyril Isaac (Carpenter) assisted his father, Evan Isaac (Stone Mason), in building a Post Office at Blaenwaun, Whitland. Measuring 5.05 m by 2.9 m it was reputed to be the smallest in Wales. The Post Master, photographed above, was Thomas Griffiths, Lamb Inn and his wife - Evan's daughter Beatrice - delivered the post on her bicycle. On the death of her husband Beatrice became Post Mistress. The building can now be seen at St. Ffagans National History Museum

"A MERRY CHRISTMAS

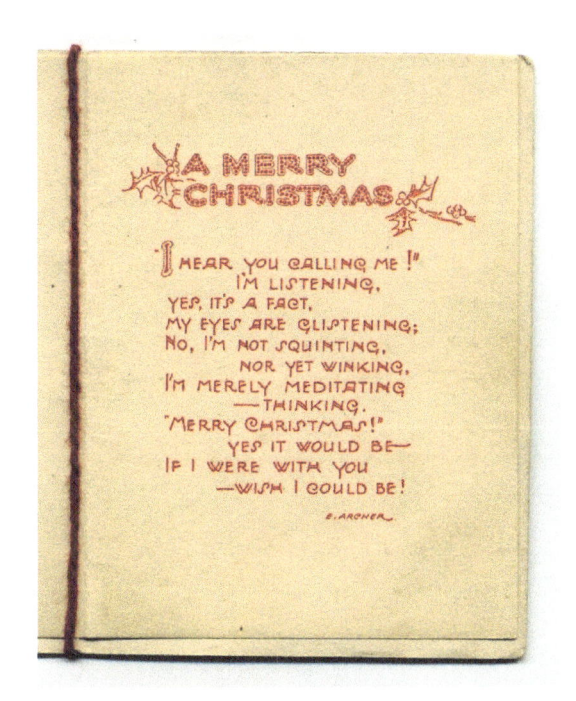

"I HEAR YOU CALLING ME!"
I'M LISTENING,
YES, IT'S A FACT,
MY EYES ARE GLISTENING;
NO, I'M NOT SQUINTING,
NOR YET WINKING,
I'M MERELY MEDITATING
—THINKING.
"MERRY CHRISTMAS!"
YES IT WOULD BE—
IF I WERE WITH YOU
—WISH I COULD BE!

E. ARCHER

LISTENING IN to Christmas Greetings

I'd give anything to be with you!

Lil received a Bible as a present from her parents when she left school and went into service in 1930.

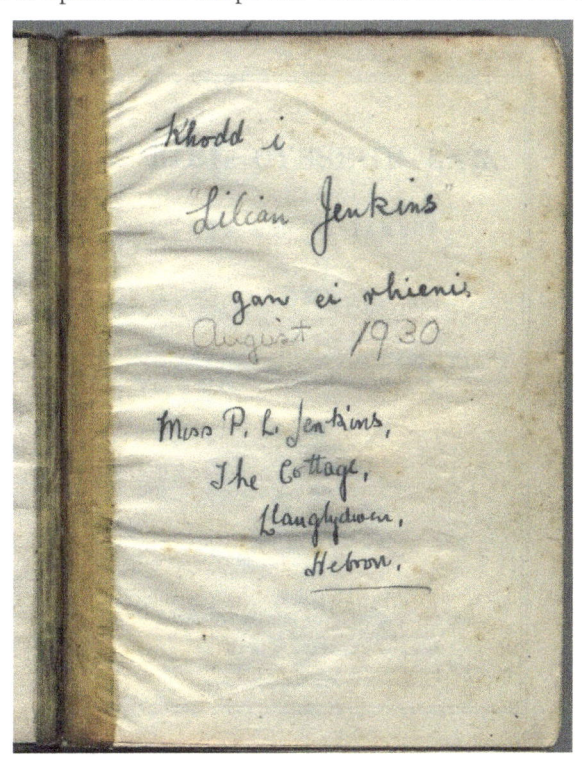

Rhodd i
"Lilian Jenkins"
gan ei rhieni.
August 1930

Miss P. L. Jenkins,
The Cottage,
Llanglydwen,
Hebron.

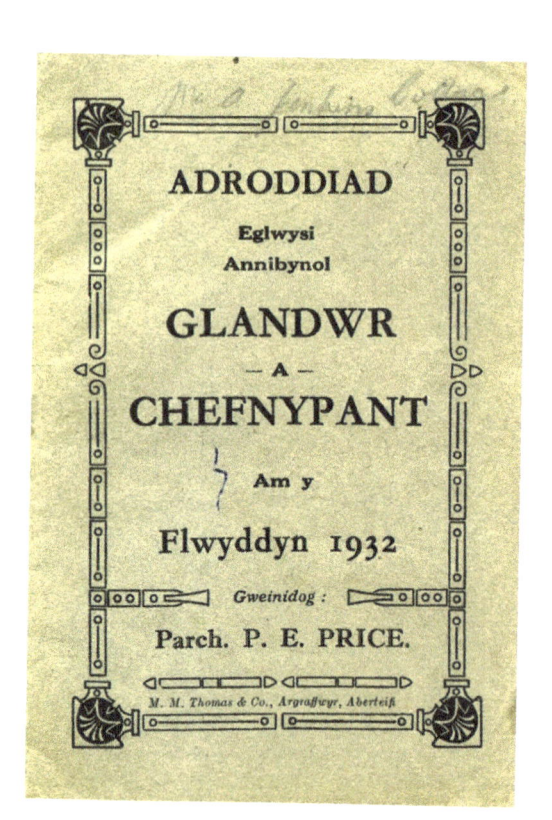

Three Taf Valley Chapels which continue to publish their annual reports.

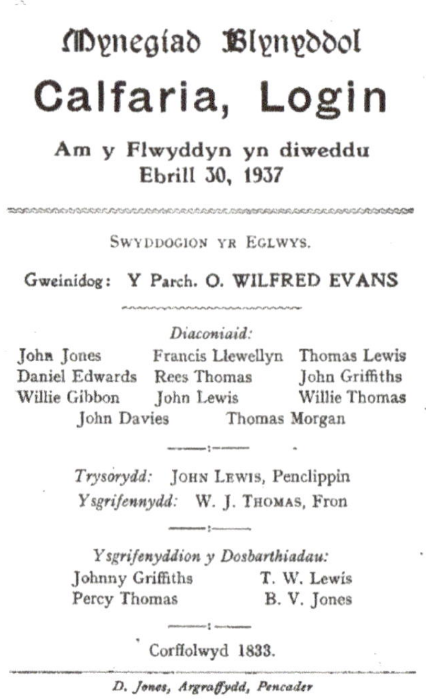

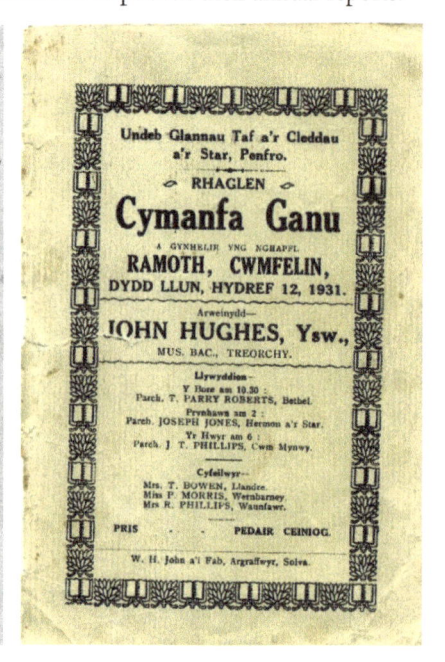

Left: This group of chapels' annual Gymanfa Ganu remains alive and well.

Right: It was Ramoth's turn to host this major Gymanfa Ganu in 1931.

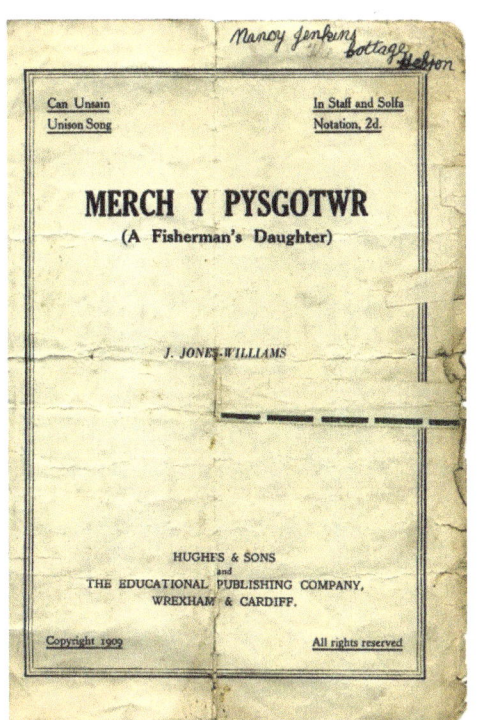

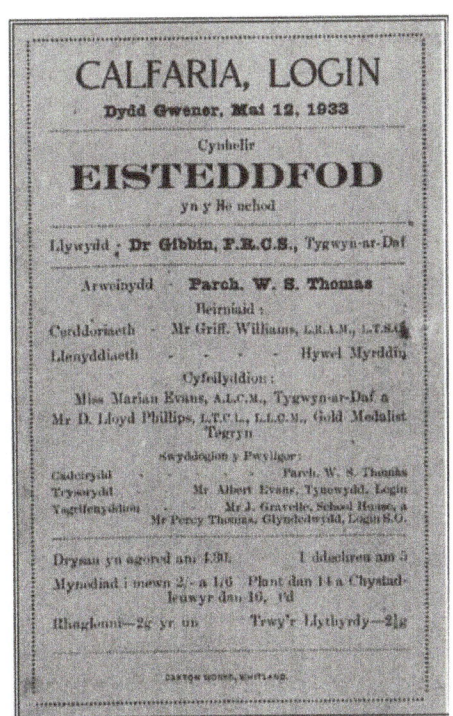

Left: Labelled 'Song for the Young' – it was sung by Nancy Jenkins in the early 1930s.

Right: An unmissable event

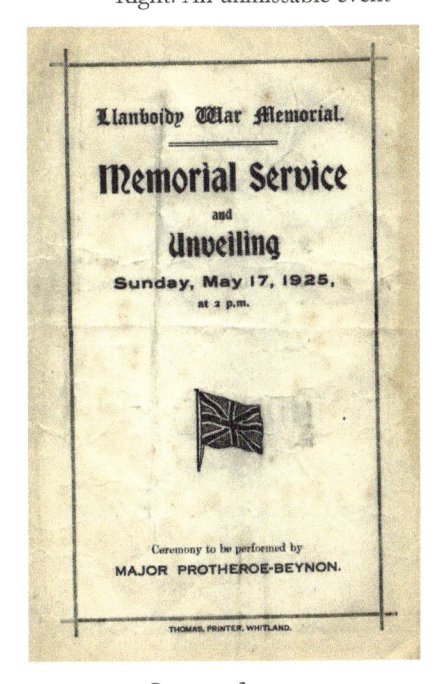

Lest we forget.

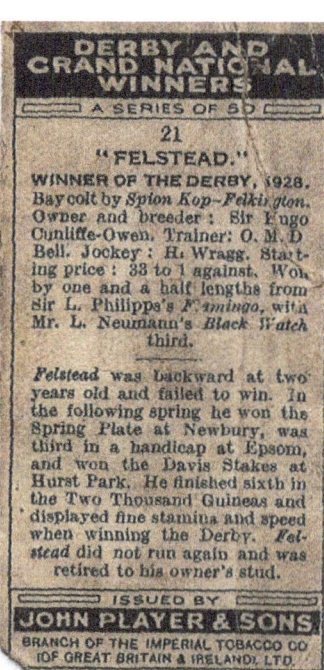

The only surviving card from Heywood's collection.

Ticket to dreamland?

Part II
1938 – 1948: BLAENWAUN COTTAGE AND CANERW
- war, toil and chapel.

2.1 1938 – 1944

2.1.1 Hazards and confinement

In 1938 Heywood and Lil got married and the practice of giving wedding presents (*cwero ty*) - being in full-swing at the time – saw them receive 82 presents which covered most of their basic needs: a Feather Bed and Bolster from Mrs Clarice Phillips of Frowen where they had recently been employed (presumably the boss W J Phillips had a say in it as well). There was a pair of blankets, a pair of sheets and three pillow cases, a hundred weight of coal, two kettles, six teapots, six tea sets, a box of four basins and a dinner service, table cloths, turkish towels, hearth rug, two blanket rugs, table lamp, a boiler from an Ironmonger, numerous jugs and basins, wine glasses, egg cups, butter dish, an American set, a Duchess set, a counterpane, trinket set and ornaments and 10 shillings (50p equivalent to about £28 today). Mr Dan Phillips, a senior deacon at Cefnypant Chapel, gave them a copy of the New Testament.

I was born in *Y Ty Rownd* on 7 April 1938 and given the names William Denley and christened at Cefnypant in July 1938. By that time I had amassed a lot of gifts including a total of £3.12s.6d (£3.625 or about £200 today) plus a few rompers, coats, shoes and socks, toys and six frocks! Two years later my brother Daniel Bryan was the recipient of similar gifts.

In January 1939 Heywood and Lil moved to Blaenwaun Cottage near Canerw Farm where lived Heywood's widowed mother Martha Owen (Mam Canerw) and her two youngest children Glenys (12) and Elfed (11) – pupils at Penygaer School - together with her eldest daughter Martha Ann (24) with her son Ernie (5). I had spent my first eleven months in Y Ty Rownd but that edifice's days as a lived-in cottage ended when my grandparents moved out in September 1939. William and Margaret Ann Jenkins again showed their enterprising nature by taking on a small General Provision Stores and small-holding called Llety on the north-west side of the Taf Valley. They sold groceries and essential goods like paraffin and kept six or eight milking cows. September 1939 was also the month that war was declared between Britain and Germany and chapel communities showed their concern by organising prayer meetings in their search for peace. At the same time community life continued as normal as possible with eisteddfodau and concerts at Llanglydwen and Llanboidy village halls.

Heywood's siblings carried on the tradition of going into service and Gordon and Morfydd found work at Cilsant and Tyisaf farms respectively to where Heywood and Lil delivered them and their boxes – containing their possessions – by trap and pony. Others not involved in farming were called-up for war service and Lil's brother Clifford, a milk-factory employee, enlisted in November 1940 followed by Heywood's brother Spencer, a carpenter, in January 1942. Heywood had a farm to manage and was not required to join the armed forces although I believe he had to make his case for exemption before some board or other in preparation for which he sought advice from a highly respected county councillor S.O. Thomas, Treparce, Trelech. Identity Cards issued during the war and required to be produced on demand by a police officer or member of the armed forces stated that the first Christian name only should be entered in full. It is interesting that 'Daniel H' was correctly entered but it was 'Lilian' rather than her first name 'Phebe' that was entered on Lil's card confirming her dislike of the name 'Phebe'.

Sometime during the early 1940s Heywood did some part-time lorry-driving taking loads of rabbits to Birmingham market. Two drivers were used, one driving to Brecon and the other from Brecon to Birmingham which was Heywood's task - passing through Clyro or through Hay on Wye which involved paying toll at Whitney to get back on to the A438 and on through Leominster and Kidderminster to Birmingham. They travelled during late evening to Brecon where they stayed overnight and then on in the early morning to Birmingham.

Heywood farmed at Canerw for eleven years until 1948 ... living with his family at Blaenwaun Cottage. The cottage was physically attached to the farm house of Blaenpant-teg and situated on the side of the road from Llanboidy to Llanglydwen at the bottom of a sharp hill (*rhiw Penrhiw*) descending from Penrhiw Farm. The lane from Canerw accessed the main road through Blaenpant-teg's farm-yard. The main road continued past Blaenwaun Cottage and a hundred yards further on the ruin of Pant-teg Cottage and its large pool of water (*llyn Pant-teg*) and in another half mile or so it reached Cefnypant Chapel and Llwynon Shop. Blaenwaun Cottage was a small abode with two down rooms (*y gegin a'r parlwr*) separated by two partitions (*palish*) between which there was a passage (*pasej*) as wide as the front door which opened into it. A step ladder led to the attic which was divided by a partition to create two bedrooms one of which had a ceiling (*wedi ei silingo*) - the other did not and was starlit on a clear night. Layer after layer of heavy blankets trapped us in bed in winter and it was a real struggle to get out into the cold-night-air if we needed to pee in the pot (chamber pot). The blankets ensured we were reasonably warm by morning. We bathed in a boat-like zinc-coated container (*badell sinc*) in front of the fire. The front of Blaenwaun Cottage ran parallel to the main road from which it was separated by a yard-wide strip of land, a low boundary fence and an open one-foot-deep drainage gutter (*gwter*) for the road's surface water. A blue flagstone bridged the *gwter* directly opposite the front door and one end of the flagstone rested on the main road! The front door was the only access to the cottage and coming out and turning right led past a corrugated zinc-sheet-clad lean-to at the side and on to a few steps up to the garden surrounded by a tall hedge. At the top of the garden was the toilet (*ty bach*). In the lean-to odds-and-ends were stored and in particular chopped wood and culm for the fire. Culm (*cwlwm*) was made from coal dust and clay mix and I remember Heywood making *cwlwm* by damping the dust and clay mix and stepping on it relentlessly to complete the process of turning it into *cwlwm*. Stored in a heap in the lean-to, when *cwlwm* was needed for the fire a bucket-full was taken into the cottage and then a hand-held device was used to make cylinders of culm of about 3inches in length and in diameter called 'balls' (*bols neu pele*). These were placed on the fire in the grate where they gave off a considerable amount of heat. Last thing before bed at night the fire was capped (*stwmo'r tan*) by covering it with a half inch layer of *cwlwm*. The fire smouldered quietly all night underneath its cap and in the morning the poker was plunged into the *cwlwm* layer and tongues of flame would burst forth through the holes and the kettle placed on them was soon boiling. The fire never went out (*y tân byth mâs*) and on one side of the fire grate there was a small oven (*ffwrn*) for cooking and it was also used to warm washed and ironed clothes (*caledi dillad*). One of my first memories is a rather sad one of returning late one evening to the cottage with Heywood and Lil from a visit to Canerw and Lil bursting into tears on realizing that the smell of burning came from scorched clothes in the oven - she had forgotten to take them out before leaving earlier in the day - a sizeable bundle of charred ashes was removed and the tone of desperation in her tearful question as to how they were going to replace them (*shwt yn y byd gewn ni rei arall*) had me struggling to keep back the tears but as always Heywood's reassuring words that they would cope (*ddew ni i ben a hi*) and the lateness of the hour soon got me off to sleep - but probably not them.

Water at Blaenwaun Cottage, piped from a Well at the top of a field belonging to Blaenpant-teg, was available from an outside tap near the shed. Electricity there was none because even though the National Grid had been in existence since 1933, only the towns were connected to it. In Blaenwaun Cottage an oil lamp lit the living room/kitchen in the evenings and a candle in its boat-like holder, which we called a *shandler*, guided us to the attic bedrooms. We had a 'wireless' (radio) which was not something found in every home in the 1940s. No doubt it was Lil's influence that ensured we had that latest means of communication to entertain and inform us. The 'wireless' in those days required a wet battery and a dry battery to reproduce the sound. The wet battery provided the energy to heat the filaments of the valves and needed regular re-charging and therefore had to be taken to someone who had an electricity generator. One such person was Gwilym Lewis, Llwyncroi

Farm, Llanboidy whose main interest was motor mechanics rather than farming and his expertise was increasingly sought-after as tractors and cars arrived in the area. Gwilym was a very genuine person and would not dream of doing what he considered unnecessary work on a vehicle. Years later when Heywood sought his assistance to locate the source of an irritating squeak in his car, Gwilym, without looking at the car, blamed the dry weather and his advice was not to worry, all would be well after a good downpour! So far as the 'wireless' was concerned there was often a problem because the battery-charging-cycle got out of sync. and eagerly awaited programmes such as the war-time favourites 'Welsh Rarebit' and 'Home Fires Burning' would then be missed. In 1945 the BBC Welsh region was revived.

In those days householders had to make their own arrangements for disposing rubbish; there was no waste collection service. Most of the waste generated was paper in the form of newspapers and bags and also a few metal cans and sauce bottles. Glass pop bottles would be returned to the shop and there were no plastic bags. Paper was useful in the toilet and to light fires. The cans and any other non-useful waste like sauce bottles were dumped in a disused quarry known as *Cware Mowr* near the village of Llanboidy.

My memories of living at Blaenwaun Cottage are rather dominated by a sense of confinement within the two-up/two-down cottage and the small garden at the side. Lil was reluctant to let us roam outside the boundaries because the main road was only a yard from the front door and she dreaded the thought of us being run over by one of the vehicles that very rarely chugged past. A little further along the road a pool (*llyn Pant-teg*) among the ruins of Pant-teg was another danger spot. The obvious 'play-ground' for us was Canerw fields, just down the lane from our cottage but one of the fields contained unfenced clay pits (*pwlle clei*) - some being 'bottomless'! - unused for at least 10 years they were by then full of water and there was no chance of us being allowed near them. Two hundred yards from Blaenwaun Cottage towards Llanboidy at Penrhiw lived Gwilym and Megan Davies and their daughter Merle who visited us to play but I was too shy or too selfish to share what toys I had with her and I spent a lot of time under the living room table. Merle was a few years older than me and our paths rarely crossed because she attended chapel and school in Llanboidy which was in a direction directly opposite to Cefnypant and Penygaer. Myrddin who lived next door at Blaenpant-teg was three years older than me but spent a lot of time with his uncle and aunt a few miles away and when he was at home he also attended school at Llanboidy.

Tragedy was never far away in those medicine-deficient times and Mary Ann Davies next door had known more than her fair share having lost a baby Thomas in 1927, her eldest son Perris age 7 in 1930, her husband Edwin age 58 in 1936 and another son Hywel age 11 in 1944. I remember Heywood taking turns with others to watch over Hywel all-night (*gwylad*) towards the end of his illness which I think was diphtheria.

During their year or so together at Frowen, Heywood and Lil clearly developed friendly relations with the boss Joshua Phillips and his wife Clarice and during the 1940s we as a family would walk the mile from Blaenwaun Cottage to Frowen once a year for supper. After the meal, Heywood and Lil and Joshua and Clarice would sit and talk and gossip in a small sitting room until late into the night. Bryan and myself would be entertained in the farmhouse dining room (*gegin*) by Megan, the maid. Or perhaps it was us who entertained Megan. The walk home invariably afforded us a wonderful opportunity to study, or at least stare at, the starlit sky and to follow the old man strolling on the moon.

Lil talked a lot about our relatives and the seeds of my interest in family history were undoubtedly sown at that time. Almost every relative was resident within the greater Taf Valley area and we visited as many as was possible in those pre-car days. I remember walking about a mile from Blaenwaun Cottage to Plasybwci, Llanboidy to call on Lil's grandmother (*mamgu*) Plasybwci, Phebe Jenkins (nee Reynolds)(1865-1956) and seeing a fairly rotund lady dressed from head to foot in black clothes. I also have a recollection of visiting Ietgoch, Garnwen to see Lil's grandfather Gad Griffiths (1870-1946). Ietgoch was nearly 5 miles from Blaenwaun Cottage and we might well have travelled there by pony and trap (*poni a bodi fach*) and had a break on the way with Lil's parents at Llety. Aunt Phebe Hughes (nee Griffiths)(1897-1976), Mamgu Llety's sister, lived in Crymych and we visited her on *diwrnod Ffair Crymych* (Crymych Fair day) at the end of August. We knew of Lil's Uncle Ben Griffiths (1895-1959) of Llangranog and her Aunt Lisi George (nee Griffiths)(1900-1976) of Glynteg, Llandisilio and also her Aunt Blodwen Griffiths (1903-2001) of Ietgoch and her Uncle Jack Griffiths (1904-1989) at Cwmfelin Mynach.

On her father's side there was her uncles Ben Jenkins (1888-1955) of Meidrim, Jack Jenkins (1896-1967) of Maesgwynne Lodge, Llanboidy, Tom Jenkins (1892-1985) of Plasybwci, Emlyn Jenkins (1904-1967) of Llangynin and Aunt Lisi Morris (nee Jenkins)(1910-1978) of Wern, Cwmfelin Mynach. And of course cousins too numerous to mention here.

Heywood had many uncles and aunts on his father's side although three out of seven uncles and one out of three aunts had died by 1945. Aunt Betsy Wheeler (nee Owen) (1876-1930) Cwmpib, Maenclochog, and uncles David Owen (1879-1940), Castell, Penffordd, Ben Owen (1889-1944), Twmpath, Maenclochog and Hugh Owen (1896-1945), Bronygaer, Llandysilio were buried in churchyards at New Moat Church, Penffordd Chapel, New Cemetry Maenclochog and Bethesda Baptist Chapel respectively and as the years went by the area's cemeteries were gradually added to by more of Heywood's deceased uncles, aunts and cousins; many at very young ages. Lil's interest in family matters never waned and as time went on an increasing number of graveyards were visited on a fairly regular basis in Maenclochog, Llawhaden, Ambleston and surrounding areas.

2.1.2 A year on the farm

To return to Blaenwaun Cottage, it was not all captivity for us in the 1940s because every summer Lil, Bryan and myself spent a lot of time at Canerw helping out with hay-making. It was the days of loose hay (*gwair rhydd*) - the baler had not yet arrived - and the whole process of hay-making was very labour intensive. Men and women worked in the fields - 'shaking' (*ysgwyd*) the hay using pitchforks (*bicwarchau*) to assist the turner (*trowr*) in the task of drying the hay as quickly as possible while the sun shone which it did for most of the summer - although my memory of long, sunny summers must be slightly flawed because I also recall talk of farmers being depressed (*siola*) as a result of the harvest being seriously disrupted by rain. When the hay was judged fit to haul to the shed (*barod i gywain*), a tractor and side-rake (*seid rec*) went into action raking the hay into rows (*tanfeio'r gwair*) which were traversed by a tractor pulling a dray (*gambo*) or trailer to the rear of which a loader would be attached to pick up the rows of hay onto the *gambo* where a man received it and built the load (*llwytho*). The loader was a clever device - simple in design - for loading loose hay onto the *gambo* or trailer and its action never ceased to amaze me and I followed it for hours watching it shifting the rows of hay from the field on to the slowly rising load on the *gambo*. Heywood had bought an Allis Chalmers tractor to do most of the pulling of implements such as the mowing machine (*mashîn lladd gwair*), turner (*trowr*), side-rake and the *gambo* and loader, but the big black Welsh Cob, Bess, was still given the task of pulling the wheeled rake (*rhaca fowr*) to rake (*crafu*) the hay that the loader had missed or that had fallen off the *gambo*. Most of the implements were designed for use with horses but Heywood was very inventive and converted the implements for use with the new tractor. In those days every scrap of hay was raked-up and women and children using hand rakes helped the *rhaca fowr* in this task. The raked hay made into small stacks (*mwdwle*) were manually loaded on to the *gambo* using pitchforks and then taken into the hay shed. Sometimes one of the shire horses would be harnessed to a *gambo* to give an additional unit for carting hay loads to the *ydlan*. I well remember a shire-horse and *gambo* carting hay down the steep hill from Penrhiw to Blaenwaun Cottage. The horse's metal shoes in contact with the tarmac did not provide enough resistance to prevent the horse slipping as the loaded *gambo* 'pushed' the horse down hill. To solve the problem a mechanical device called a *scwt fach* was used as a brake on one of the *gambo's* wheels which resulted in the horse having to exert a gentle pull to overcome the braking and take the load down the hill. The *scwt fach* consisted of a curved metal plate on to which one of the *gambo's* wheels was run and whose other end was fixed to an axle joining two small metal wheels. As the *scwt fach* carried the *gambo* wheel down the hill sparks flew as the metal plate was dragged along the tarmac road.

In the hay yard (*ydlan*) at Canerw the dray (*gambo*) load of hay was pulled up at one end of the hay shed. A mechanical, four pronged metal grabber (*pige*) was lowered on to the hay load by rope and pulley from a small carriage (*carriage bach*) running on a beam fixed along the length of the shed under the corrugated zinc roof. A man, sometimes two, standing on the loaded *gambo* opened out the *pige* and pushed the four prongs as deep as possible into the hay. At the other end of the shed the rope ran off the end of the beam, over a pulley and vertically down to another pulley fixed a yard above ground level suitable for the rope to run horizontally to be attached to a *camren* pulled by a horse whose power lifted the *pige* with its load of hay up to engage with the *carriage bach* and then to be pulled along the beam into the shed. A trailing light rope attached to the *pige* would on instructions from one of the two or three men in the shed be jerked to open the *pige* so as to unload the hay which was then spread evenly to build up the hay in the shed. The light rope was then pulled and pulled so as to return the *carriage bach* and *pige* to the hay load and the whole process repeated until the *gambo* was empty with the hay transferred to the shed. I remember leading Bess as she pulled the *pige* - a prized occupation for children - and I still wonder how I managed to keep my feet clear of her trampling hooves. When it was required to deliver the hay to the far end of the hay-shed Bess was led as far as possible from the shed and the mare's path finished up in a narrow cul-de-sac. The return journey for Bess required reversing out of the cul-de-sac, something that horses do not like doing and Bryan still remembers his horsemanship being tested to the limit as he struggled to get Bess back to square one. At the same time the person pulling back the *carriage bach*, using the light rope, would be exhorting him to get a move on!

When the hay-shed was full (or if a farm had no hay-shed) a hay rick (*rhic wair*) was built in the *ydlan* on a base of tree branches. The rick was covered with a roof of rushes (*brwyn*) and after it was allowed to settle for some weeks the sides of the rick were plucked by hand to remove loose hay leaving the rick with firm sides and water-tight roof. In the 1940s not every farm had all the machinery described above and many did not use a loader but raked by hand the rows (*tanfeie*) of hay into stacks or cocks (*mydylau neu mwdwlau*) and these were lifted using pitchforks (*picwarchau*) on to the *gambo*. Even after the arrival of a loader many an old-stager did not trust such an awkward looking device and continued the time-honoured practice of lifting the hay on to the *gambo* in competition with the mechanical pitchfork! Heywood kept up with developments in the farming world and he dug a silage pit in the *ydlan* at Canerw in the mid 1940s at a time when silage-making was a comparatively new process for storing grass for winter feed. As summer turned into autumn it was time to harvest the corn. A clever device called a binder (*beinder*) cut and bound the corn into sheaves (*ysgubau*) which were collected and stood together in groups of four (*stacane*). After a few days the *stacane* were gathered into groups of 12 and built into a *tâs*, a small rick of 48 *ysgubau*. The *teisi* were left on the field for some time before being carted to the *ydlan* and built into a large *tâs* or rick ready for threshing. A contractor did the threshing and his implements consisted of an engine pulling a massive threshing machine (*dyrnwr*) which he parked at a suitable distance from the corn rick. The engine operated the threshing machine by a pulley and belt system. It was an amazing sight to observe the corn fed into the machine and reappear from three outlets having been threshed into three parts - straw (*gwellt*), chaff (*ûs*) and corn (*llafur*). The straw was built into a rick, the chaff was left in a heap under the machine and the sacks of corn - filled directly from the machine - were carried up steps to a storehouse (*storws*), above the cattle or the horses, and emptied on to the floor. The centre of the loft space was isolated by flat metal sheets (*sinc fflat*) fixed upright about two feet from the walls to prevent rats getting at the mound of stored corn. Threshing was very labour intensive and throughout the day the workers quenched their thirst on home brewed beer - there was no Health and Safety Executive in those days - and as a result, the mood of many was a happy one and the day ended with a crowded room of hungry people enjoying a big super. Unfortunately for me the day ended in the same unhappy way as did the hay-making days with the dust associated with the threshing process triggering my allergy symptoms of itchy-eyes and runny-nose accompanied by violent sneezing. But there was no sympathy, indeed I was a figure of disdain to some of those hard bitten folk and it is little wonder that R. S. Thomas' poetry about his rural parishioners struck a chord when I first came across it and still does! But after laying bare his characters, R. S. Thomas admired greatly the people of the soil, as in this verse from 'A Priest to his People':

> *I have taxed your ignorance of rhyme and sonnet,*
>
> *Your want of deference to the painter's skill,*
>
> *But I know, as I listen, that your speech has in it*
>
> *The source of all poetry, clear as a rill*
>
> *Bubbling from your lips; and what brushwork could equal*
>
> *The artistry of your dwelling on the bare hill?*

Canerw was a dairy farm with a Freisan herd and a surviving Ministry of Agriculture and Fisheries 'License for Bull' shows that in March 1945 a Freisan bull named 'Hebron Advance' born on April 17th 1944 was kept there. The herd was milked by hand twice a day. For this purpose the cows were collected from the fields (*hol da*) and tied in their stalls in the cow-shed (*glowty*) - each cow invariably knew which stall was its own - and drinking water was piped to each stall since plenty of water was essential for milk production. The hind legs of the friskier cows were tied together before the milking-stool (*stôl odro*) was placed in position and the milker took his/her seat, placed a bucket between his/her legs into which milk from the squeezed and pulled teats flowed. Buckets-full of milk were carried to the cool-house (*ty cwler*) which was a corrugated zinc-sheet-clad-shed built on a part of the yard where the ground behind the shed was naturally higher than that in front enabling running water to be piped in at the rear into the top part of the *ty cwler* and there to fill and flow inside a metal device made of two corrugated stainless steel sheets about two ft wide by two ft long and about two inches in depth and mounted vertically. The warm milk from the buckets was poured into a large container from which it ran down and over the water-cooled corrugated surfaces and was thereby cooled and then collected by a funnel containing a muslin or paper tissue filter placed in the opening of a 10 gallon milk churn. When the milk-soaked filter was discarded after a milking session, the farm dogs were waiting to pounce and the first to snap his jaws around the filter would swallow it more or less in one gulp! Once filled, the churn was lifted into a concrete cold-water bath to keep the milk cool. There were about six to ten churns in the bath after the night and morning milking sessions and these were taken by horse and cart to the milk-stand at the entrance to Canerw by Blaenpant-teg from where a milk-lorry collected them once a day for processing at the United Dairies Factory in Whitland. After every milking-session the cowshed (*glowty*) had to be rid (*carthu*) of the dung (*dom da*) produced by the cows while being relieved of their milk. The *dom da* was shovelled into a wheelbarrow (*whilber*) and taken to the dung heap (*y ddomen*) where it remained until the annual dung-spreading (*hala dom*) when it was spread over the fields as nourishment for the grass which as feed for the cows was turned into milk and dung and so on ...

In winter the cows were kept in the cowshed (*glowty*), tied in their stalls, (*côr*) all day and were fed twice a day which involved carrying hay from the hay-shed to the walk (*wâc*) in front of the mangers (*manshieri*) into which the hay was placed. In winter, *carthu'r glowty* was a very physically demanding job. Evening milking in the winter required half-a-dozen oil lamps to light-up the *glowty*. As I remember the lamps were a mixture; a few were the so called hurricane lamps in which a wick soaked in oil burned inside a glass globe; the others were oil pressure-lamps in which oil issued into a mantle and burned brightly with a hissing noise. The pressure in these lamps gradually decreased with time and every so often they had to be 'pumped up' to regain their brightness. Dairy farming was the main industry in west Wales in the 1940s and it involved heavy manual work and long hours. In winter Bryan and myself went for days without seeing Heywood because he had gone to Canerw before we got up in the morning and we were in bed asleep before he got home at night!

A few days before Christmas the geese at Canerw were killed, feathered and trussed ready to be sold for Christmas dinner tables. Their wings were kept for use as feather dusters. Lil and other helpers joined Heywood, Elfed, Morfydd and Mam Canerw and they worked all day in an outbuilding which gradually filled with fine feathers and at the end of the day the workforce emerged like large feathered birds, tired but pleased with a good day's work.

Every Christmas Day while living at Blaenwaun Cottage we spent in Canerw where we took our presents of an orange, dates, pencil, notebook and a few other odds and ends and enjoyed a goose dinner, played games in the afternoon, had Christmas cake for tea and cold meat for supper. I remember an unusual present we had one Christmas of a toy horse and cart. They had bought two plastic horses about four inches long and Heywood had made two carts out of plywood and the horses were taped between the shafts. We had hours of pleasure with the home-made model of something that was very familiar to us in those pre-car days. During Christmas day meals Heywood would keep us laughing with stories, some made up as he went along such as the tale of how footprints of slightly deformed feet in snow identified the person who made them and revealed that the person had been forced to 'reverse' into a farm entrance when he met a car on the road. Boxing Day we also spent at Canerw and in the afternoon Heywood joined other men from nearby farms ferreting for rabbits and shooting them.

On the morning of New Years day Bryan and myself went around our neighbours wishing them a happy new year in song:

Mae'r flwyddyn newydd wedi dod

Y flwyddyn orau fu erioed

O hapus flwyddyn newydd

O hapus flwyddyn newydd

A blwyddyn newydd dda!

This was repeated until someone from the house answered the door with their donations (*calennig*). The performance was called-off at mid-day because continuing into the afternoon was supposed to bring bad luck all round. I was never convinced of the truth of that rule because as far as I could make out the only effect on children that did not obey it was that their pockets were much heavier than ours at the end of their performance!

During the war, food shortage was a spur to increase agricultural production. The County Agricultural Committee insisted on more land being ploughed and the 215,000 hectares of arable land in 1939 was more than doubled by 1944. Corn and potatoes were the main crops. This extra work called for more machinery and for more agricultural workers. The number of tractors on Wales' farms increased from 1,932 in 1938 to 13,652 in 1946. The day of mechanized farming was dawning in Wales. There was no great increase in numbers of farm servants but their numbers was added to, temporarily, by the 'land army' of girls and of conscientious objectors as well as prisoners of war. I remember hearing about Italians and Poles working somewhere in the area. Agricultural Wages and Farm Incomes shot up; the minimum wage increased from £1.14s.0d (£1.70) in 1939 to £3.5s.0d (£3.25) in 1943. It was estimated that net incomes of farms in Britain increased by 207% between 1938 and 1942. Since many farmers were involved in the 'black market' the figure was most certainly an under estimate. Food was rationed and by 1942 'points' were required to buy ordinary food except bread and potatoes. The following year a person was allowed 1lb of meat, 4 oz of bacon, 2 oz of butter, 1 oz of sweets and $6/10^{th}$ of an egg every week which worked out to be 3 eggs every 5 weeks. The rationing continued after the war and it was 1954 before butter, cheese, margarine, cooking fat, meat and bacon came off rationing. Bread rationing was introduced after the war, in 1946, because Britain had run out of money and could not afford to import wheat from America! But things improved and bread came off rationing in 1948. I do not think that we were too worried by rationing, after all, farmers were well placed to get round the rationing limits but perhaps it explains our diet being high in bread-and-tea (*bara te*) and rabbit meat and rabbit soup (*cawl gwningen*) which were not rationed.

In the spring, during the war, the Allis Chalmers was hard at work at Canerw ploughing (*aredig*) a field or two and after further treatment with a disc (*disg*) and a harrow (*oged*) the fields were re-seeded with grass or/and sown with corn. Heywood walked back-and-fore across the fields spreading seeds by hand from a bucket hanging around his neck. Later he bought a device called a 'fiddle' for doing this work - the fiddle still had to be hung around his neck and he still had to cover the fields on foot but instead of spreading seeds by hand he now moved a lever back-and-fore continually - this caused the seeds to be mechanically dispersed over the land. Heywood seemed to undertake this extremely tiring work in his stride. In later years he let-on that he was hired by other farmers to do jobs like this because they were too lazy to do the work themselves!

The barn (*ysgubor*) was another busy place where for example, chaffing of straw (*gwellt*) and gorse (*eithin*) took place to feed Bess and the other horses. The chaff-cutter was a dangerous implement consisting of a large flywheel with knives forming one diameter mounted on a structure allowing feeding of straw and gorse into the path of the spinning knives. It was driven by a pulley-and-belt system connected to the Allis Chalmers. In earlier years a water wheel (*rhôd ddwr*) was used to operate the chaff-cutter. The danger arose from the fact that it was relatively easy for a hand to get trapped and dragged with the straw into the cutter and then systematic chopping of hand and arm proceeded until the contraption was stopped by some means. I knew a man who had lost half his forearm in such an accident.

2.1.3 Mishtir

I started at Penygaer School in 1943. The school stood on its own in the middle of the country on a plot of land donated by a farmer (Mr Gibbin, Penrallt, Login) and was opened in 1883 by W.R.H. Powell M.P. Apparently I gave everyone much trouble when starting school. Heywood had a motorbike and on some mornings I was taken to school riding on the bike's tank, facing backwards burying my face in Heywood's chest. The headteacher was W Rhydderch Evans and we called him *Mishtir* (Master). I created a first for him in that I was the first child to start school with him at Penygaer whose father had also started with him. I well remember being taught to print using chalk on a framed one-foot-square slate. Two years after I started school Bryan joined me on the daily trek. We walked in our clogs – wooden soles with leather uppers - about two miles to school along the same path followed by Heywood a generation earlier. We walked down the lane to Canerw and then across a few fields where we were joined by Marina of Frowenfach and on to Frowen (Davies) where Barbara met us and from there we followed a river through some fields and a wood to reach Plasbach where we emerged on to a road leading down-hill to Lanafon where after crossing the river we joined-up with another group from the Cefnypant area - Gareth and Roderick Reynolds, Glasfryn and Gwen, Eifion , Evelyn, Desmond and Glenmary Griffiths, Waungron – and then we had a 300 yard hill to climb to the school. Halfway up the hill there was a small quarry which had a two-foot diameter hole near its top. In this hole there was a curious purple powder and the story was that it was used to make ink but I never got to the bottom of that tale!

Half-a-mile from the school was a cottage called Clyndedwydd where lived a character called Jack and his family. Jack decided to build himself a new small cart (*bodi fach*) to put behind his pony. He built the cart in the barn and only after completing the job did he realize that the door was not wide enough to get the finished cart outside! Part of the barn wall was demolished to enable Jack to hitch up and make use of his new cart!

On the way home from school we usually walked a route on the opposite side of the river to the one we followed in the morning. This took us past Brynafon where one of my class mates Bertie Davies and his many brothers lived. After that we negotiated a narrow footbridge over a stream or walked through the stream if the water was low and on to the cottage of Cwm where Dafi and Lisi Reynolds lived. They were the grandparents of Gareth and Roderick, Glasfryn and Lisi was always there with a hearty greeting of welcome. She was a very kind woman and occasionally she would provide us with a real treat - slices of fresh bread and syrup. We loved that quick picnic and it soon caught-on that the first to arrive at Cwm would have the prized slice of a crust. I never seemed to be the first and when I moaned about my bad luck Lisi told me not to grumble as she would cut off the loaf's back-side for me to have my crust! (*paid cintachi ... tora i thîn hi bant i ti 'nawr!*). Dafi Reynolds was a farm labourer at Frowen (Phillips) which was where this route from school reached the main road and where the parting of the ways took place; those living near Cefnypant bearing left up the hill past Tower (*Dyffryn Tawel*) and the rest of us going right up to Frowen (Davies) and then left through the fields towards Canerw and Blaenwaun Cottage.

Penygaer was a two-room, two-teacher school and I remember the little-room (*rhwm-bach*) teacher, Miss Gibbon, reading a story about a giant chasing children in a forest. When I found myself one morning on the way to school on my own in the forest I was terrified of meeting the giant and actually crept around every turn in the path to check that it was all clear ahead! In the big-classroom (*rhwm-mowr*) there was an enormous wood and coal burning stove around which we congregated on a cold day. Hanging on one wall of this classroom was a huge framed picture composed of the heads of all of England's kings and queens. The land on one side of the school building was a reasonably flat strip 10 yards wide and 50 yards long and part of it was cultivated as a garden by the older boys. The rest of the land sloped markedly down towards a stream but was walled off well short of the water. There was a circular track in the middle of the sloping playground which we referred to, mysteriously, as *y gôls* around which we ran our runs during the endless games of rounders. I remember a group of us accompanied by *Mishtir* climbing over the playground wall on to a flat field to do some training in relay running prior to the area sports meeting at St Clears. I think the four runners were Eifion, Gareth, Rhythwyn and myself and we were not a bad outfit. But it has to be realised that attending such a major event was an experience well outside our normal environment and I for one felt bemused and lost before we arrived at St Clears. *Mishtir* took us around the running track to get us acclimatised and placed us in the appropriate positions to receive the relay baton. He left me - the final runner - at the side of the track near the final take-over station saying '*arhoswch chi fan na*' (you stay there). I still do not know whether I should have known which lane to stand in or whether some official was supposed to sort things out. I did not have the confidence to ask anyone and the result was that I became one of the crowd and our third runner could not find me and needless to say we did not win!

When I started school I took sandwiches for the mid-day meal which was eaten in the classroom and we continued to eat in the classroom when, later, hot lunches were delivered by car from the canteen of Llanboidy School. A few weeks before the end of my last term at Penygaer in the summer of 1949, Henry Thomas a builder from Llandisilio arrived to build a canteen on the land previously used as a garden.

The war with Germany was in full swing during my early years at school and I remember evacuees arriving in the area and many English pupils attended the school for a short time. One day an aeroplane was circling overhead and *Mishtir* evacuated the school and led the pupils about 200 yards down the road to shelter under a road bridge at Lanafon. We stood in the water for a few hours before the aeroplane moved off and *Mishtir* sounded the all-clear and the wet-footed army returned to barracks. Next day's attendance was down because many had developed colds! Over the war years I dreaded the morning-break at school because during it we were 'forced' to drink a milk-substitute made by adding hot water to a yellow powder which resulted in a glass-full of yellow liquid topped by a slimy yellow-green crust. Even though I was reduced to bouts of vomiting Miss Gibbon insisted that every drop be drunk. Every night I prayed for fine weather so that we would be allowed outside to have our drink. It was fairly easy to wander with glass in hand over to the low boundary wall and pour the stuff into the field and to this day there is a bare patch where the concoction landed! One boy professed to liking the yellow liquid and often volunteered to drink other pupils' milk but invariably he dashed to the toilet and be violently sick before returning to the classroom!

An incident I remember well happened after I had progressed to the big-room (*rhwm-mowr*). A big commotion was heard in the small-room (*rhwm-bach*) which attracted a visit from *Mishtir* and he soon returned with a concerned look on his face and announced that Bryan, whom he was half carrying, had swallowed a button. *Mishtir* carried him outside and instructed me to follow. He then got hold of his bike and put Bryan on it and wheeled the bike down the road glancing around to check that I was in tow. As I trotted after them I assumed from what I'd seen that it was vital that Bryan's feet did not touch the ground and I was intrigued as to how *Mishtir* would negotiate the style that awaited the convoy about 400 yards further on at Plasbach where our way home left the main road. But when we reached the style *Mishtir*, unceremoniously, took Bryan off the bike and dumped him on the road and put me in charge of walking him the one and three-quarter mile to Blaenwaun Cottage with clear instructions for Lil to keep him home until the button was found in the 'thing' (*y peth*) that he passed. It took a day or two for the button to come through after which Bryan resumed his school attendance having enjoyed a short holiday.

Another incident involving Bryan became the core message of one of *Mishtir's* sermons - he preached most Sundays in one of the areas' numerous chapels. It happened that a piece of writing produced in class by Bryan was covered in blots of ink which often happened when writing with a pen repeatedly dipped in a bottle of ink which was the practice in those days. *Mishtir* was very displeased and tore out the blotted page and instructed Bryan to take it home to show Lil. Next morning *Mishtir* asked Bryan for Lil's response to which the reply was that Mam thought it was very good ! 'Very good!? - but what did she say about the blots? Oh! Mam did not see the blots, Sir !' The exchange delighted *Mishtir* as it was a marvellous example of the truth of the Welsh proverb: '*Gwyn y gwel y frân ei chyw*' ! (A mother sees only the best in her child). He commemorated the incident in verse :

Llygad Mam

Un diamynedd oeddwn
Yn 'f ysgol, 'slawer dydd,
'Roedd gweled blots ar lyfr
Yn gyrru mellt yn rhydd.

Un dydd mi roddais draethawd
I blant bach "Standard Two",
'Sgrifennu am eu cartref
A'r oll ynglun a nhw

Gan un mi gefais draethawd
Y gorau er's mawr dro,
Ond O! y blots oedd arno
A'm gyrrodd i o'm co'.

Mi dorrais mas y ddalen
A'm tymer megis fflam,
Gorchymyn wnes i'r bachgen
Ei ddangos ef i'w Fam.

A thrannoeth daeth y bachgen
A'i wyneb fel y wawr,
Yn dweud, fod Mam, 'rol darllen
Yn rhoi canmoliaeth mawr.

Ond beth am yr holl flotiau
A'i dweud wnaeth hi, 'sdim ots?
Na, Syr, atebai'r bachgen'
Ni welodd Mam y blots.

W Rhydderch Evans [Mishtir]
Ysgol Gynradd Penygaer, Login

Any misgivings I had about starting school soon gave way to eagerness to be there on time for the first lesson which was a story from the Bible narrated and acted by *Mishtir*. I was engrossed in his performance and well remember glancing upwards as Samson brought down the Temple and being relieved that the roof, despite all the pulling and grunting, was safely in place. Today *Mishtir* would, probably, be a successful actor or perhaps a writer. A humorous column appeared in the *The Weekly News*, circulating mainly in the Whitland and Narberth areas, which recorded the adventures of a Wanderer (*Y Crwydryn*) roaming the Preseli hills from his base in a small zinc shed (*y shed fach sinc*). The author described the antics of identifiable characters in that wonderful rural area and every article was signed '*Y Crwydryn*'.

Eventually his long suspected identity was confirmed as being *Mishtir*. The articles appeared over a period of more than 20 years. W Rhydderch Evans was born in Abergwili near Carmarthen and I remember him organising a trip for parents and children to visit a special garden in Abergwili called *Gardd Eden* (Garden of Eden) where Biblical characters from the Old Testament had been formed from box shrub hedges. It was an eye opener and a slightly frightening experience for me to be confronted around every corner by another of the Old Testament patriarchs who, from what I had read and been told about and had seen pictures of in Sunday School, seemed to be most unattractive characters.

At Penygaer School we were taught reading, writing and arithmetic through the medium of our first language of Welsh although the arithmetic terms were a mixture of Welsh and English ones. 'Addition' was 'adio', 'subtraction' was 'tynnu i ffwrdd' or 'subtracto', 'divide' was 'rhannu' or 'divido' and 'multiplication' was 'multiplio'. We had to learn the multiplication tables up to 12 times and in arithmetic we were taught how to work out fractions and to add, subtract, multiply and divide money in pounds (£), shillings (s) and pence (d). We used 'imperial units' to measure length (inches, feet, yards and miles) and mass (ounces, pounds and tons). Calculations had to be computed in our heads and all our workings, including crossings- out shown on paper; there were no pocket calculators in those days.

2.1.4 That telegram

Growing up during the war meant gas masks, blackout, rationing and very little activity outside of attending school and going to chapel on Sunday morning and afternoon. I can vaguely remember having to try on my gas mask and of being unhappy at the thought of having to wear it for any length of time. Bryan was young enough to qualify for a contraption in which he was completely enclosed to protect him from a gas attack but as far as I remember the device never arrived. Every night in Blaenwaun Cottage a thick grey blanket (army blanket) was fixed with drawing pins over the living-room window to prevent light 'leaking' to the outside world to make us a target for German bombers. One Sunday I watched the Home Guard training in the fields opposite Blaenwaun Cottage and felt that it was all rather mysterious and slightly frightening. There was another organization called the Local Defence Volunteers one of whose duties was monitoring traffic movement at night. There were very few cars around so I would imagine the volunteers' main problem was keeping awake. There was talk about an incident when a car ignored signals to halt at Cefnbrafle cross-roads and was allowed to continue although the LDV had the right to shoot to enforce their orders. I think the organization was soon absorbed into the Home Guard. I have a recollection of talk about bombs falling on Swansea. I now know that the Lufftwaffe made 44 sorties on Swansea between 1940 and 1943 and 369 people died with 230 of them killed on the three nights of blitz on 19, 20, 21 February 1941. The centre of the town was flattened and it was still in a derelict state in the early 1950s when I went there on a bus trip with Cefnypant young people.

It goes without saying that the outbreak of war had a depressing effect on people's morale. They worried about what lay in store for the men called up to fight and they wondered how long Hitler was going to delay before invading. Community leaders did their best to raise people's spirits. Local ministers produced booklets of light verses and limericks for use by chapel groups and village parties, such as *Seiniau'r Sien* (Sounds of the Sien) from Cwmbach, Llanwinio, to entertain audiences in vestries and halls. The Reverend T. Elfyn Jones of Llanboidy was the author of *Y Bibell Glai* (The Clay Pipe) and the Reverend S. L. Owen of Cwmbach wrote *Go 'With a Go Dde* (The Wrong Way About and The Right Way About). A schoolmaster from Bwlchygroes near Crymych, W. R. Evans, produced a booklet of light entertainment *Pennill a Thonc* and established what became the most well known and highly regarded concert party in west Wales *Bois y Frenni*. Lil's brother Vince was a member. W.R. was called-up and served in the Air-force but he still found time to write a second volume of verses, sketches and limericks, *Hwyl a Sbri*, for his beloved *Bois y Frenni*. In 1996 a stone monument in memory of W R Evans (1910-1991) was erected at Glynsaithmaen, Mynachlogddu where he was brought up. Foel Cwm Cerwyn, the highest peak in the Preseli Hills forms an appropriate backdrop.

In early 1944 Clifford, Lil's elder brother, visited us in Blaenwaun Cottage in his army uniform. He was home on leave but 3914425 Private Clifford Jenkins was soon to rejoin The Monmouthshire Regiment's 3rd Battalion and the likelihood was that he would be part of the long awaited invasion of mainland Europe. He was doing his rounds saying good-by to the family. Before joining-up Clifford worked at St Clears Milk Factory. I was 6 years-old but I remember being scared of the soldier. A few days later he walked from his home to St Clears Rail Station calling on the way at Llangynin School to give his children 13-year-old Joan and 10-year-old Bertie a final hug. In July a letter dated 11/7/44 arrived at Blaenwaun Cottage from Clifford in which he wrote that he had been in the front line for a few days but had then returned for a rest. He asked about the progress of hay-making and wondered if

Heywood was still following the sports meetings. He added that Dinah (his wife) sent *The Welshman* (a local weekly) to him so he could keep-up with current news. He asked to be remembered to Denley and Bryan, writing that : 'They will hardly know me when they see me next', and finished with : 'Hoping to see you quite soon with the war over. Drop me a line some time. All the best, Clifford'.

In another letter on 27/7/44 he wrote: '3914425 Private Jenkins, D Company, 3rd Battalion, The Monmouthshire Regiment, British Western Expeditionary Force.

My dear Sister and all,

Thanks very much for the letter I received this week. It was very interesting to hear from you again. I am sure you are having a good time in all those sports. I wish I was following them myself. I was pleased to find that you are all quite well. Remember me to Denley and Bryan. Can they recollect seeing me? I expect Denley can. Do you remember how he used to gather all his toys together when he saw me coming? Canerw seem to have had good luck with their hay. I was very sorry to hear about Heywood's cousin. He was very unfortunate. It is just a matter of luck. Mine has held good so far. I am now in a rest area behind the line. We have our old choir going again and were recorded by the B.B.C. today. Frank Gillard the reporter was here as well. Sounds as if we are here for a holiday but you can take it from me we do our share in between. If the news is right the war should not last much longer. It can not finish a moment too soon for me. I am fed up with it all. I have no news. Write again soon. Cofion gore , Clifford.'

That was the last letter we received from Clifford.

About a week later I overheard Heywood and Lil say that Cliff was reported missing in France. And then one day in early August Lil, Bryan and myself were returning from shopping in Cwmfelin Mynach when we were met at Penrhiw Farm by our neighbour Gwilym Davies. I heard mention of a 'telegram' and Lil was suddenly in tears as we continued the short walk to Blaenwaun Cottage. Eventually she was able to tell me to go to Canerw to tell Heywood that *wncwl* Cliff had been killed in Normandy. Heywood came home to comfort Lil and later the sadness was interrupted when a hired car stopped outside Blaenwaun Cottage and Lil joined her parents William and Margaret Ann Jenkins in Eben Jones' car to go to visit Clifford's widow Dinah and her children Joan and Bertie who lived about four miles away in Bodathro, Llangynin.

It turned out that Clifford was killed by a sniper in the bocage area of Normandy. His battalion was involved in heavy fighting on Le Perrier Ridge around Sourdeval south of Vire. It seems that Clifford survived the bloody fighting around Perrier Ridge because he was more likely to have been shot by a sniper (which was the claim) during the pursuit of the retreating enemy.

Clifford died of his wounds on the 14 August 1944 in a hospital and is buried in St Charles de Percy War Cemetry, 6 miles north-east of Vire on the road towards Caen in bocage country. He is commemorated in perpetuity by the Commonwealth War Graves Commission as follows:

In Memory of Private Clifford Jenkins,
3914425, 3rd Bn., Monmouthshire Regiment
who died age 32 on 14 August 1944.
Son of William and Margaret Annie Jenkins;
husband of Dinah Olwen Jenkins, of St Clears, Carmarthenshire.
Remembered with honour
St Charles de Percy War Cemetry.

His name is also listed on the War Memorial at St Clears, Carmarthenshire.

Thankfully many soldiers survived the war and concerts were organized to welcome them home. Heywood, Bryan and myself attended one or two welcome-home concerts in Cefnypant but Lil stayed away (*alla i byth mynd*). But we all attended a Memorial Service to Clifford held at Rhydyceisiaid Chapel, Llangynin on Sunday 10th Sepember 1944 and Lil also attended a Memorial Service to Welsh Forces at Brecon Cathedral held at 3pm on Thursday, September 19th, 1946. The ticket for the service was with the letters.

2.2 1944 – 1948

2.2.1 Motorbikes, buses and cars

After the war the numbers of eisteddfodau, penny readings, plays, concerts and fairs returned to their pre-war levels. We only competed in the Cefnypant penny reading; having a go at the recitations, answering ten questions and reading aloud an un-punctuated paragraph and trying to make it sound sensible. We did not meet with much success but satisfied ourselves that it was not winning but taking part that was important. I enjoyed seeing the entries in the drawing competition and some wonderful drawings of a wheelbarrow were held up by the adjudicator for the audience to appreciate. We went to Crymych eisteddfod on motorbikes. I was sitting on the tank of Heywood's motorbike facing backwards with Lil on the pillion and Bryan was in a similar position on auntie Alice (Heywood's sister) and her fiancé Stan's motorbike.

Heywood's motor bike was a Royal Enfield, built by the Enfield Cycle Company in the north London Borough of Enfield. The company also manufactured rifle parts for another Enfield company the Royal Small Arms Factory and this allowed it the use of the word Royal and from it developed the company motto of a canon with the words 'built like a gun, goes like a bullet'. About 300 yards along the lane from Blaenwaun to Canerw Heywood had built a shed from corrugated zinc sheets to keep his motor bike. There was no room for the bike at Blaenwaun so the shed, half-way down the lane, was convenient for him to get to his motor bike from both Canerw and Blaenwaun. The shed had been built when Heywood was single and had moved from Frowen to take over the farming at Canerw and the location, 300 yards away from the farm house, might well have been chosen so as not to disturb his mother when returning after a late night out. Every now and then the motor bike's engine had to be 'taken down' (tynnu lawr) - I guess that today we would call it a 'service'. Heywood performed that operation himself but his first attempt at servicing the Royal Enfield resulted in a surplus of bits when he reassembled the engine! The situation that he found himself in was similar to that of the character Will Bryan when reassembling a clock in Daniel Owen's (no relation) classic novel Rhys Lewis. Heywood collected the bits of his motor bike, placed them in a sack and carried the load on his back to the nearest mechanic who put the Royal Enfield together again!

More common than Royal Enfields were motor bikes made by the Birmingham Small Arms Company and the bikes were called B.S.A. They were also referred to as 'Blydi Slow Articles'. Other makes of motor bike in those days were A.J.S or '*Asyn Jac Sâr*' made by the A.J. Stevens Company in Wolverhampton and the Triumph Twin. But I have an idea that yet another make, namely the Norton, made by a company founded in 1898 in Birmingham by James Lansdown Norton, had a bit more prestige than the others and Uncle Garfield (Heywood's brother) had one of those.

What with vehicles rolling past within feet of Blaenwaun Cottage's front door, the bottomless pools in the Canerw clay pits, the German bombers overhead and the unconventional motor bike rides, we did well to survive our early years in the 1940s!

Carnivals were very popular after the war and Clarice Phillips of Frowen, where both Heywood and Lil were servants before the war, was somehow involved in me becoming a carnival competitor as an 'Ancient Reaper'. I was dressed in a specially made flannel shirt and a waistcoat and breaches made of homespun cloth. I wore a pair of leggings and boots together with an appropriate hat and sucked at an unlit pipe. Thrown nonchalantly over one shoulder was a model of a scythe with a frame. The moustache, stuck on just before joining the line of competitors, made my eyes water. Bryan was dressed up as 'Little Boy Blue' and carried a carved-out cow's horn which he blew with gusto. Whitland Carnival and Fun Fair organized by the Chamber of Trade in aid of the Town's Improvement Fund was held on Saturday 10 July 1946 in brilliant sunshine according to the *Weekly News*. The paper reported that the ankle competition judge was Dr G. M. Evans of Gwynne Villa. He was better known as *Doctor Bach* (Little Doctor) because he was short and as small of body as his partner in the practice at Whitland, Doctor Phillip Gibbin, was large. Was it his shortness that got him the job of judging ankles? The same report describes how all the carnival competitors led by Pontyberem Silver Band paraded around the town before returning to Parc Dr Owen for judging. In the Class for 6-12 year-olds the first prize was shared between 'Ancient Reaper' (Denley Owen, Llanboidy) and 'Make-do and Mend' (Brenda Mary Davies, Mayfield, Whitland) and the second prize went to 'Nigger Boy' (Owen Griffiths, Whitland) - how times have changed! Later in the year the 'Ancient Reaper' won first prize at Llanboidy Carnival and there must have been other successes which I cannot recall because the celebratory mood at Blaenwaun Cottage lasted for a period longer than seems justified by one success and a half.

It was during those years that Lil suffered terrible toothache. At that time only school children made any sort of regular contact with a dentist and that was on a yearly basis. In general it was as difficult then as it is now to find a dentist on the NHS although for different reasons. It was Doctor Gwyn M. Evans (*Doctor Bach*) who recommended extracting the lot as a cure to Lil's aching teeth. I do not know whether alternative treatment was offered but even if it was it would not have been uncharacteristic of Lil to take a kill-or-cure approach. One day *Doctor Bach* arrived at Blaenwaun Cottage and Bryan and myself were ushered into the *parlwr* and the door closed. Eventually the ordeal in the living room (*gegin*) was over and half the teeth had been extracted. *Doctor Bach* came back a week later for the other half. I do not know where the false teeth came from but Lil was fitted with a complete set before she was 30 years of age.

In the mid-1940s a bus-service started from the Taf Valley to the county town of Carmarthen. The first bus that went past Blaenwaun Cottage had an oval shaped rear window and passengers sat on wooden seats. The service was run by a local bus company called *Thomas and Jones* - Clodwyn Thomas of Efailwen and Idwal Jones of Login. Later the company was known as *Preseli Motors* and today it is run by a grandson of Idwal Jones and is known as *Jones Login*. A prominent local figure namely Dan Phillips of Frowenfach, deacon at Cefnypant and author of an early history of the chapel, was one of the first to make regular use of the bus service to Carmarthen. He walked, with assistance from his walking stick (*ffon*), from his home to Blaenwaun Cottage and sat in the passage to wait for the bus. I also recall Dan Phillips telling us on VE day, when Bryan and myself had found a *Union Jack* to wave, that the war was not yet over and that it was a bit premature to celebrate.

A little earlier the first car arrived in the Llanboidy area and the owner's first major outing was to Whitland but on arrival he had forgotten how to stop the vehicle so he drove round the town and noticed a family taking delivery of a large load of culm which was being tipped on to the pavement. He decided to go round the 'circuit' again and to drive his car into the pile of culm, stalling the engine and sending the family diving for cover! Very few people in the area owned cars in the 1940s and when a car was needed, for example for a marriage or a funeral, people would hire one. The best known car-hirer in the area was Eben Jones from Efailwen and Eben must hold the record for the number of appearances in wedding photographs! It was by hired-car that James (Jim) Owen and members of his family from Felinfoel, Llanelli visited Canerw in about 1945. Jim was Heywood's uncle and had fought in the 1914-1918 World War and it was he that suggested the name Heywood for my father. Lil, Bryan and myself were invited to Canerw to meet Jim, his wife Lizie Mary, their daughter in law Phyllis and her children Jean and Mair. Jim's son Mervyn Heywood was unable to accompany them because of work commitments. Jim was very keen to record the occasion and the chauffeur was clicking a camera all afternoon taking photos of various groups and a special one of Jim sitting with Heywood on the Allis Chalmers tractor.

In the 1940s lorries became increasingly important for transporting goods. But we were into the early 1950s before a friend, Gareth Glasfryn, was able to claim to have seen a six-wheeler in the Cefnypant area! Today, you need look on one side only of many a lorry to see six wheels!

2.2.2 Labour landslide

On the 5 July 1945 a General Election was held - the first for ten years. Because ballot boxes had to be collected from battlefields all over the world the results were not declared until the evening of 25 July 1945. Heywood and Lil listened to the results on the wireless and they were clearly Liberal supporters. They were disappointed by the outcome although my recent check on what actually happened revealed that the eight seats won by the Liberals in Wales was the same number as they had won ten years earlier. Liberal Sir Rhys Hopkin Morris managed to hold on to Carmarthen with a small majority over Labour as did another Liberal Roderick Bowen in Cardiganshire. Lloyd George's daughter Lady Megan retained Anglesey (over Labour's Cledwyn Hughes) and her brother Gwilym held on by 0.4% in Pembrokeshire. At the same time Labour in Wales increased their number of seats by 7 to a total of 25 and in Britain as a whole Labour won a landslide victory winning a total of 393 seats (+239) to the Conservatives 197 (-190), the Liberals 12 (-9) and the National Liberals 11 (-22). Farmers and tenants in rural Wales at that time hung on to the belief that their interests were best served by the Liberals and they must have hoped for a Liberal revival at the 1945 election to restore them to the glory days when Lloyd George ruled the roost. But the near annihilation of the Liberal candidates in England put paid to those hopes. Winston Churchill, the hugely popular war-time Prime Minister and Tory leader, was left wondering what hit him! Before the election he was in a meeting with the USSR Dictator, Stalin, and the USA President, Truman, trying to divide the spoils of victory and he expected to rejoin them after the election. But it was the Labour leader Clem Attlee, an unassuming man of few words, who returned to the meeting to the surprise of both Stalin and Truman.

Bevin, Morrison, Cripps and Aneurin Bevan became household names as they strove to re-build war-ravaged Britain. 'Nationalisation' was a word often heard and it was supposed to be good for railways, coal-mines and steel-works. We felt some pride in that Aneurin Bevan was Welsh and was prepared to stand-up and demand affordable health treatment for ordinary people. Eventually, in 1946, the National Health Service was established to provide for 'free universal medical care'. But Bevan had to give-in to doctors and allow them to treat the rich privately and in N.H.S. Hospitals if necessary.

Despite their obvious interest in the result of the 1945 election I never heard Heywood or Lil talk about the turbulent politics of their youth in the 1930s. They were in their teens as the rise of Fascism in Europe brought Franco, Mussolini and Hitler to the fore while in Britain the Fascist hope Oswald Moseley a former Tory, Independent and Labour MP felt unready to compete in the 1935 election and urged his supporters to abstain under the slogan

'Fascism next time'. Lil was interested in the royal family and they had had their troubles in the 1930s. In 1936 the heavy smoker King George V became very ill and was advised to go for some sea air to Bognor Regis to which he replied 'Bugger Bognor'. Secret papers released in 1986 revealed the startling information that his doctor, Lord Dawson, speeded up his death in-order to get the obituary notice into the morning papers rather than have it mixed-up with the racing results in the evening ones. This information made headline news in the Western Mail on 27 November 1986 and the article was duly cut out and filed away by Lil. Dawson gave the King a lethal injection of morphine and cocaine and the King's last words were 'God damn you'. Technically speaking he was the last English king to be murdered although it was done out of respect for the monarchy. But it could be argued that another way of respecting the king might have been not to kill him. His son succeeded him as Edward VIII about whom George V had despaired of his affairs with married women. He said of him 'After I am dead, that boy will ruin himself in twelve months'. He was wrong, it took only eleven. During that time Edward VIII was forced to choose between the throne and his American companion Mrs Wallis Simpson. He chose the twice divorced Mrs Simpson, abdicated in favour of his brother George VI, and was given the title of Duke of Windsor. I recall Lil talking about the scandal but always in hushed tones reflecting the seriousness with which divorce was viewed in those times.

2.2.3 Chapel events

During our last few years at Blaenwaun Cottage I was trusted to walk with Bryan along the main road, keeping close to the hedge, for a mile to the shop at Llwynon by Cefnypant Chapel. It was before the days of ready packed goods and Mrs Thomas measured the requested quantities of various ingredients on the shopping list such as tea, sugar, butter and if there was flour and margarine on the list we looked forward to Welsh-cakes for tea. Recently, in a second-hand bookshop in Tenby, I came across a Llwynon Shop Invoice made out to an unknown customer.

We walked the same stretch of road to Sunday School. And on most Sundays Heywood, Lil, Bryan and myself would walk to Cefnypant for the afternoon service, often accompanied by Mam Canerw, Morfydd, Elfed and Ernie. Tom Williams, Frowenfach, a neighbouring farm to Canerw, was the Sunday School teacher and we read selected bits of the Bible verse by verse, year after year. Tom was also the precentor (*codwr canu*) in the Sunday afternoon service and he also conducted the chapel choir. The organist was Yvonne Phillips of Cilhernin. Chapel attendance was serious business in those days and I well remember the minister the Reverend Philip E. Price arriving at Blaenwaun Cottage one Monday morning and giving Lil a bit of a telling-off for missing the previous day's service! A major yearly activity associated with the chapel was the door-to-door collection for the missionary movement. Cefnypant Chapel records reveal that door-to-door collection was started in 1942 and was carried out by children, usually one from a household. At the same time all the Sunday School children made a yearly donation to the missionary movement. The names of Bryan and myself appeared on the Sunday School list for the first time in 1944. We made donations of 6d (2.5 pence) each. My name also appeared on the much shorter list of collectors but considering I was only six years old it must have been a team of Lil, Bryan and myself that succeeded in amassing 25 shillings (£1.25) for the missionary cause. Whoever did the collecting it was I that received the book prize which, unlike Heywood's book in 1929, was in Welsh and was entitled *Deuddeg Apostol Arall* gan T. Glyndwr Jones. A year later it was five-year-old Bryan's name that was listed as having collected £1.12s.0d (£1.60). My name was listed for 1946, 1947 and 1948. In 1948 and afterwards the collection was recorded as being for the Missionary Ships (*Y Llongau Cenhadol*). A further two prize books have survived but they are undated. Both books were specially published in 1939 to commemorate the 300th anniversary (1639-1939) of the Independent Chapels. One book, with Bryan's name on it, was entitled *Storiau am yr Annibynwyr* gan E. Curig Davies. It contained pictures of etchings by R. John Petts. The author E. Curig Davies was a native of Glandwr. The second book, with my name on it, was called *Arweinwyr yr Annibynwyr* and its author was J. Rees Jones. We did not take part in collecting in 1949 and 1950 and no one did in 1951. Bryan's name was listed for the last time in 1952 having collected 56 shillings (£2.80). But we continued to attend Sunday School and Bryan did not miss a single Sunday in 1954 for which he was rewarded with yet another book prize. As a mater of information, Glandwr Chapel Sunday School did not take part in door-to-door collections for the *Llongau Cenhadol* until 1950. The practice of door-to-door collections ceased at Cefnypant in 1986 but continued at Glandwr until 1993.

Another religious mater taken very seriously was denominational-ism. I remember Lil's father William Jenkins, a Baptist and member at Calfaria, Login, visiting us at Blaenwaun on a Sunday and accompanying us to a Communion Service in the afternoon at Cefnypant Independent Chapel. When it came to the Communion 'ceremony' he made a quick exit and sat out the 'ceremony' in the lobby. All very mysterious!

The Reverend P. E. Price passed away in 1946 at 70-years-of-age after serving the chapels of Cefnypant and Glandwr for 42 years. The following year a student from Carmarthen College, Edgar J Phillips accepted an invitation to become minister for the two chapels and soon he established a young people's group in Cefnypant which met monthly in the vestry. We listened to others reading 'papers' on various topics and practised sketches and learnt some poetry and songs all of which was presented as entertainment at our Christmas concert.

The star item at the concert every year was a duet sung by Mrs Sarah Ann Phillips, Rosehill and Mr Thomas Williams, Frowen-fach called 'Larboard Watch' although it was much later before I realized the first word of the title was not 'cardboard' but rather it was an archaic word for the port side of a ship! I remember the Reverend Edgar Phillips calling to see us at Cefn just after we moved there. Heywood, unusually, was sporting a day or two's growth of whiskers and Edgar Phillips' enquiry as to whether razor blades were in short supply went down very well with Heywood who enjoyed such familiarity from the Minister!

Lil was caretaker of Cefnypant Chapel for a year or two 1947/1948 and Bryan and myself enjoyed wandering around inside the chapel and delivering a few sermons from the pulpit. It was Lil who brought out from the store-room under the pulpit the bulbous globes to fit over the lamps on either side of the pulpit - they are still in use today!

The pre-war pattern of a chapel-dominated society prevailed in the Taf Valley during the 1940s. In addition to the Sunday services there were three annual events associated with the chapel, namely the *Gymanfa Ganu* (Singing Festival), the *Gymanfa Ysgolion* or *Gymanfa Bwnc* (Sunday Schools Festival) and the Sunday School trip. For the *Gymanfa Ganu* members from seven Taf Valley Independent Chapels - Cefnypant, Glandwr, Hebron, Nebo, Llwyn-yr-hwrdd, Brynmyrnach and Moriah - drew up a programme of hymns in three sections - one section suitable for children was sung in the morning session and the grown-ups had an afternoon and an evening session of singing. It would come-off on a Monday in October under the baton of an invited, renowned conductor and accompanied by a group of violinists (Luther Lewis' group from Drefach in the Gwendraeth Valley) seated in the main pew (*cor mawr*) below the pulpit. The whole proceeding was rehearsed in a big rehearsal (*rihyrsal fawr*) on the preceding Sunday and on several Sunday evenings prior to that rehearsals under the baton of one or two of the chapels' own choir conductors were held over a few months. Cefnypant and Brynmyrnach chapels were too small to accommodate the numbers attending the *rihyrsal fowr* and the *gymanfa* which meant trips for us every year! Admittance to the gallery was by ticket only and queues formed outside the vestry at lunch and tea times. Attending the *rihyrsal fowr* and the *gymanfa* were particularly exciting occasions for the children because after their morning session they would be free to roam and explore the particular area. At Glandwr a 400 yard walk up the road towards Pentregalar led to a field full of goats and much fun was had teasing the unfortunate animals. At Llwynyrhwrdd it was a short stroll to the famous but by then un-worked Glogue slate quarry. Many a new suit of clothes was soiled if not spoiled by frantic games of chase and the occasional fisticuffs between rival chapel gangs in the haunting surrounds of the quarry.

The origin of the festival can be traced to one held in Aberystwyth in 1830 although it was after a *gymanfa* in the Temperance Hall, Aberdâr in 1859 that the festival took-off and in subsequent years singing festivals organized on a denominational basis were held all over Wales. In 1895 the Non-conformist denominations held 280 singing festivals with an average attendance of 500. The total of 140,000 singers was 10% of Wales' population. The *Gymanfa Ganu* had become a National Institution. Looking back it is probably true to say that the late 1940s and early 1950s were the final years of the golden era of the *Gymanfa Ganu* in the Taf Valley and we were highly privileged to be part of that unique festival in that era.

The *Gymanfa Ganu* held at Nebo on Monday 6 October 1941 was a special occasion in that it was dedicated to the memory of Dr Joseph Parry (1841-1903) musician and composer born in Merthyr Tydfil who worked as a miner before his parents took the family to America in 1854. He returned in 1864 to study at the Royal Academy of Music in London and in 1874 he was appointed Professor of Music at the University College of Wales, Aberystwyth. The programme that survived with 'L Owen, Blaenwaun' initialled on the cover contained a brief summary of the composer's life written by the Reverend Elvet Lewis (Elfed). The *Gymanfa* was concerned with Joseph Parry's contribution to hymn singing and the programme contained twelve hymns for children, nineteen hymns for adults and one anthem. The tunes for all the hymns and the anthem were composed by Joseph Parry and included the well known 'Aberystwyth', 'Blaenycoed', 'Sirioldeb' and the anthem 'Teilwng yw'r Oen'. The guest conductor was Edward Lewis from Aberdâr. To their credit the seven chapels mentioned above still hold their *Gymanfa Ganu* in October but the reduced attendance means that Cefnypant and Brynmyrnach are now able to take their turn in holding the event.

The *Gymanfa Ysgolion or Gymanfa Bwnc* (Sunday Schools Festival) involved the children of a chapel learning about a character or an incident from the Bible in the form of questions and answers prepared by the chapel's minister and gone through and rehearsed in Sunday School for about a month prior to the day of the Gymanfa Bwnc. The children's choir was formed and practised a number of children's hymns under the baton of the chapel's children's choirmaster - Edward Eynon (*Ted Penrallt-fach*) in my day who was a wonderfully kind man. At the same time the grown-ups studied some section or chapter from the Bible, practised some hymns and, as the star item, they mastered a new anthem every year. On a Sunday in May three chapels, Cefnypant, Glandwr and Moriah got together for a final rehearsal and in the morning two of the chapels climbed to the gallery in turn to go through their programme (*mynd trwy'u gwaith*) and the third did so in the afternoon. During these sessions each group of grown-ups was questioned in depth by a minister about their understanding of their chosen Biblical topic and sparks sometimes flew as arguments developed into angry exchanges!

Cefnypant's Sunday School trip's destination was invariably the subject of lengthy discussion at a meeting held immediately after Sunday School early in the year. But the end result was always the same -Tenby! And a wonderful day out it invariably was. After an initial tour to pick up the passengers a bus-load headed for the coast and as it got near it's destination the sea eventually came into view and the shout went up - ' '*co'r mor!*' (there's the sea !). From the bus park, families with children made for the North Beach while the elderly prefered the South Beach which we referred to as '*sans Mam Canerw*'. By the time everyone was settled in family groups on the sands it was time for food and arms suddenly plunged into shopping bags and sandwiches were extracted which unavoidably became peppered with sand and as they were being crunched into empty stomachs the mothers tracked across the sands and up some steps to the tea-selling shanties bordering on to the beach to buy pots of tea and of hot water as well as jugs of milk all of which were placed on trays and carried in a careful balancing-act down the steps to the beach where cups of tea soon washed down the sand which had refused to go down with the sandwiches. And that would complete the North Sands picnic for another year! In the afternoon we went for a dip and watched more adventurous youngsters from somewhere else climbing up to the diving board on Goscar Rock which we of course had been lectured not to go near, which was sensible advice considering that we could not swim let alone dive from a great height! During this time and without realising it many of us were lightly cooked in the burning sun and by late afternoon turned colour from the normal whitewash to a pinkish hue which became bright red on the bus home where on arrival sufferers were plastered with pink calamine lotion (if there was any in the cupboard) before suffering a painful and sleepless night and it took several days to fully recover from the annual Sunday School trip to Tenby!

2.2.4 Pony express

Bryan and myself had our first holiday away from home on our own during our last years in Blaenwaun Cottage when we stayed for a few days with our grandparents (Lil's parents) William and Margaret Ann Jenkins, Llety, Hebron. We walked the 3miles from Blaenwaun Cottage to Llety and no doubt were a bit apprehensive when Lil left us there for our vacation because *Mamgu* (grandmother) could be a bit strict with us. Perhaps she had too much work on her hands running the shop and the small dairy farm while *Tadcu* (grandfather) maintained his length of road for the council. He was always very kind to us. Our nervousness manifested itself the first night we were there in the act of one or both of us wetting the bed! Although we decided to report the matter to *Mamgu* I do recall that my attempt to draw her attention away from milking the cows was a pretty feeble inaudible 'shout' from the bedroom window which failed to register. So we decided to forget the whole thing and hope for the best! Nothing was heard about the mishap and the bed was made up and was dry when we next retired there. The toilet at Llety was unusual in that two people could use the place at the same time because the wooden seat had two round holes in it, one larger than the other. But I never saw two people enter or leave the toilet together so the two holes in the seat seemed an unnecessary luxury. The Llety toilet was sited over a small stream and as far as I know did not require cleaning out. The Environment Agency had not been thought of at that time. *Wncwl* (Uncle) Johnny, who also lived at Llety, was a cobbler and we spent most of our days in his shed observing him repairing shoes and making clogs. He was also skilled at making wooden spoons which were always used in those days for drinking *cawl* (soup). Johnny was Sunday School secretary at Hebron from 1941 to 1948.

Owen Jenkins who farmed at Tower (Dyffryn Tawel) was a stalwart at Cefnypant Chapel where he was a deacon and conductor of the choir. He was a horse-man through- and-through; there was no tractor at Tower. His powerful build was a great asset because he travelled to Clunderwen mart in a *bodi fach* (small cart) pulled by a horse he was going to sell. After the sale he himself pulled the cart all of the six miles home! I well remember Owen sitting in his *bodi fach* outside Blaenwaun Cottage offering to take Bryan and myself for a ride. The mare between the shafts of the *bodi fach* was to be served by a stallion at Plasnewydd, Llanboidy about a mile form Blaenwaun Cottage. We were delighted when Lil gave her consent and on the way Owen told us about two new foals born to two of his mares. He had named them Simon Jehosophat and May Queen. After the encounter with the stallion the mare was put between the shafts and we were soon on our way home at a good gallop. Owen started singing and after he spelt out the words the three of us sang-our-heads-off all the way home:

> *Hold the fort for I am coming*
> *In the donkey's cart,*
> *The wheel came off and the shaft was broken*
> *And the donkey stopped to fart.*

Another trip by *bodi fach* and pony around 1946 must have been a terrifying experience for Heywood and Lil and Mam Canerw who would have fully appreciated the dangers that might not have been quite so clear to Bryan and myself. Heywood was very interested in horses and often bought a new horse which he broke-in to pull the *bodi fach*. He may well have bought one from a Mr R S Belton, Trewern Farm, Velindre, Crymmych from whom he received a letter dated April 15th 1945:

'Mr D H Owen, Canerw, Login S.O., Carm.

Dear Sir,

Re yours to hand requirements of Pony I have some now but I have no time for 7 or 8 days and will write you when to come along as I have in view one of the fastest Ponys in wales and have not the time to go and buy same as we have a lot of contract work not finished but will certainly write you when to come along .

Yours faithfully

R S Belton.'

It might well have been 'the fastest Pony in Wales' that Heywood used with a *bodi fach* to take Mam Canerw to Llanglydwen station to catch the train for Cardigan to visit her sister. Lil and Bryan and myself went along for the ride. After passing Trevilla the horse speeded up and Heywood could not stop it galloping - it was out of control (*wedi rhedeg bant*) - and we flew along at full speed past Trehir and along the level road towards Talygarn where the road became a steep hill (*Rhiw Bont*) for a good half-mile down to Llanglydwen. At the top of the hill at Talygarn there was a road leading off sharply to the left and it was vital for the horse and *bodi fach* to be guided on to this road because if the horse did gallop down the hill then a catastrophe was unavoidable. The grown-ups must have been terrified as the runaway approached Talygarn at full speed with Heywood pulling desperately at the reins in an attempt to steer the combination away from the hill - miraculously he succeeded and soon afterwards the incident was over as the horse tired and came to a stop on the flat road. Heywood led the horse and *bodi fach* and we walked down the hill to Llanglydwen Station and Mam Canerw caught the *Cardi Bach* for *Aberteifi* (Cardigan). By then the horse had had its fling and we were able to ride home in the *bodi fach* in comparative calm.

Another incident with another young horse which Heywood was in the process of 'breaking in' occurred when he was trying to put a collar on the horse and the animal swung its head away and in doing so failed to avoid dragging its head through some brambles. It's subsequent behaviour was odd and then it was realised that the horse had lost an eye. It had been pierced in the brambles and the fluid escaped. I recall Heywood saying '*ma un llygad wedi rhedeg*' and being very upset at the mishap but I do not recall what became of the unfortunate animal.

In the 1940s in the Taf Valley and in west Wales in general the horse still played an important role in farming and the training of young horses or 'colt breaking' (*torri ceffyle miwn*) was a skill possessed by only a few practitioners. A well known 'colt breaker' and jockey lived about half a mile from Blaenwaun Cottage at Cwrte Bach. His name was *Dafi Jams* (David James) and I remember seeing him guiding a frisky colt with guide-ropes attached to the colt's halter (*ffrwyn*) along the road past Blaenwaun Cottage - a wonderful sight. 'Colt breaking' could be a dangerous business and *Dafi Jams* suffered a serious accident when the colt he was riding across Cardigan Bridge (*Pont Aberteifi*) suddenly leapt over the side, landed in the river Teifi and caused *Dafi Jams* to break both of his legs. He recovered and resumed his work as 'colt breaker'.

There was a tradition of horse racing in the area and Heywood talked about a racecourse that had existed at Cefnbrafle although it had ceased to be used before his time. In the nineteenth century Llanboidy was listed with Abergavenny and Carmarthen among the main centres of steeplechasing in Britain. The Llanboidy racecourse was at Cefnbrafle, as Heywood had said, and was built in 1851 by W R H Powell of Maesgwynne Mansion whose famed Llanboidy Races had a golden era between 1856 and 1865. The final race meeting at Cefnbrafle took place in 1871.

In the 1940s and 1950s there was horse racing on the flat in the area and at a meeting held at Trehir Farm, Llanglydwen in early 1949 I saw a very promising local rider called Aneurin Evans, a comparatively small and slightly built youngster, mounted on what appeared, at least in comparison, a massive race horse. In June of that year at Carmarthen Races Aneurin's horse fell and a following horse kicked Aneurin in the head and he was killed. It was a terrible tragedy.

As previously mentioned the day-to-day maintenance of roads was the work of 'length men' but major resurfacing was carried out by a gang and the final rolling of the road was performed by a steam roller. I remember a steam-roller pulling a caravan similar to the old Romani caravans going past Blaenwaun Cottage and parking in a lay-by about fifty yards from the cottage. The driver was called Wil *Rhowler*. At the end of the day's work we gathered around the caravan and steam roller and Wil let us have a good look over both - we were fascinated! He was parked there for about two weeks travelling to-and-from work by roller! Eventually he moved to a more convenient parking spot as the resurfacing work gradually moved further away.

In September 1947 the Local Education Authority decided to provide transport for all children living more than two miles from school. By road it was about three miles from Blaenwaun Cottage to Penygaer School but the Authority decided that we did not qualify for school transport because our track to Penygaer through fields and woods was just under two miles! If we were prepared to walk the half mile to Cefnypant we could get into the school car there provided it had room in it! As far as I can remember there was always room in the car and we enjoyed a few months of car trips before disqualifying ourselves by moving to live within a mile from school.

2.2.5 Homework the priority

It was during our last year in Blaenwaun Cottage that a defining moment for our future occurred. One of the best farms in the area, Bronyscawen Farm, Llanboidy, came up for sale. I was about 9 years old and was able to catch snippets of conversation which indicated that Heywood and Lil had decided to seek financial help to make a bid for Bronyscawen. It must have been an attempt to secure a future in farming not only for themselves but for Bryan and myself as well. Their former boss at Frowen, Joshua Phillips, agreed to fund a bid up to a certain limit. On the day of the sale there was a higher bid and that was that. As far as I know Heywood and Lil never again thought about setting us up in farming and I feel sure they had decided or at least hoped consciously or subconsciously that our futures would be secured through education. During the war the Tory minister R. A. Butler took on the task of reforming education. His 1944 Education Act offered free grammar school education to all 11-year-olds who successfully overcame the 11+ (eleven-plus) examination. The outcome was that about a quarter of 11-year-olds went to grammar schools and three-quarters went to secondary modern schools (the proposed third branch of technical schools based on the German model was largely forgotten). Perhaps the idea of buying Bronyscawen Farm indicated Heywood and Lil's doubt about our ability to clear the 11+ hurdle although Lil would not have entertained the idea of 'failure' for long; her favourite saying was 'where there's a will there's a way'. In any case neither of them encouraged us to take too much interest in farming - except later-on during hay-making at Cefn where we actually got to do some milking by hand so that Heywood need not be called from the hay fields to attend to the chore of milking. On the other hand Lil did her best to encourage us to read and despite the difficulty of the nearest book-shop being in Carmarthen - which was rarely visited before 1946 when *Thomas and Jones* began their bus-service - she managed to get hold of the Reverend Joseph Jenkins' Welsh language booklets recounting the adventures of youngsters in a rural environment such as *Meic ac El*, *Ianto a Straeon Eraill*, *Y Llwybrau Gynt Lle Bu'r Gan* and *Helynt Coed y Berw*. Others included Moelona's classic *Teulu Bach Nantoer* and her early-reader about a cat *Mimi* and Kate Roberts' *Deian a Loli*. (Moelona was the pen name of Mary Elizabeth Owen younger sister of the Reverend O.R.Owen sometime minister at Glandwr and Cefnypant Chapels). Bryan and myself devoured these stories as soon as they were handed over. The weekly *Children's Newspaper* was ordered and collected from Cloth Hall Shop, Llanboidy and some of it we were able to read which, on reflection, was proof of the effectiveness of *Mishtir's* weekly English lesson because that was our only encounter with the English language in those days.

Heywood and Lil were avid readers of the local weekly newspapers which were sold in local shops such as Cloth Hall, Llanboidy. Two of them, the *Carmarthen Journal* and *The Welshman* were taken regularly at Blaenwaun. The *Journal* had been established in 1810 and was Conservative in outlook. *The Welshman and General Advertiser for the Principality of Wales* was launched in about 1830. It was considered to be the mouthpiece of the Carmarthen Reform Club and was Whig (Liberal) in outlook. It changed its name to *The Welshman* in 1943 and was bought by the *Carmarthen Journal* in the late 1940s. It ceased publication in 1984.

Once we started to have school homework Lil made sure that it received top priority and every night we sat on the *ffwrwm* (bench) with our backs to the *palish* (partition) separating the kitchen from the passage leading to the front door. And there we stayed until the work was done! No stone was left unturned to ensure that the work was completed even if, a few years later, it meant a late night visit to Plascrwn, Login to seek our Primary School Headmaster's (*Mishtir*) help with Grammar School Algebra !

Lil was very interested in cultural matters. She listened to wireless commentary from the National Eisteddfod at Mountain Ash in 1946. In addition to the cultural content I think she particularly wanted to hear about the visit of Princes Elizabeth to that Eisteddfod because she followed the antics and activities of the Royal Family with considerable interest. I recall seeing in the Western Mail in November 1947 pictures of the wedding of Elizabeth and Philip Mountbatten and reading or being told about some of the guests at the 'do' and being puzzled as to how a 12-year-old boy called Faisal could really be king of Iraq. (Faisal's reign lasted until 1958 when he and his family were murdered in a military coup.) Lil was an alto in Cefnypant Chapel choirs. She took us to most of the eisteddfodau, penny readings, concerts and plays held in the area's chapel vestries, Llanglydwen Village Hall and Llanboidy Market Hall. Like her father and brothers Lil was fluent in Tonic sol-fa having been taught the scale at home and in the chapel vestry. Fluency in Tonic sol-fa was a huge aid in learning the music for four-part singing. Lil with Heywood's help also enjoyed composing verses for special occasions; fitting them to a popular air and having a group to sing them on the occasion. Unfortunately none of the early ones that I know were composed in Blaenwaun Cottage have survived. Although not fluent in Sol-Fa, Heywood was a keen fan of hymn singing and when the BBC started broadcasting *Caniadaeth y Cysegr* on the wireless - half an hour of hymn singing at about 5 o'clock on a Sunday afternoon - he would most surely be listening. The Sunday morning religious service on the wireless was also regularly listened-to while Bryan and myself were packed-off to Sunday School. The four of us attended the Sunday afternoon service (*cwrdd*) at Cefnypant at which four hymns were sung and at least one of them enabled the congregation to generate sound approaching choral standards of harmony and volume. Four-part singing came naturally to most in those days and I remember being roused from deep sleep late on some Saturday nights in Blaenwaun Cottage by the sound of hymn singing from the *parlwr* beneath. Heywood's brother Garfield (no singer) who rode a Norton motorbike had called, together with a few friends such as Chris Pentair-rhiw, Gelliwen and Arthur Pensarn, Cefnypant and they and Lil harmonised some well known hymns. A favourite was a German tune known as Dolwyddelan matched to Penllyn's words:

> *'Nid ar deganau'r llawr*
> *Yn awr y mae fy mryd;*
> *Sylweddau tragwyddoldeb mawr*
> *Yw nhrysor drud;*
> *Rhy wan yw braich o gnawd,*
> *Rhy dlawd yw gorau dyn;*
> *Mae'r Hwn a anwyd i mi'n Frawd*
> *O hyd yr un.'*

It was a wonderful sound (*swn bendigedig*) that was created in our *parlwr* all those years ago in the 1940s.

Lil tried her best to teach Tonic sol-fa to Bryan and myself and we were actually slowly acquiring the skill together with that of playing the mouth-organ during our last year in Blaenwaun Cottage. Unfortunately the practice of teaching Tonic sol-fa in a class in the chapel vestry had ceased by that time in Cefnypant and our own efforts petered out as we turned our attention to preparing for the 11+ exam. Why did we not continue to develop our home-grown musical abilities? Looking back now I feel that the 1944 Education Act changed people's or at least some people's perception of what the future might hold for their children. Before the Act the vast majority of children left school at 14-years-of-age and faced a lifetime of labouring, mostly on local farms. Not surprisingly they hung-on to and developed those skills gained in the home, chapel and primary school environment as a welcome diversion from their daily toil. The 1944 Act changed all that by giving 11-year-olds the chance to break with tradition and enter another world and the key to this new world was to pass the 11+ examination. This challenge must have weighed on parents' minds, to a greater or lesser degree, as their children prepared for the 11+ and unfortunately, but understandably, the activities and practices of a previous age were, perhaps, viewed as unnecessary distractions to the crucial business of ensuring examination success and were allowed to lapse, to the detriment I feel of the fuller development of the children.

2.2.6 Recreation

Heywood was interested in all kinds of sports including the traditional country sports of fox hunting, ferreting and shooting rabbits. He enjoyed reading in the *The Welshman* and the *Carmarthen Journal* of the thrills and spills of motor cycle racing on Pendine Sands and on Eppynt Mountain in Breconshire. Eddie Stephens from Llanarthne was a local hero who had competed in the Isle of Man Grand Prix in the 1930s. In the 1940s and 1950s Fred Rist from Middlesborough with his awesome 650cc 'Golden Flash' BSA capable of 140 mph was a frequent winner at Pendine. He has been referred to as 'the last king of Pendine'. Bob Berry, a garage proprietor from Manchester, made Pendine Sands famous for his attempts on the World Land Speed Record from the late 1940s to the early 1960s. Lack of resources prevented Bob Berry from achieving his dream. He retired from his back-street-garage in Manchester to a remote small-holding in Tegryn in the foothills of the Preseli Hills. He died in 1970 at the age of 62.

Heywood won a silver cup for sheep shearing at the 1952 shearing match in Llanglydwen. He was also a fast runner and won the over 40's sprint in the August Bank Holiday Sports meeting at Llandygwydd near Newcastle Emlyn on three consecutive occasions in 1957, 1958 and 1959. The Llandygwydd Bank Holiday meet was a long established event and drew competitors from all over west Wales and beynd. Heywood's success was quite outstanding.

Quoits was a popular sport in those days and Heywood built two quoit beds in Penrhiw field opposite Blaenwaun Cottage. Men would gather there on summer evenings to throw quoits and smoke their cigarettes. Heywood smoked 'Players' in those days and his younger brother Elfed (1926-2008) who worked with him at Canerw recalled being sent to Llwynon Shop on a fairly regular basis to buy 20 Players. Heywood eventually became a 20-cigarettes-a-day man and developed a dreadful retching cough which resounded around the cowshed (*glowty*) in Cefn every morning as we left to catch the school bus. But suddenly he gave up the costly habit before it did him serious damage.

Heywood and Lil were keen gardeners and they created flower borders to run along the boundary fence in front of Blaenwaun Cottage. There were flower beds in the garden as well although most of the garden was used to grow vegetables. Every spring without fail Heywood turned the soil (*palu'r ardd*) and prepared beds and rows (*pame a rhychie*) containing plenty of cow dung (*dom da*) for potatoes, cabbage, peas, carrots, runner beans, shallots, onions, parsley, lettuce, cress and radish and plenty of horse manure (*dom ceffyle*) for the rhubarb bed. They tended the garden diligently although I do remember the weeds getting a bit out of hand at times and an extra long session of weeding would be called for (*ma' ishe whini'r ardd 'na!*). Although we were allowed to help with the weeding, we were kept off the long-rooted Dandelion (*Dant y Llew*) because we tended to snap its long root and leave it in the soil from where another yellow flower would soon appear. Heywood was a more skilful operator and was able to completely remove the lengthy root. *Dant y Llew* was a particular nuisance in the flower borders at Blaenwaun Cottage and I well recall a poetry lesson at Penygaer School and being amazed at Crwys' knowledgable description of flower beds in his *Y Border Bach* but perplexed at his assertion in the final verse that *Dant y Llew* only became a problem when Mam grew old.

> *Hen estron gwyllt o ddant y llew,*
> *A dirmyg lond ei wen,*
> *Sut gwyddai'r hen droseddwr hy*
> *Fod Mam yn mynd yn hen?*

Gwilym Davies, Penrhiw sometimes called for Bryan and myself in Blaenwaun Cottage and one spring day he took us with him to burn the trash (*llosgi trash*) that he had cut-off in tidying the hedges in the autumn and had gathered in heaps around the fields. He poured black fluid over the heap of trash before putting a match to it. *Beth yw'r stwff du 'na?* (What is that black stuff?) was our question; *pisho blac* was the answer!

Another Gwilym Davies kept a shop called Portland in Hermon Village. Gwilym Portland's shop was a kind of emporium selling groceries, ironmongery, boots and shoes, bicycles and so on. But the place was unbelievably untidy with shoes mixed up and bicycles without wheels which were usually found buried under a pile of Wellington Boots. It was from Gwilym Portland that Heywood got Bryan and myself our first bikes and after much falling off on the lane to Canerw (*ar hewl Canerw*) the bikes eventually broke us in and we were able to stay on-board for a considerable time. I do not recall that we made much use of the bikes at Blaenwaun although we often turned them up-side-down and got the back wheel spinning like mad by turning the pedals as fast as we could. We sometimes fixed a piece of cardboard so that the spinning spokes hit it making a noise like a revd-up motorbike. On one occasion Bryan got a finger jammed between the cogs and the chain. I was able to release it by turning the pedals backwards. The jamming had damaged the finger enough for me to be sent packing to get Heywood from Canerw to take Bryan to the doctor. But my reward for releasing the finger and shattering myself by sprinting to Canerw was to be accused of causing the extensive damage to the finger in the first place! It was reckoned I must have turned the pedal in a direction that carried the finger all the way around the cog wheel ... completely untrue but I learnt there and then that justice is hard to come by in this world!

A favourite past-time was hoop-playing (*whare cylch*). The hoop was an iron rod about six foot long and quarter inch thick, bent into a circle and the ends welded together. A length of wire with one end shaped into a hook was used to push and guide the hoop over the ground at as fast a pace as possible.

Early in the year of 1947 we had a very heavy snow-fall and Heywood had to dig his way out of the cottage to find the snow filling the road up to hedge level for about half a mile on both sides of Blaenwaun Cottage. School was closed for a few weeks. Milk collection from farms was impossible for many weeks and during that time farmers took their milk-churns as best they could with tractors and carts to particular places where collecting-lorries managed to reach. Peering through the window of Blaenwaun Cottage I saw someone walking high up on top of the snow and suddenly he disappeared into the 10-foot-high drift. It turned out to be Mr Christie who had brought his wife and children Sheila, Bobi and Georgi as evacuees to live in a small cottage, Canerw Cottage, a couple of miles from Blaenwaun. He had walked on top of the snow but had been careful to place his feet over the hedge position to avoid sinking into the depth; he miscalculated outside our cottage but resurfaced and continued on his way in search of bread. The following notice which appeared in *The Welshman* under 'Llanboidy and Cwmfelin Mynach' gives an idea of the disruption caused by the snow and also indicates the activities taking place under the auspices of the chapels in those days. (Note the anglicized spelling of Llanelli and the practice of giving printed information in English about events which were, naturally, Welsh language events since they served a community which was effectively 100% Welsh speaking!):

'Postponements: The Welsh drama, "Abel Simon" by Tom Griffiths and party, Llanelly, has been postponed until April 19th 1947; Cwmfelin Mynach Eisteddfod to April 3rd; and Rhydyceisiad Eisteddfod to April 8th.'

Other famous drama parties in those days were Edna Bonnell's party from Llanelli and Dan Mathews' group from Pontarddulais. They performed on an annual basis at the Market Hall, Llanboidy where 'Abel Simon' would have been performed.

Eventually things returned to normal and 1947 gave way to 1948 and a big change in our circumstances. Our home Blaenwaun Cottage was owned by Mary Ann Davies who lived and farmed next door at Blaenpant-teg. In 1948 her daughter Phebe Mary married David Owen (no relation) of Lan, Cefnypant and they wished to make their home in Blaenwaun Cottage. Heywood decided to take the tenancy of a small-holding a mile and a half west of Blaenwaun and his unmarried brother Garfield came home to Canerw to run the farm for his mother.

The year 1948 could not be described as the year of the car in terms of numbers on the road but it was the year in which the revolutionary Morris Minor designed by Alec Issigonis appeared. Although described by Lord Nuffield as 'that damned poached egg designed by that damned foreigner' it would become the first British model to sell over a million and would still be in production as late as 1971. Alec Issigonis had another brilliant brain wave in 1959 when he produced the Mini.

Blaenwaun Cottage today. Apart from porch and boundary wall, not much has changed since the 1940s.

The wall-clock needed winding once a week.

Bess ready to take a cart-load of milk-churns from Canerw's cool-house to the milk-stand

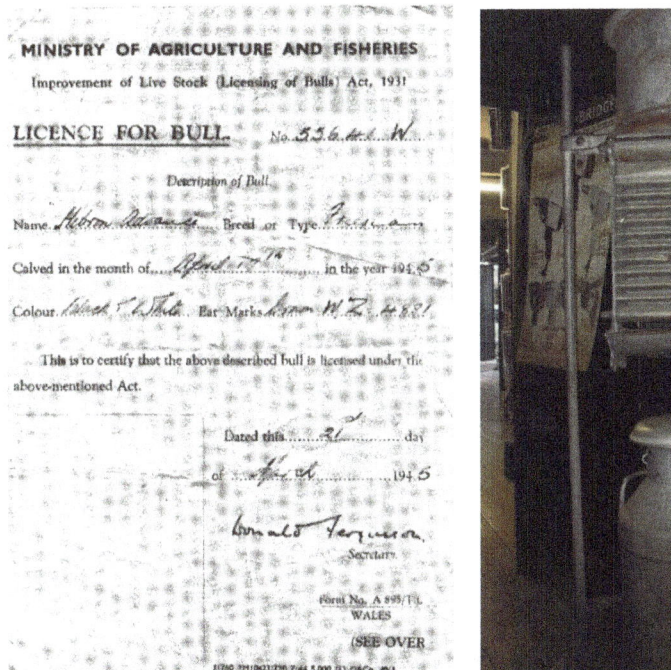

Right: Milk Cooler: milk flowed over the corrugated surface cooled by water flowing inside the device
Left: License to keep a bull at Canerw in 1945

A 'fiddle' – played like a violin – sprayed seeds and, after much walking, a field was re-seeded.

Rabbits at Llanboidy with L/R: Churchill y Lamb, John Thomas, Brynderwen and son William (Wil Bach).

Harvest time at Tower Farm, Cefnypant in 1939 with Owen Jenkins, wife Blanche and daughter Meima restraining a 'helper'.

Haymaking at Dolwilym Cottage 1938. L/R standing: Glyn Evans, Rhos; Albert Howells, Glyntaf; Benjamin James, Penbobtbren; Margaret Ann Jenkins, Cottage; Eunice Davies, Parc-y-rhos; in front: Joan Davies, Butt; Lil and Denley; Johnny Jenkins, Cottage; Dorothy Davies, Butt; Rowina Davies, Butt; Margaret Mary James, Penbontbren.

'Sgwt fach' used to brake one wheel of a loaded gambo when descending a steep hill so as to assist the horse.

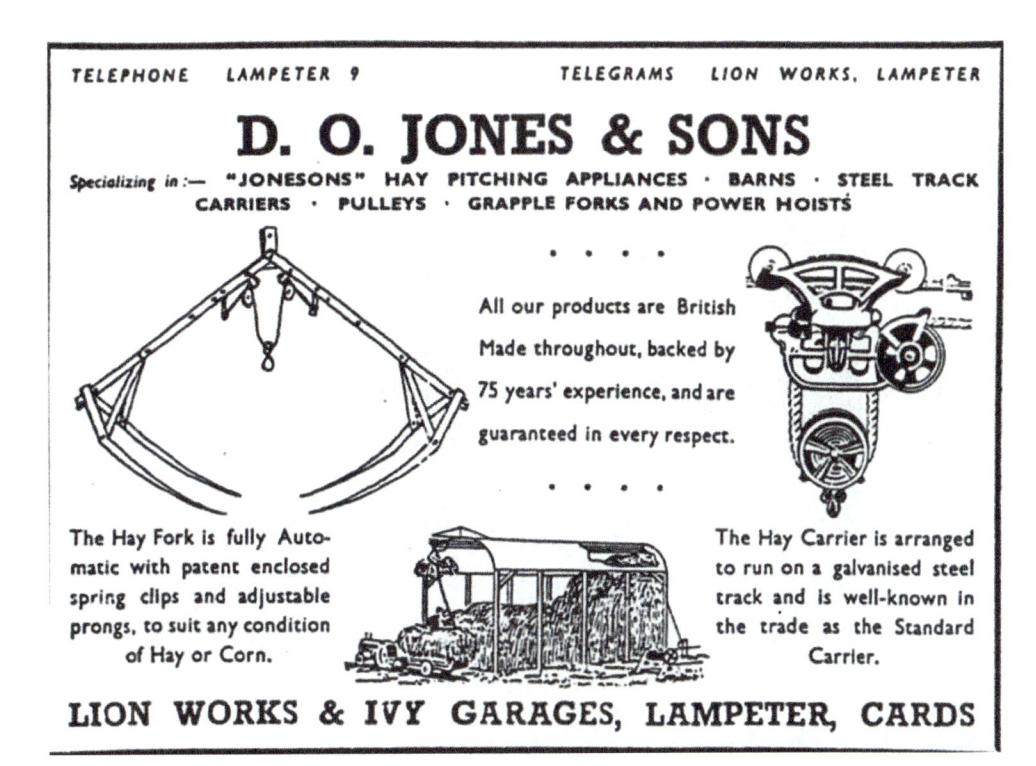

TELEPHONE LAMPETER 9   **TELEGRAMS LION WORKS, LAMPETER**

D. O. JONES & SONS

Specializing in:— "JONESONS" HAY PITCHING APPLIANCES · BARNS · STEEL TRACK CARRIERS · PULLEYS · GRAPPLE FORKS AND POWER HOISTS

All our products are British Made throughout, backed by 75 years' experience, and are guaranteed in every respect.

The Hay Fork is fully Automatic with patent enclosed spring clips and adjustable prongs, to suit any condition of Hay or Corn.

The Hay Carrier is arranged to run on a galvanised steel track and is well-known in the trade as the Standard Carrier.

LION WORKS & IVY GARAGES, LAMPETER, CARDS

At the hay-shed fork-fulls of hay were lifted off the gambo by a hay-fork (pige) lowered on to the gambo load. The lifting was done by a horse pulling a rope attached via a system of pulleys to the hay-fork which was lifted to engage with the hay-carrier (carriage bach) which was then pulled along a track under the roof of the shed (see below) and the fork-full of hay deposited where required.

Threshing in full swing.

Fred Sage, a London evacuee, rides the horse during haymaking time at Harry Jeremy's (standing) farm. (*Photo courtesy of Nansi Jeremy.*)
Courtesy Gomer Press, Llandysul.

Raking hay into rows

Hay-making at Cilhernin, Cefnypant in 1947. Hugh Phillips, Cilhernin on the tractor. L/R standing: Gwynfor Phillips, Trehir-isaf; Muriel, Cilhernin; Glyndwr Phillips, Rosehill; L/R sitting: Leila; Yvonne; Nansi and Jean … all of Cilhernin.

Corn-harvest at Penrhiw, Llanboidy 1941. L/R: Eben, Ffynnon-wen; Megan, Penrhiw; Phebe Mary, Blaenpant-teg; Annie, Cwrte-bach; Lizzie, Penrhiw; John, Cwrte-bach; Mrs Christie, Canerw Cottage (evacuee); Glyn, Ffynnon-wen; Dan, Rhos. In front: Bobbie and Georgie Christie.

Ploughing at Canerw 1947. Heywood having to accommodate his uncle James visiting from Llanelli.

Llanglydwen Home Guard. L/R: Front row: Bryn, bysis; Tom, Argoed; James Ifor Jenkins; Gwynfor Parry; Tomi, Llysaeron; Stanley Young; Lewis, Minefield; Griff, Ty-coch; Thomas John, Manordaf; Emlyn, Marchgwyn; Johnny Jenkins; Jack, Marchgwyn; Tom, Lleine-bach. Second row: Gwynfor, Trehir-isaf; Dai, Tanner; Gwyn, Postman; ----, Nebo; Jack, Llwyn-yr-ebol; Keni, Penbontbren, Login; Vincent Griffiths; Ben Owen; Jack Owen; Gordon Owen; Owen, Rhos; ---------. Third row: Vince Edwards; Dai, Llety; Tom, Post Office, Hebron; Garfield, Felin; Oliver, Goodwin's Row; Cecil, Berllan; Cliff, Maes-y-ffynnon; Arthur John, Post Office, Hebron; Jos, Penback; Dennis, Llysmyrddin; Will Reynolds, Glasfryn. Fourth row: David, Rhosnewydd; Lloyd Wheeler; Ingli, llwynglas; Ben Wheeler; Trefor, Ffynnon; Tom Rees; Albert John, Brynbedw; Herbert, Drefach; Idwal Jones; Gwilym Bowen, Pencraig; Dai Morris, Llwynmynydd.

Home Guard Officers group: L/R standing: ----------; Griff, Tycoch, Rhydwilym; ----------; Samuel Sweet, Danllan, Llanwinio; Gwilym Davies, Penrhiw, Llanboidy. L/R seated: Stanley Young; Tomi ………, Llanboidy; George Evans, Nant-yr-eglwys; Wilmot Vaughan, Maesgwynne; Lewis Evans, Minefield; William Goodwin; William Morgan, Rhydvilla, Cwm Rhyd.

Llanwinio Home Guard. L/R front row: William Hughes, Hafod-y-pwll; Jack Edwards; Ivor James, Clun; Jim Saer, Penclippin; Gwilym Nicholas, Goitre Isaf; Dai Lewis, Blaenffynnon; Wil Morgan, Rhydvilla; Tomi Davies, Pencraig Isaf; Hywel Lewis, Blaenpant; Bryn Rees, Felin, Gelliwen; Gwyn Jones, Huanfryn; Elfed Davies, Leon. L/R middle row; Rev. T.O. Evans; Ifor Rees, Ffynnonlas-isaf; Gwilym Hughes, Rallt Goch; Cyril Isaac, Rhyd-y-parc; Glanville Davies; Eirwyn Davies, Fforest; Wil Rees, Crossland; Gwyn Walters, Pencraig; Trefor Davies, Fron-uchaf; Percy Rees, Bush; William Davies, Orvil; Emrys Thomas; Dewi Davies; J.S.N. Evans, Cwmfelin Mynach. L/R back row: Bernice Phillips; Emlyn Davies, Frondeg; Haydn Thomas, Alba; Dewi Edwards, Pwll Trap; Tom, Brynelwyn; Wil Evans, Ffoshelyg; Emlyn Davies, Gilfach; Ronnie James, Bwmper; Jimmy Davies, Frondeg; Johnny Evans, Cware; Dennis Lewis, Awelon; Samuel Sweet, Danllan, Llanwinio.

Llanboidy Home Guard: L/R standing: David James, Tanner; Elwyn, Clungwyn; Hywel Phillips; Ben, Felin; Ronnie James; Jimmy Davies; William Thomas; Dewi Davies. L/R seated: Gwyn Evans; Emlyn Morris; Henry Rees; Killa Jones; Bryn, Rhydgaled; Johnny Jenkins; Jack Jenkins.

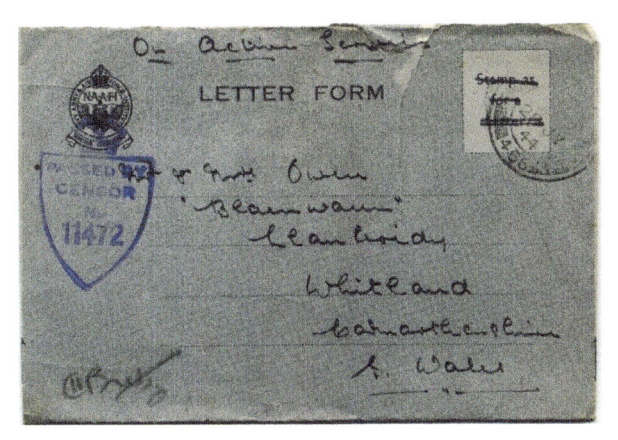

Clifford Jenkins (wncwl Cliff) (1912 – 1944).

Clifford's last letter to his sister Lil and family. Fourteen days after date of postage he died of his wounds in Normandy.

MEMORIAL SERVICE
BRECON CATHEDRAL
Thursday, September 19th, 1946, at 3 p.m.

PLEASE BE SEATED BY 2.45 P.M.

You Enter by Garth Door
See Reverse

THERE WILL BE A COLLECTION FOR THE WAR MEMORIAL FUND DURING THE SERVICE

Service of Remembrance and Unveiling

(Arranged by the British Legion and Parish Council, St. Clears)

Remembrance Sunday, 9th November, 1947

AT

CAPEL MAIR

At 2 p.m.

CONDUCTED BY

The Rev. T. C. JONES, B.A., Chaplain
The Rev. O. C. JENKINS, Capel Mair

Names of the Fallen : 1939-1945

GWYN MORRIS
WILFRED AUSTIN LEWIS
ELLIS LYN HOWELLS
HAMLYN PHILLIPS
JOHN LLOYD JAMES
CLIFFORD JENKINS
GERWYN BOWEN

"Lest we Forget"

THE UNVEILING AT THE CENOTAPH BY
Lt. Col. W. H. BUCKLEY, Branch President
At 3 p.m.

Capel Mair, St Clears remembers

Logo which headed *Y Crwydryn's* column in the *Weekly News* for over twenty years. Y Crwydryn turned out to be the headmaster of Penygaer County Primary School, W. Rhydderch Evans.

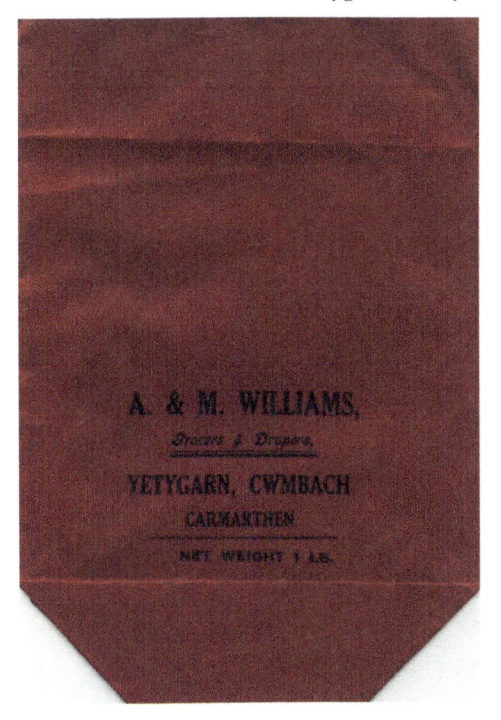

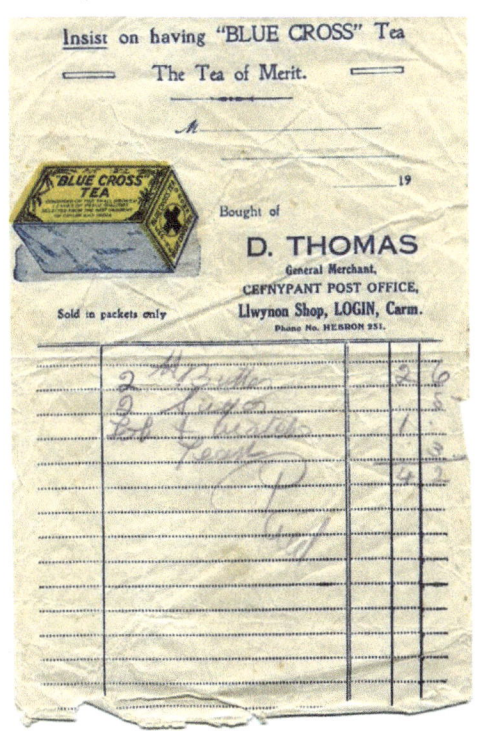

Groceries bought in local shops were packed in sturdy bags.

On wncwl Garfield's Norton in 1947

Heywood and boys 1947

Carnival time 1946.

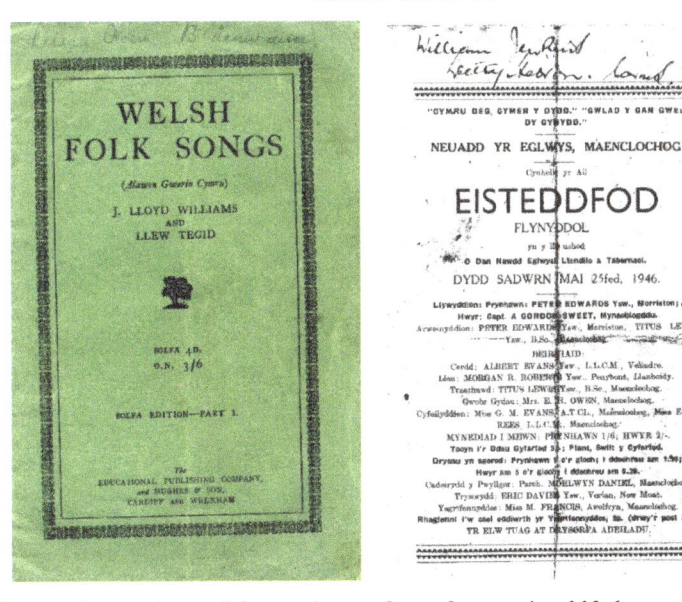

A source of songs for soloists and for parties.   One of many eisteddfodau eagerly looked forward to.

121

RHAGLEN GOFFA

DR. JOSEPH PARRY
1841 ·· 1941

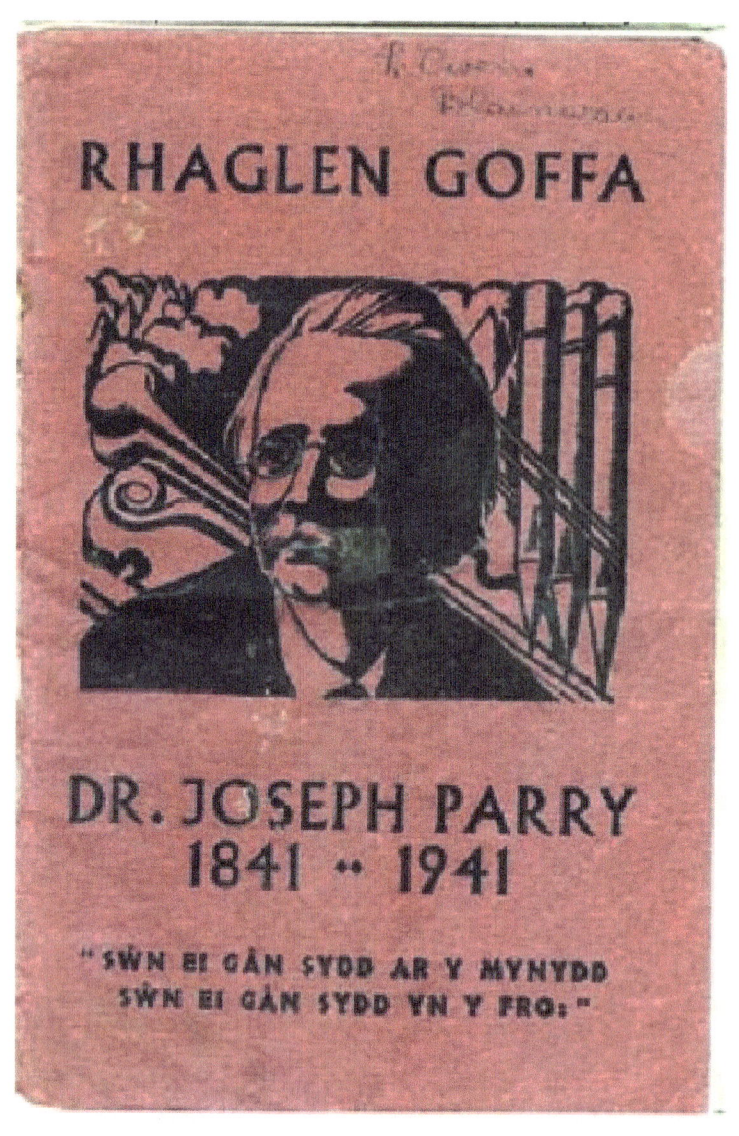

"SŴN EI GÂN SYDD AR Y MYNYDD
SŴN EI GÂN SYDD YN Y FRO:"

Programme of hymns sung in the Gymanfa Ganu held at Nebo Independent Chapel, Efailwen on Monday 6 October 1941 in celebration of the birth of Welsh composer and musician Dr Joseph Parry. Born in Merthyr Tydfil, Joseph Parry worked in the mines and in Cyfarthfa iron works before emmigrating with his parents to Danville, Pensylvania in 1854. He was exceptionally talented musically and competed regularly at eisteddfodau in America and in Wales. At the National Eisteddfod of 1865 at Aberystwyth he was received into the Gorsedd of Bards. Public financial support enabled him, in 1868, to study at the Royal Academy in London. He was the first from Wales to receive the degree of Mus.B. from Cambridge University. In 1874 he was appointed the first Professor of Music at University College of Wales, Aberystwyth. Later he became Head of Music at the new University College, Cardiff. He is best remembered for his numerous hymn tunes, especially 'Aberystwyth' and the famous male choir song 'Myfanwy' with words by Richard Davies (Mynyddog) who also worked with Joseph Parry on his opera 'Blodwen'. The duet 'Hywel a Blodwen', from that opera, remains an immensely popular concert piece. In his later years he lived in Penarth and is buried in that town's St Augustine Church graveyard.

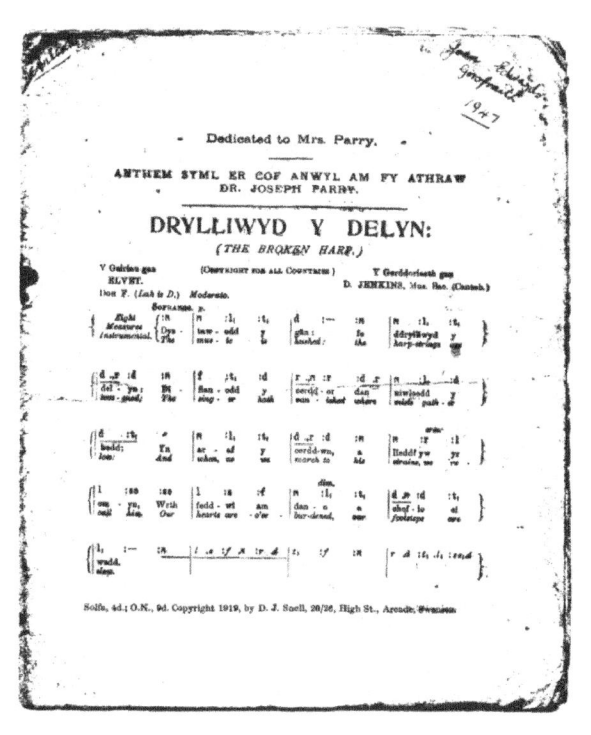

'Drylliwyd y Delyn' – anthem performed by many a chapel choir. Music is by David Jenkins in memory of his mentor, Joseph Parry, whom he succeeded as Professor of Music at Aberystwyth.

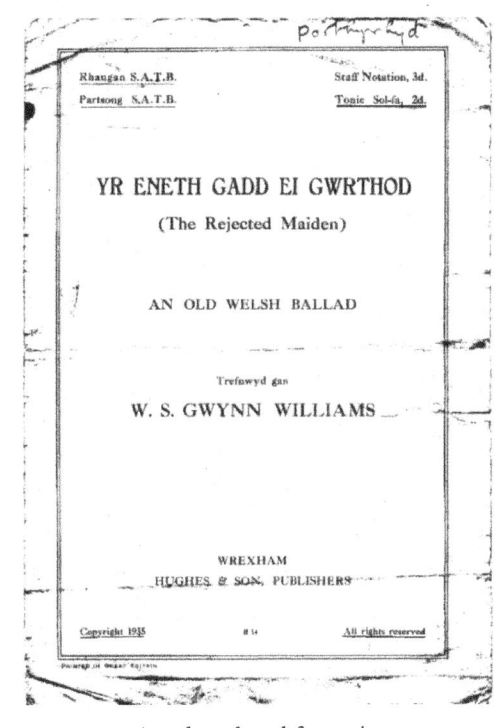

Another choral favourite

Dan Phillips, Frowen-fach, Cefnypant, reluctant farmer, prolific reader, occasional essayist, subscriber to 'The Listener'. Elected deacon at Cefnypant Independent Chapel in 1906, he was chapel treasurer from 1928 to 1930 and again from 1944 to 1949 and was chapel secretary for 10 years until his death in 1952. One of his surviving essays is a record of the history of Cefnypant Chapel up to 1939; another is a learned treatise on the question 'Beth yw Cerddoriaeth?' (What is Music ?). Both essays won first prizes for Dan in eisteddfod competitions

On their way to a service at Cefnypat are Gordon Owen, Canerw and Thomas Williams, Frowen-fach.

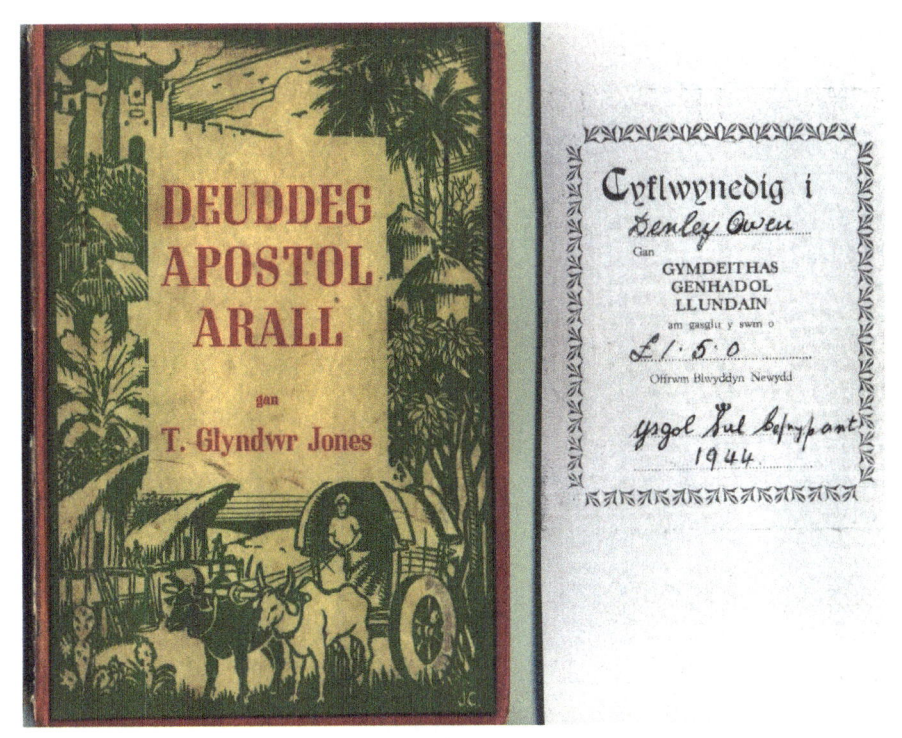

Collecting money in support of the London Missionary Society was an annual 'chore' for many.

Regular attendance at Sunday School was a prize-winner at Cefnypant in the 1940s and 1950s.

Reading material received through the Sunday School

Rev. Edgar Phillips, B.A.,B.D. minister at Glandwr and Cefnypant Independent Chapels with his deacons in 1947. L/R seated: William Thomas, Rhydcoed-bach; Rev. Phillips; Dan Phillips, Frowen-fach. L/R standing: Robert James, Derlwyn; Edward Eynon, Penrallt-fach; Tom Nicholas, Glandwr; Tom Williams, Frowen-fach; Idwal Davies, Danderi; John Thomas, Gwarllwyn; Stanley Phillips, Rosehill; Joshua Phillips, Frowen; Albert Howells, Glyntaf; Sion Philip, Caerdaf; David Williams, Pengamell; Willie Mathias, Pencnwc.

Llanboidy Market Hall was the venue for eisteddfodau, concerts, dramas and the Hunt Ball.

An early photo of Bois y Frenni. L/R standing: Vince Insiwrans; Dan Sa'r; Idwal Danderi; Ianto Shop; Dai Garreg-wen; Stan Mans; Emrys Bach. Sitting: Wil Cwm-hir; Sam Post; May Cole; 'W.R.' Pati Cole; Dai Dyffryn; Glyn Twmpathog. Formed by Bwlch-y-groes, Llanfyrnach schoolmaster W.R. Evans in March 1941 'Bois y Frenni' held about 350 concerts until the end of World War II and raised £5,000 towards good causes, helped keep-up morale and proved that humour and entertainment were part of Welsh language culture.

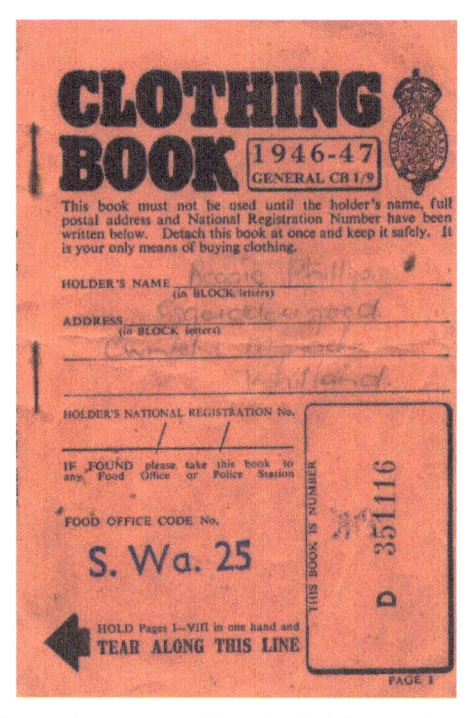

Clothes rationing came into effect from 1 June 1941 and lasted, albeit in a gradually reduced format, until March 1949.

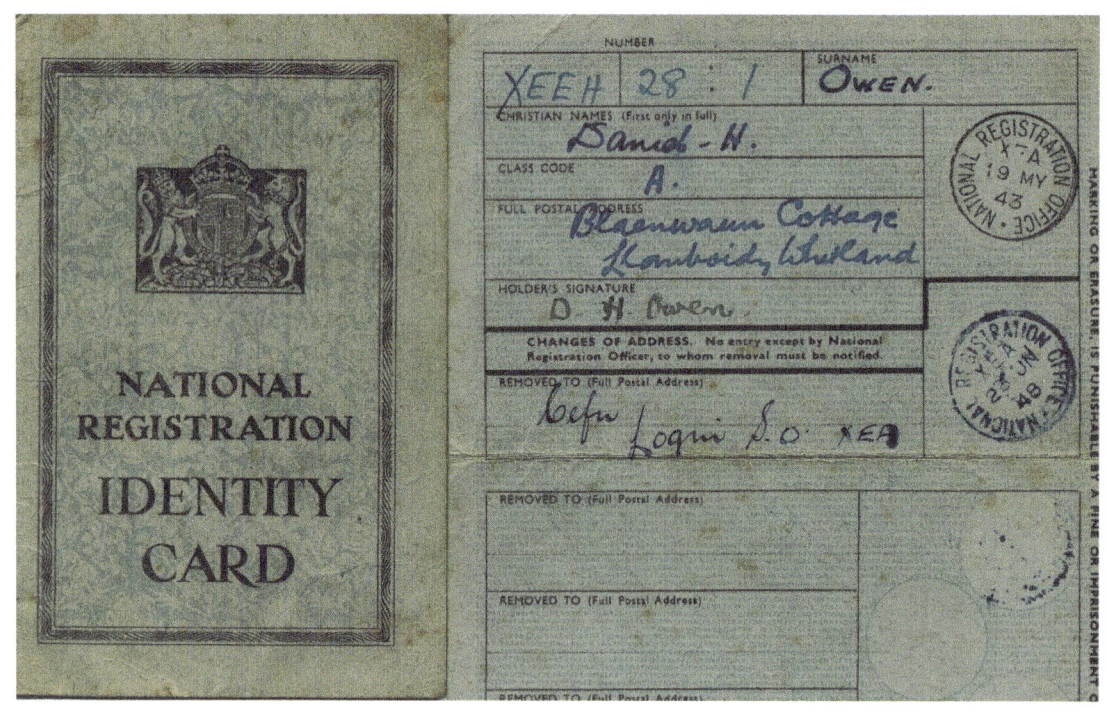

Identity Cards kept track of changes of address.

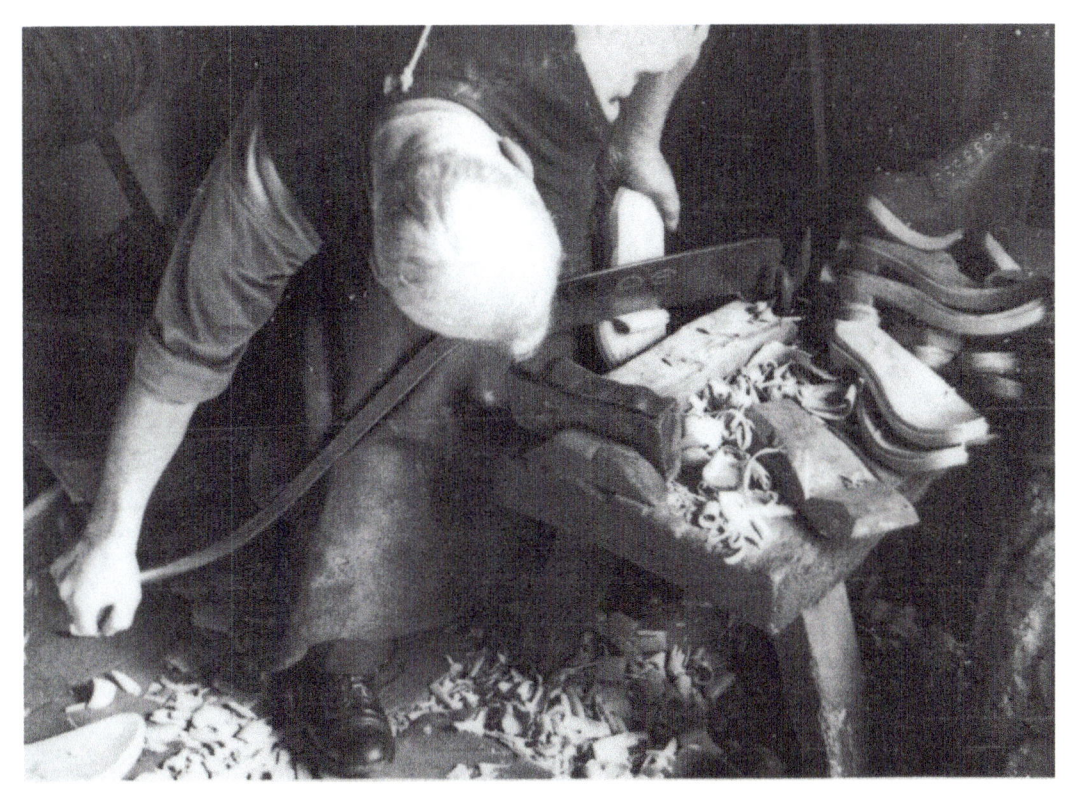

Preparing a wooden sole for a clog. *Courtesy Trefor Owen, Clocsiwr, Cricieth.*

Left: Pair of clogs typical of the sort made by Johnny Jenkins at his workshop in Llety, Hebron. *Courtesy Trefor Owen, Clocsiwr, Cricieth.*

Right: Wooden ladle and spoons (lledwad a llwyau pren) made by Johnny Jenkins (author's uncle) with which cawl was served and consumed

Part III

1948 – 1958: CEFN – toil, chapel and 'isgol Whitlan'

3.1 1948 – early 1950s

3.1.1 Hazards and freedom

In the spring of 1948 during the Easter school holidays Heywood and Lil with their children, Denley (10), Bryan (8), moved to Cefn, near Llanglydwen although the address was Cefn, Login S.O., Carms. Our furniture was loaded on to a trailer and the Allis Chalmers did the rest. A Milk Marketing Board contract effective from 18 April 1948 directed D. H. Owen, Esq., Cefn, Login, S.O., Carms to supply milk produced at Cefn to the United Dairies factory at Whitland. The number of cows and heifers in milk entered on the contract was just three – after a few years a dozen milking cows were supported on the 40-acre small-holding rented from Haydn Harries, Abertigen.

Moving-home led to a funny incident on our return after the Easter break to Penygaer School. Before the school broke-up we were learning about mutation and, as a test, each member of the class had to announce - with the correct mutation - where he or she lived. In my case it was: '*Rwyf yn byw* **ym M***laenwaun*' (I live in Blaenwaun). For some reason the 'sharp' Miss Gibbon was taking the class rather than Mishtir. After the holidays she got us off again on mutations and when my turn came I started to say: '*Rwyf yn byw* **yng Ngh***efn*' but I only got to uttering '**yng**' before Miss Gibbon tore me to bits shouting '**Nage! Nage! Nage! ... ym ym ym (No! No! No! ... ym ym ym)**'. After she cooled down I explained that I'd moved-home and she allowed me to finish the perfectly correct mutation for Cefn ... and then we all had a good laugh!

One person who knew that we had moved and was rather disappointed by the end of 1948 that Bryan and myself had not cycled over to see her was our 83-year-old great grandmother Phoebe Jenkins , Plasybwci and she let us know her feelings in a letter.

' Dudd Iai   Plasybwcy

Anwil Oll

Wele fi in anfon gair in fir gan fawr obeithio eich bod in iach yna i gud fel ag ir ydim nine ar i Banck yma wel wif wedy bod in dishgwl i Boys draw ond nid ydint wedy dod ag wif in hala bobo necloth bach iddint in galenig yw nw fawr o beth fe nan i tro i sichyr slat in ir ysgol

Wel ir wif in mind draw ir Wern dywedd ir withnos may Emlyn a Lizzie in mind i Llunden i weld Sibbie a Stan gobeitho na anw ddim ar goll yna may Llunden in dipin o seis cofiwch chy

Terfinaf nawr gida dimuniade gore a llwiddianis i chwy oll am i flwiddin newy 1949

O ie cofiwch ddod am dro ar ol i fi ddod nol or Wern'

(Thursday   Plasybwci

Dear All

Here I am sending a word hoping to find you in good health as we are here on the Bank.

Well I have been expecting the boys over here but they have not come and so I am sending them a small hankerchief each as New Year's gifts they are not much they'll do to wipe the slate in school

Wel I am going over to Wern end of the week Emlyn and Lizzie are going to London to see Sibbie and Stan I hope they do not get lost London is quite a size after all

I will finish now with best wishes for a successful new year 1949 to you all

O yes remember to come for a visit after I come back from Wern).

The letter was written in Welsh which suggests that Lil's Mamgu Plasybwci, born in Cwmfelin Mynach in 1865, had received most of her education in the Sunday School where she would have learnt to read in Welsh. In the 1871 Census she was not listed as a 'scholar' and probably did not attend Ysgol Powell Bach two-and-a-half miles away at Llanboidy thus avoiding the anglicising influence of that school's monolingual headmasters. It is more likely that Mamgu Plasybwci had taught herself to write and since the Bible was probably her only regular contact with written words it is not surprising that she wrote in Welsh.

To me Cefn was a heaven of freedom after the confinement of Blaenwaun Cottage. It was sited about half-a-mile from the river Taf and the Cardi Bach railway, Dolwilym Mansion, Cromlech Gwal y Filiast and Cottage (Y Ty rownd). Cefn was about 200 metres from the road running from Cefnypant to Login and the access was about 600 metres from Tal-y-garn bungalow at the top of the hill leading down to Llanglydwen (Rhiw Bont). A few evenings after we arrived in Cefn a neighbour, Stanley Phillips, Rosehill Farm, paid us a visit to welcome us to the area. Stanley was a deacon at Cefnypant and we knew him well but it was a fine gesture on his part to spend the evening helping us to settle in our new home. In fact Stanley and his wife Sarah Ann had lived in Cefn from 1933 to 1935. One of the first jobs undertaken by Heywood at Cefn was to lay a track from the main road to the farmyard. Once again he showed his incredible strength and toughness in digging out soil to a depth of about one foot over the 200 meters distance from the road to the yard and over a width of about 2 meters. He was helped by some neighbours but the remark of one of them that it was a 'ffwc o job yw hi' was reflected in a lack of 100% effort from anyone except Heywood. The dug out space was filled with shindrins (cinders as used on railway tracks) and rolled with a tractor-pulled farm roller. The result was an excellent roadway that was in first class condition ten years later.

Our nearest neighbours were the Evans family, Glyn and his mother at Rhos about 300 metres along but on the opposite side of the road towards Llanglydwen. They ran a small farm and Glyn was also a cobbler and had a work-shed set on the side of the road nearer to Tal-y-garn. 'Planning guide lines' would rule out such a location today. Also on the opposite side of the road and about 300 metres towards Login was Cilhernin, one of the largest farms in the area, home of Percy Phillips, deacon and secretary of Cefnypant Chapel, and his family. Another neighbouring farm was Penbontbren where lived Benjamin James who was more interested in books than in farming. He was a member of Hebron Chapel so we did not benefit from his knowledge at Sunday School and other gatherings at Cefnypant. I am pleased to have picked-up in a second-hand bookshop *Crwydro Sir Benfro (Y Rhan Gyntaf)* bearing his signature and the name of his retirement home: 'B James Brynfedwen'.

A few large fields on the Login side of Cefn Farm were retained by our landlord Haydn Harries for sheep-grazing and in the spring and early summer many Curlews built nests on those flat fields. Our name for this magnificent bird was *Chwibanwr* derived from its beautiful whistling as it flew to a great height and hovered majestically before descending to earth and landing well away from its nest so as not to provide a marker for any watching egg-snatchers. It would zig-zag its way to its nest and sit on the eggs or feed the chicks. We were so used to seeing and hearing Curlews in those days that it is difficult to believe that they are now almost extinct. Haydn Harries' fields (*perci* Haydn) bordered on to land belonging to Glyntaf House where lived Captain David Garrick Protheroe. Born in 1869 he was a bachelor who had spent his working life in the Army and had inherited the Dolwilym Estate in 1908 on the death of his brother Baldwin. He had lived with his sister M Katherine Protheroe - the one that insisted on being saluted by Lil and Vince all those years ago – until her death in 1945 and thereafter was reliant on a housekeeper. The following note headed Glyntaf, Login, S.O.,

Carmarthenshire and addressed to Mrs Owen, Cefn, Login suggests that Captain Dai was into butter-making and that we were well into the post-gentry age:

'Dear Mrs Owen,

I have another churning for you if you can let D Evans know when it is convenient for you.

Yours

D G P'

The butter milk (*llaeth enwyn*) left over from the 'churning' was to be collected by Dai Evans, Parcyrhos and delivered to Lil to be added to the pig-swil at Cefn. A pig was fattened and killed every year for the first three or four years that we were there but the practice was then discontinued as food became more plentiful and cheaper in the shops. In 1950 Captain Dai employed a German housekeeper who specialized in making home-brewed-beer. Heywood and Lil were invited over to taste her produce one Christmas and on the return journey found it rather difficult to follow the path! Captain Protheroe was then in his eighties and we sometimes saw him being driven in a taxi to somewhere-or- other but he was no longer able to enjoy his life-long passion of hunting. He passed-away in 1951 and was buried at St Cledwyn's Church, Llanglydwen with all the other Protheroes.

The annual meet of the Carmarthenshire Hunt at the Bont, Llanglydwen was a popular community event and those able to do so followed the Hunt for the whole day. On one occasion a gang of us children found ourselves in a clump of trees with the hounds not too far away sniffing around trying to pick up the scent. We tried to get away from the scene but a red-coat rode up flashing his whip and commanded us to stay-put so as not to disturb the hounds' concentration! We were 'trapped' there for what seemed like hours until at last the hounds picked up the scent and were on their way with the tally-ho! gang in tow. We followed as fast as we could and saw the riders clearing a hedge ahead of us but on the other side - where they landed - there seemed to be a bit of a commotion. When we arrived at the scene the reason for the commotion was clear: a mounted huntsman had managed to land his steed in a bog into which the horse sank up to its belly! The fact that the huntsman concerned was our earlier tormentor made our glee all the more delightful! Over the summer months some of the hunters took part in Point-to-Point races and Heywood's interest meant that we attended two meetings every year. One was the Carmarthenshire Point-to-Point at Cana near Bancyfelin and the other was the South Pembrokeshire Point-to-Point at Lydstep Haven near Tenby. There was also a Pembrokeshire meeting held at Scoveston Fort near Haverfordwest.

A big attraction at those races was the bookmakers (bookies) and many a shilling was lost to their big bags.

Haydn Harries who rented the Dolwilym lands had a lot of ponies there during the early 1950s and he lent us one that had been broken-in. It was a beautiful animal with a light brown body and blond mane. We referred to it as *y poni melyn* (the yellow pony) but 'yellow' meant light brown in the same way as 'blue' was used to describe what is actually green hay (*gwair yn las*). We rode *poni melyn* in the fields but not having a saddle we soon discovered we were not of Red Indian origin. Our interest in the *poni melyn* soon faded and he was returned to the Dolwilym fields.

Near the access gate to Cefn, there was a large sand pit (*pwll sand*) dug amongst trees where we scrambled on our bikes. A more sensible use of the bikes was to get us to Penygaer School which was just over a mile away although we usually walked there. We cycled to get bread and other essentials from Pretoria Stores, Llanglydwen but this involved walking and pushing the bikes back up the steep half-mile-long hill (*rhiw Bont*) to Tal-y-garn and we preferred the flatter route to Llwynon Shop, Cefnypant. We also cycled the 2 miles or so to Llety to visit *Tadcu a Mamgu* (William and Margaret Ann Jenkins) and *Wncwl* Johnny. Traffic was very light in those days and did not pose the danger it does these days. But we created our own danger ! On one particular journey home we cycled too fast down the sloping road from Llety and Bryan could not take the sharp right turn at Penygawse and his bike finished in the river although he hung on to a bush and saved himself from getting his feet wet! After fishing-out the bike we set off again at a more sensible pace, largely dictated by the hard work of pedalling up the slope to the T junction at the entrance to Dolwilym Mansion and St Cledwyn's Church. On reaching the junction and turning down-hill towards Llanglydwen we completely forgot the earlier encounter with the river and set-off at a searing pace to a right-angle-bend which I completely failed to negotiate and crashed head-on into the solid 7 ft high hedge onto which I was tossed leaving my bike with a bent front-fork lying on the road. After slithering off the hedge I set about straightening the bent front-fork assisted by Bryan. We managed to make the bike usable and continued our journey at a gentler pace - this time all the way home. On other return journeys from Llety we followed the lane past St Cledwyn's Church down to Dolwilym Mansion. After exploring the place and admiring the magnificent staircase we cycled across the bridge over the Taf and then pushed the machines up the incline past *Bwt* Cottage (a name derived from it having been a storage for wine and ale butts when Dolwilym Mansion was in its hey-day in the previous century) and on to *Carreg Llech* (Gwal y Filiast Cromlech). After failing again to dislodge the capstone we proceeded across the fields to Cefn.

3.1.2 The house of Cefn

Cefn was a small two-up/two-down house with a small pantry added at the rear of the living room/kitchen. There were two bedrooms but only one had a ceiling although both had a window which iced-up on the inside in winter. The bedrooms were accessed by a step-ladder from the living room. As in Blaenwaun Cottage, the Sunday night bath took place in a *padell sinc* in front of the fire. There was only one access door, which opened into a passage (*pasej*) formed by two partitions (*dou balish*) through which two doors accessed the parlour (*parlwr*) on the left and the living room/kitchen (*gegin*) on the right. Sited against the partition in the living room was a bench-seat (*ffwrwm*) on which Bryan and myself were destined to spend most of our sitting-time during the years we lived in Cefn either eating our meals or doing our homework on the table in front! The dresser (*seld*) was placed against the back wall of the living-room and the big wall clock mounted on the partition ticked loudly and struck louder every half hour. We had a settle (*sgiw*) by the fire-grate and a few chairs, two of which were by the table opposite the bench-seat. In the parlour there was a three-piece-suite, a table and chairs and a glass cabinet. All the furniture had been acquired during our time in Blaenwaun Cottage. A dart board was sometimes mounted on the wall in the living-room and occasionally a few men would turn up on an evening to play a few games. Bryan and myself were told-off after one session for embarrassing Heywood with our cheers for his success! In the early 1950s the fire-grate in the kitchen/living room was replaced with a Yorkseal cooker. At about the same time gas-lighting was introduced into the two downstairs rooms. A gas cylinder was sited in the shed at the side of the house and connected via copper tubing to the lamps fixed to the ceilings of the living room and parlour. Oil lamps and/or candles were still required in the pantry and in the bedrooms.

About three metres away from the front of the house and running parallel to it was a hedge behind which was the garden as well as the toilet and a shed. Inside the garden, running parallel to the hedge, was a row of black-current bushes (*llwyni cwrens du*) and the first time they bore fruit I ate more than my fill of black currents resulting in violent retching and vomiting and I've never eaten black-currents since. A few apple trees provided enough fruit for a number of apple tarts (*tartenni 'fale*) which Lil taught us to eat by starting with the hard crust and refuse the temptation to go straight for the fruity middle! It soon became the natural way for us to devour the delicious apple tart and remains so to this day. But there was more to it than how to munch a slice of apple tart because whether she realised it or not she was in fact expressing her approach to life in general - get stuck in to the difficulties and then go on to enjoy the rewards.

There was a corrugated-zinc-sheet-clad-shed in the garden where day-old chicks were reared with the help of an oil heater and many sheets of newspaper to keep their feet warm and collect their droppings. The chicks were obtained from Thornbers Chicks Ltd the Mytholmroyd-based business in the Upper Calder Valley in Yorkshire. Although tiny and apparently fragile the day-old chicks easily withstood transportation in cardboard boxes by fast passenger trains and were delivered to Llanglydwen Station. One year there was an accident involving the heater and the paper and only the corrugated zinc sheets survived. For many years egg production was a serious undertaking at Cefn and Heywood constructed three corrugated zinc bottomless hen coops mounted on wheels so they could be moved around the 'Ffald' field which was therefore thoroughly fertilized by the regular moving of the coops. Lil did most of the feeding and egg collecting but she often roped-in Bryan and myself to look-after the beautiful silver leghorn hens. At that time I was quite at home amongst hens - it was about 10 years later I discovered they gave me the creeps. For a time we kept a few black and white pet rabbits in a hutch built by Heywood but their high rate of reproduction and the work needed to keep their environment clean and to feed and water them got us down eventually. We gave some away and others escaped into the wild and although we occasionally caught a glimpse of them for a few months, they then disappeared and left us wondering whether they were able to cope with their new freedom.

There was no piped water at Cefn but there were at least three sources from which we obtained drinking water. One was a spout (*pistyll*) on the way down to the yard (*clôs*), another was a spring on the other side of the cowshed (*glowty*) and the third was an ice-cold spring in one of Haydn's fields – this one never dried-up. Usually we filled a metal pitcher (*stên*) from the *pistyll* and stored it in the small dairy (*llaethdy*). Naturally there were times when there was no drinking water in the house. I recall such a moment when a local carpenter was working at Cefn and Bryan and myself were in the house on our own. It was a very hot day and the carpenter kept knocking on the door asking for a drink of water. Eventually the drinking water ran out but rather than trundle out to the *pistyll* to replenish our supply, Bryan noticed some peeled potatoes soaking in water and the next time the carpenter knocked he was given a cupful of the 'potato water' (*dwr tato*) to quench his thirst! He downed his drink in one and praised the water's refreshing taste and when he did not return for more we realised that we should have filled his first cup with *dwr tato*!

It was in the *llaethdy* that Lil skimmed the surface-cream off the milk which had stood in a bucket over night. The cream was poured into a metal pitcher (*stên*) after which, with the cap (*caead*) tightly in place, the pitcher was shaken in a rhythmic motion by hand (*corddi*) until, about an hour later, a clunking noise from inside the pitcher signalled the presence of butter. The butter milk (*llaeth enwyn*) was drained-off and eagerly sampled by Lil, Heywood and Bryan but to me its taste was quite sickening. The butter was for our own use and we soon acquired a small glass butter-making churn (*budde*) in which a paddle, mounted through the cap of the vessel, was turned by a handle making the process of *corddu* more bearable.

A stone-built out-house, with a corrugated zinc roof, extended from one side of the house and this served as a general store mainly for logs and coal needed to feed the Yorkseal cooker. Another important use for the shed was as a place to hang the pig's carcass after it had its life unceremoniously extinguished by slashing its throat and its wiry body-hair removed by scraping them off with metal scrapers after soaking the body in boiling water.

3.1.3 Pigs, cows, fish and rabbits

Diwrnod-lladd-mochyn (literally: 'pig-killing-day') was an annual occurrence on most farms up to the early 1950s. Early in the morning at Cefn a large metal cauldron was mounted on a *dribe* (three legged metal tripod) inside a shed at the top of the *clôs* (yard) and was filled with water. Kindling underneath the cauldron was ignited and the fire fed with more kindling and fire-wood as required until the water boiled and thereafter kept at boiling point. A specially constructed *ffwrwm-lladd-mochyn* (pig-killing-bench) was positioned on the yard outside the shed. In our first year at Cefn the *dyn-lladd-mochyn* (literally: pig-killing-man) was a local farmer Thomas John Thomas, Ietgoch, Cefnbrafle, who had learnt the skills of the job from his father. Other *dynion-lladd-mochyn* in the Login area were John Rhydgaled, Gwilym Pencraig and Dan Wernddu. Heywood had helped the butcher every year for many years when it was *diwrnod-lladd-mochyn* at Canerw and after helping him again in our first year at Cefn, Heywood had picked up sufficient knowledge to carry out the job himself in succeeding years.

Any farming-related job that Heywood was able to acquire experience of doing, he mastered with comparative ease. As already mentioned he learnt a lot of farming skills from his co-worker at Frowen, Dafi Reynolds, but his mastering of the procedures of butchering a pig based on a few observations and no proper training was a remarkable achievement.

The butcher's first task was to lay out his knives and scrapers and select a particularly dangerous-looking knife which he sharpened as the unsuspecting pig was ushered to his presence near the *ffwrwm*. After sizing up the situation, the *dyn-lladd-mochyn* plunged the knife into the pig's throat severing the main artery and blood gushed out. The pig's scream was ear-piercing but he quickly weakened and when his legs started wobbling the *dyn-lladd-mochyn* and Heywood tripped the pig towards the low level *ffwrwm* and lifted it on to it. Boiling water, brought from the cauldron, was poured over the body and we were invited to join in the work of scraping off the pig's body hair using *a caead sten* (metal pitcher cap) until the body was shining clean. The corpse was then suspended by its hind legs from a beam in the shed and the *dyn-lladd-mochyn* opened it up and removed the entrails. The bladder was blown up and used as a football but it soon burst. Next day the butcher returned to remove the *cig mân* (small bits of meat) such as the liver, kidneys and the *cwningen* (rabbit), also known as *llygoden* (mouse). He cut the body into six large pieces of two hams, two sides and two shoulders (*palfeisiau*). Lil had the mincer out and soon some of the *cig mân* was minced and formed into faggots each one wrapped in the *ffedog*. It was customary to share some of the faggots and the *cig mân* with neighbours and the job of delivering the stuff fell to Bryan and myself. Over the following few weeks the sides and the other parts, laid out on stone slabs in the *llaethdy*, were rubbed with salt and finally the salted parts were hung from the ceiling in the *llaethdy*. The pig's head including the ears and also its feet were made into brawn, a kind of pate, and allowed to settle in basins. When required, brawn was extracted from a basin on to a plate where it settled like a big pink jelly. It was brought to the table at meal-time and sliced and those who fancied it helped themselves.

Mention of soaking the pig's corpse in boiling water reminds me of an occasion when boiling water was used to send a pig packing! Soon after we moved to Cefn a pig from a neighbouring farm found its way to Cefn and in addition to eating everything that was to its taste it messed-up the place by digging everywhere as pigs do unless their snouts are pierced with a metal ring. We chased the pig back to the farm several times and informed the farmer of the need to make him secure (*ishe ti gau'r mochyn 'na miwn Glyn*) but nothing was done and the pig continued its unwelcome visits. Heywood's solution was to throw boiling water over its backside which resulted in the squealing pig heading for home at full speed. A few days later Heywood met the pig's owner who mentioned that his pig was behaving very strangely: he had not moved from his sty for days ('*sa i'n gwbod be sy'n bod ar y blydi mochyn 'co, so'r diawl wedi symud os dou ddiwrnod*', *medde Glyn*). The pig made a full recovery but never again did he pay another visit to Cefn.

Heywood planned to keep a dozen milking cows at Cefn but the four-cow *glowty* (cowshed) which he found there in April 1948 left him short of eight places. This need was solved when our landlord Haydn Harries told Heywood he could dismantle the corrugated zinc-clad eight-cow *glowty* at *Y Ty Rownd* and re-erect it at Cefn. This was the first major job that I remember helping with at Cefn. It was prior to Heywood buying a *Ffergi bach*, as the popular grey Ferguson tractors were called, so a tractor and trailer were borrowed from Stanley Phillips, Rosehill to complete the work. A mason from Glandwr, John Phillips, who wrote poetry under the pseudonym 'Sion Philip', was called in to prepare the concrete foundations and floor of the new *glowty*.

The herd was built-up gradually through buying older, and therefore more affordable, cows inorder to get the business started. Two cows bought in Carmarthen in 1948 were named 'Gert' and 'Daisy' after the characters created in 1930 by Elsie and Dorris Waters who achieved success on the wireless and went on to be stage stars too. Their brother Jack Warner was famous as T.V.'s 'Dixon of Dock Green'. Heywood's undoubted talent for assessing the quality and potential of animals was amply demonstrated when he bought a heifer from one of the first non-Welshman to buy a farm in the area. His surname was Rabaiotti and the heifer was duly known by that name. After developing into an outstanding milker she fetched the highest price of the day when sold at Carmarthen Mart. At Cefn milk stored in 10-gallon-churns, cooled by standing in a concrete cistern of cold water, was collected daily from the farm gate by lorry.

Cefn had a wonderful setting high above the Taf river. In Welsh the valley was known as *Dyffryn Taf* and never to my knowledge as *Cwm Taf* which seems to have infiltrated into use today. *Cwm Taf* simply does not have the resonance that *Dyffryn Taf* has to describe the beauty of the valley. Many a time Bryan and myself would run down over the narrow sloping fields that formed a branch valley hemmed in on both sides by trees and leading from Cefn down to the railway on the other side of which and close to it was the river. As we approached the railway and the river the area became thickly wooded although a few fields stretched out on one side of *Y Ty Rownd* which was still standing and its massive central chimney was an object of great curiosity to us. We would peer through the trees to try and locate another cottage, Dan-y-coed, on the other side of the river, tucked away in the undergrowth and the home of a loner called Twm Dan-y-coed. We did not linger too long although I do not recall ever setting eyes on Twm. There was a deep pool in the river opposite *Y Ty Rownd* called '*Pwll Dan-y-coed*'. We fished there once or twice but did not have the patience for the task and preferred to take a dip in the pool on a hot summer's day. A few miles away at Rhydyparc, Lon and her brother Brian, practised the art of catching fish by 'tickling' ones trapped in a pool created a few days earlier by diverting part of the river to form a fish-trap. A path climbing through woods away from *Y Ty Rownd* and the river enabled us to reach the track from Glyntaf to Dolwilym along which, a generation earlier, Lil and her brother Vince had encountered the redoubtable 'Miss'. Walking towards Dolwilym we passed Bwt Cottage - sometimes occupied, sometimes not. About 20 metres past Bwt was the railway which required care in crossing to reach the bridge across the Taf over which the track continued and in a further 200 yards or so we were at Plas Dolwilym. Unoccupied, it contained a massive central staircase which we climbed rather warily and tried to prepare ourselves for the fright of our lives as birds suddenly and noisily escaped from their cosy perches in the rafters. Outside near the walled garden there was a dogs' graveyard with stone slabs carrying the deceased dogs names marking their last resting place: a reminder of the vanished golden age of the aristocracy. Returning to the bridge over the River Taf and walking along the track towards Glyntaf would bring us to a thickly wooded area and the prehistoric monument of *Cromlech Gwal y Filiast* known locally as *Carreg Llech* which was surrounded by an eight-metre-radius circle of trees. We scrambled on to the massive capstone and for a few minutes ruled the world. Leaving the *Cromlech* and the track to Glyntaf, a walk up the slope out of the woods led into a field belonging to Haydn Harries at the top of which was the boundary hedge of the farthest Fron field (*Fron nesa draw*) belonging to Cefn. We proceeded along the top of three successive fields sloping away down to our right: *Fron nesa draw, Fron ganol* and *Fron nesa 'ma* with the long and narrow *Ffald* on our left. The final walk home was a diagonal across a squarish field behind and to the side of the house.

Heywood had a narrow escape on *Fron ganol* (the middle Fron) when, one morning as he collected the cows for milking, he found that Haydn's bull had broken through the boundary hedge and was sizing up his new-found harem at the top of *Fron ganol*. When Heywood tried to drive him towards the boundary the bull suddenly turned and charged at him. Heywood ran down the slope and remembered that a bull finds it difficult to run down-hill because of its short front legs. Half way down the field Heywood turned sharp left and jumped over a gate into *Fron nesa 'ma* (the nearest Fron). The bull skidded past the gate but recovered its footing, charged at the gate and lifted it out of its way and charged after Heywood again! By now Heywood had sprinted home and was panting outside the door as we were leaving to catch the bus to school. The bull was on the other side of the hedge bellowing and churning up the soil with its front hooves but was not making any attempt to remove the gate which would allow him access to the farm yard. We left to catch the bus but Heywood, after getting back his breath, got hold of his double-barrel-shot-gun and with a stock of cartridges in his pocket went after his adversary to settle a few scores. By then the bull had re-joined the cows and Heywood went round the back way and got the bull in his sights and within range from the comparative safety of the top of a hedge. He shot the bull a few times in his back side which was enough to drive the creature through the gap in the hedge back to his own abode. After a few days the bull was fully recovered but he never again showed any interest in the cows over the hedge.

The Taf was a great river for fish and the Water Bailiff, Mr Murphy, had his work cut out trying to prevent *potsian* (poaching). Heywood owned a Driver and a Gaff and a Carbide lamp – the gear for poaching. One night Heywood and one or two others were searching for fish at a well-known pool near Llanglydwen fully armed with all the gear when Eia Rees, Yr Efail, Llanglydwen came along the river bank towards them shouting the warning '*'Ma Murphy yn Llanglydwen*!' Unfortunately her warning was answered immediately by a voice from across the river announcing 'Murphy is here!' And so it was that Heywood and the rest were caught poaching and were later fined by the Magistrates Court. But, in those days of salmon-filled rivers, Murphy stood no chance of stopping the supply of fresh fish reaching most households' tables during the poaching season.

There was no hay-shed at Cefn and at the end of the harvest a rick of hay in the *ydlan* had to be plucked of loose hay (*plwco'r rhic*) and thatched (*toi'r rhic*). Thatching a rick was a skilled craft which Heywood had learned, as previously mentioned, from Dafi Reynolds his co-worker at Frowen in the late 1930s. There is a classic photo of Heywood and an assistant, Ben Lewis, Llwyncelyn enjoying a cigarette-break surrounded by mounds of loose tinder-dry hay! At least for that particular hay-rick only an outside agent - like a match - could set it alight but ricks of unfit hay sometimes burst into flames as a result of slow internal combustion. Hence the endless examination and turning (*troi'r gwair*) of mowed hay to ensure it was dry and free of traces of green (*'bach yn las mae e*) before carting it to the hay-shed or rick. We never experienced the catastrophe of a hay-rick fire but I remember Heywood pushing a long metal rod deep into a rick to take its temperature. When the rod was too hot to handle a few uncomfortable days and nights would ensue until the rick showed signs of cooling. Hay-making was still labour intensive in the early 1950s and neighbours got together to manhandle the loose hay in the field and in the *ydlan* (hay-yard). Ten or so men and a few children turned up at Cefn and Heywood would suggest a job for each one. Lunch-time and tea-time were welcome rest periods when sandwiches and Welsh-cakes, tea and home-brew were served in the *ydlan*. On one occasion about six of us children were detailed to do some *crafu* (raking strands of hay left on the field after the bulk had been carted away) but were not missed when we did not stick to the task. We took a few bottles of home-brew to a quiet corner and sampled them until they were empty. As the last *gambo* of hay was unloaded some of us were violently sick in *pwll sand* and no more *crafu* took place that evening.

Heywood dug a silage pit which, for one thing, meant that the harvest was not so dependent on having good weather. Digging the silage pit was another back breaking task which Heywood thought nothing of undertaking such was his fearless approach to hard physical work.

A constant threat to crops was the large population of rabbits that plagued the countryside. Grass and other crops were eaten-away for distances of up to three metres from field boundaries. The rabbit population was controlled by trapping. A rabbit catcher was contracted and he would carry loads of Gin traps on his shoulders from one field to another. He examined a rabbit track leading from a hole (*twll gwningen*) in a hedge and noted a worn spot on the track where the rabbit landed. He pressed a shallow depression into the worn spot and set a Gin-trap into it and covered it with grass. This exercise was repeated for all the holes in a field's boundary hedge and in an afternoon traps would be set around as many fields as possible. During the night the unsuspecting rabbits emerged from their warrens only to step on a trap, spring it and have their legs trapped in its jaws. Rabbits' screams were heard all through the night but no one showed any undue concern because it was part-and-parcel of living in the countryside. Wil Coedfryn (William Williams), Cefnbrafle was the rabbit catcher in the area and he was sometimes assisted by Sid Felinfach. Early morning the rabbit catcher and assistant went round the traps, broke the rabbits' necks and collected the bodies for gutting after which their hind legs were spliced together enabling the body to be hung on a convenient holder. The bodies were taken to a centre like Y Bont, Llanglydwen from where they were collected by lorry and sold in markets as far-a-field as Birmingham. Heywood had some Gin-traps of his own and he as well as Bryan and myself were well versed in the business of trapping and breaking necks.

To supplement the trapping of rabbits we had a ferret, kept in a *cwb* (coop), and a bundle of nets. Ferreting on a Saturday morning was something to look forward to. As a starter we had to sew the ferrets lips together to prevent it killing a rabbit underground, eating its fill and sleeping in the warren for the rest of the day. After finding a warren, we set nets over the holes and put the ferret in one of them. Soon the rabbits would attempt to bolt from the holes only to be caught in the nets. We then broke their necks and after bagging a goodly number we got Heywood to gut them before taking them to Y Bont, Llanglydwen and selling them to Dai. No! I could not do it now but in those days it was a way of life in the countryside. Some of our ferreting was to supply live rabbits for Mansel Davies, of Llanfyrnach, founder of the now famous Haulage Firm, Mansel Davies and Son. Mansel in his youth had been a top class cyclist and motorcyclist and in the 1950s his sporting interest was racing greyhounds and part of their training was chasing live rabbits.

The Taf Valley with its overgrown terrain was ideal for hunting with Spaniel dogs and the fleeing rabbits and pheasants provided targets for the hunter with a gun. Wil Reynolds, Glasfryn, Cefnypant was as keen a hunter as anyone in the area.

Rabbit meat was part of our diet, especially in the form of stew but the rabbit plague of Myxomatosis which hit the area in the spring of 1954 removed rabbit from our menu but on the positive side crops now grew right up to the boundary hedges for the first time for 2,000 years. Mole skins were also in demand in those days and we trapped those blind burrowers as well, skinned them and pinned the skins on to a board to dry before once again walking or cycling to sell them to Dai Bont, a larger-than-life bachelor who was the landlord of the Penybont Inn. A maid looked after the house and milked his cows. He owned a greyhound, 'Old Judge' - a regular winner at the Fforestfach track near Swansea. Dai enjoyed betting but 'Old Judge''s winning habits had shortened his odds so that it was not worth betting on him. Dai decided to act. It was alleged that he took a box of paint with him to Fforestfach and put a few large spots on the dog's back and entered him under another name. The 'novice' runner attracted very favourable odds and as rain began to fall Dai rushed to collect his winnings and was on his way home before the rain could change the appearance of the 'novice'!

At a concert in Llanglydwen Hall Dai Bont was President for the evening. Presidents usually sat up front and said a few words at half time. However there was no sign of Dai until the interval arrived when he suddenly appeared at the back-door of the Hall and made his way down the centre aisle flanked by two friends just like a boxer and his seconds shuffling their way to the ring. When he reached the stage he simply repeated 'I'm here to tell my tale' a few times and then returned to his place behind the bar at Bont!

The Bont Inn was a doctor's surgery on one day a week. Two rooms were set aside: one as a waiting room and the other as the consulting room. Patients would turn up to see the visiting G.P.s; Gib (Dr Phillip Gibbin) or his partner Doctor Bach (Dr Gwyn Evans). Some people attended the surgery at Bont in order to meet and gossip with friends and never missed the weekly meeting unless they were ill! Dr Gibbin was born and brought-up locally at Penrallt, Login and in addition to his G.P. duties he also acted as a specialist for the Health Authority. He was a big man with a large head and was a prolific eater. He enjoyed brawn which was always in good supply on the farms after a pig-killing (*lladd mochyn*) when several basins-full would be made. Dr Gibbin was reputed to eat a basinful of brawn in one go. One day in Cefn I suddenly found myself unable to move my legs: some sort of paralysis had suddenly hit me. I was bundled into the van and taken to Dolycwrt Surgery, Whitland to see Dr Gibbin. I was better by the time I saw him but he insisted that I needed to see a specialist in Haverfordwest Hospital. A week or so later, we travelled in the van to Haverfordwest where, at the hospital, I was ushered into a curtained-off enclosure and a little later the curtains parted and there stood the specialist: none other than Dr Gibbin! He gave me a thorough examination but since I was not suffering from anything it is no surprise that no treatment was recommended and thankfully I never experienced paralysis thereafter.

3.1.4 The 11+ and a new world

In the spring of 1949 I sat the 11+ examination at Whitland Grammar School. Heywood took me to the school in the van and left me to find my way around the place which was an unnerving experience for a country boy. I eventually teamed-up with a room-full of children I'd never seen before and we were herded by two or three teachers into a large classroom to face the ordeal. The exam required some writing in Welsh and in English and working out a few sums. A few months later the results came through and our world changed again as I prepared to enter Whitland Grammar School (commonly referred to as 'isgol Whitland'). I well remember my last few weeks in Penygaer School because Harry Thomas a builder from Llandisilo started building a canteen where the school garden had previously been cultivated.

An information leaflet from Whitland Grammar School itemized requirements for a pupil entering Form 2W. There was no Form 1 which explained why, later on, we spent two years in Form 5 to avoid arriving early and unqualified in Form 6. The W stood for Welsh speakers; the other first year entrants went into 2E. In this way did the powers-that-be set about converting us Ws into English speakers. The listed requirements included a leather satchel and the smell of new leather in the shop in Whitland really put me off the whole business. A pair of gym shoes and shorts and a pair of football boots were other essentials. I got a new pair of daps but a pair of boots belonging to Lewis Eynon, Brynawel was bought second hand and Lil cut up an empty flour sack to make a pair of gym shorts, carefully avoiding displaying the blue 'Spillers' name across my backside. We had been a close-knit 'family' of 20 children at Penygaer County Primary, so it was a bit of a culture shock to suddenly be part of a 300-pupil-school at Whitland Grammar – a number which had doubled following the implementation of the 1944 Education Act.

I had suffered from tonsillitis in Blaenwaun Cottage and the severity of the attacks increased as I got older. The fever woke me up in the night and I claimed all sorts of outrageous 'visions'. The most talked about was my excited claim that the Sun was trapped in the corner of the bedroom! On that occasion the doctor was called by Heywood who travelled to the kiosk in Bont and Dr Bach climbed the ladder to the oil-lamp-lit attic and had as good a look down my throat as was possible using his torch. He gave me some medicine but more importantly he advised that I should have my tonsils removed. In the autumn of 1950 I was admitted to Hospital at Carmarthen for the operation and was there for about a week and in the same ward was Gwilym Davies our neighbour in Blaenwaun Cottage days. I do not know what was wrong with him unless it was hernia which was a common complaint with farmers except that they called it 'rupture'. After coming out of hospital, recovery was a slow process and I was confined to the house for a week or two. I re-read some books such as Daniel Owen's *Straeon y Pentan* and Elizabeth Watkin Jones' *Luned Bengoch*, *Lois* and *Esyllt*. Bryan was still at Penygaer School and he brought home two books by W E Johns which described the adventures of a pilot called Biggles. It was a very thoughtful gesture by *Mishtir* considering I had ceased to be his pupil for over a year. Lil reacted by finding out on her next trip to Carmarthen what books were available for boys of our age to read. She brought home one *Famous Five* and one *Secret Seven* and from that day on we became keen fans of Enid Blyton. It was around this time that we started buying the *Beano* and the *Dandy* on a fairly regular basis. Reading Comics had been encouraged by *Mishtir* who used to bring piles of *Beano* and *Dandy* comics to school and our weekly English lesson on a Friday afternoon sometimes consisted of reading about Desperate Dan and Korky the Cat. And then a new comic, The *Eagle*, was launched with its leading character Dan Dare – pilot of the future. We took that too.

Heywood's and Lil's thirst for local news continued and the *Carmarthen Journal*, *The Welshman* and *The Weekly News for Pembrokeshire and Carmarthenshire*, known locally as the *Narberth News*, were bought every week. Other weeklies which appeared at Cefn from time-to-time were the *Western Telegraph*, a paper based in Haverfordwest and founded in 1854, and the *Cardigan and Tivy Side Advertiser* founded in 1866 - both are still in circulation.

Our expanding world was not limited to acquiring more reading material. It must have been an advert in the *Western Mail* that alerted us to the existence of Meccano construction sets and once we showed an interest Lil, with Heywood's full backing, wrote to David Morgan, The Hayes, Cardiff to place an order. In due course the postman delivered the goods and we were soon at work joining together metal pieces to make all sorts of mechanical models from buildings and bridges to cars and tractors. However we also found out that getting the electric motor to drive a device as shown in the advert was far from easy to accomplish in practice.

In 1952 Bryan passed the eleven-plus and in September both of us were on the bus at 8.00 a.m. heading for 'isgol Whitland' (Whitland Grammar School). After entering the grammar school we were, in a way, leading a double life of, on the one hand, experiencing the 'new' at school such as non-Welsh speakers from Laugharne and Pendine, English-medium education, geometry, algebra, science, rugby, cricket and athletics and on the other hand, continuing with the 'traditional' at home such as attendance at Cefnypant Chapel, ferreting, haymaking and enjoying the natural environment and being part of the monolingual Welsh community of Dyffryn Taf. As the years went by more and more of the 'new' was brought home and the 'traditional' was gradually squeezed out. But not the language. Whilst English was the language of the classroom at Whitland, Welsh was the language of the playground and, at home, belonging to the local community was only possible through the medium of Welsh.

But the traditional activities took quite a knock as in addition to the mounting homework we were also by the mid-1950s spending time improving our athletic prowess on a running track we measured out on one of Haydn's fields and also on the natural slope of the Fron fields. Furthermore, Heywood and Lil must have been mystified by our antics when the best county-cricket-team in England played the best and only team in Wales in the field next to *pwll sand*. We knew the names of the eleven players in both the Surrey and the Glamorgan sides through intense study of the *Western Mail* sports pages. One of us assumed a different name, eleven times in-order to complete one team's innings, unless a declaration was made, and the other played the roles of the other team's range of bowlers. Surrey was led by Stuart Surridge and included Peter May, the Bedser twins, Jim Laker, Tony Lock and Peter Loader and Glamorgan was captained by Wilfred Wooller with Emrys Davies, Phil Clift, Gilbert Parkhouse, Allan Watkins, Jim McConnon, Don Shepherd and the rest making them a formidable team. But there was a clear lack of variety in batting and bowling styles in both teams when they played at the Cefn Oval!

From 1953, six days of every week during the autumn and spring terms were taken-up by school studies and rugby playing, leaving only Sunday as the day when we could switch-off from school work except that usually we had homework to do! However, at the same time I cannot think of any other child from the Cefnypant catchment area at that time that followed such a committed timetable in terms of school sport as well as studies. The majority of children, not only in the Cefnypant area but throughout the country, had no homework, no Saturday sport and finished at their Senior Centre Schools at 15-years-of-age. Such was the divisiveness of the 11+ examination.

Of course it was the system that divided us and when the system was absent, for example during school holidays, there was no division. But it is interesting to note that even during school holidays playing football and rugby took up more and more of everyone's time: the influence of the grammar school was all pervading. On one occasion about eight of us from the Cefnypant/Llanglydwen catchment area got together and organized games of rugby and soccer against a similar number of boys from the Llangolman area. We got permission to use one of Haydn's fields at Cefn and cut-down suitable trees for goal posts. The encounter took place on a Saturday and a few weeks later we cycled the five miles or so to Llangolman for the return matches.

3.1.5 Heywood's odd-jobs, newspapers and boxing

As already mentioned, Cefn was a 40-acre small-holding and although Heywood and Lil did as much as possible to maximize the income from milk and eggs, Heywood was always on the look-out for jobs to supplement his income. In 1950 he took on the work of planting trees on sloping land (*bryst*) near Login on behalf of Vincent Williams, Cilowen. Bryan and myself assisted and soon discovered how hard the job was and lunch-time was a welcome break. We quenched our thirst with drinks of water and Heywood had a few swigs from a flagon of ale. Mrs Margaret Williams, Vincent's daughter-in-law, still recalls Heywood's put-down of a self-righteous observer of the scene who declared that the contents of a flagon had for him a dreadful taste. 'No doubt it has' said Heywood ' you have to generate some sweat to appreciate that taste'!

He also drove a baker's van for Will Lewis of Login and delivered bread to homes in the north of the Taf Valley.

A few months after moving to Cefn, Heywood applied to the Ministry of Agriculture for the job of Calf Certifying Officer for the parish of Llanboidy. The appointment was decided on a vote between two applicants which Heywood won. Farmers were paid a subsidy by the Ministry of Agriculture to rear calves: £5 for a steer and £2 for a heifer. The farmers had to fill-in an application form printed in bilingual format and return it to the County Executive Agricultural Committee which redistributed the forms on a parish basis to the Certifying Officers. A batch of forms arrived at Cefn every month and Heywood and Lil planned a route around the farms listed, decided on a day to visit them and worked out the approximate time at which each farm could expect Heywood to call. Lil undertook the secretarial work and filled-in the appropriate information for each farm on a card and on the reverse side she entered the appropriate address. The completed batch of cards were posted at Cefnypant or at Llanglydwen. On the agreed day or days Heywood toured the farms inspecting and cutting out a small slot from one ear of every calf using a pincer designed for the job. He did this work on average about two days a month. The largest number of calves certified by him in one day was 122 on 25 August 1951. In 1948 he certified 401 calves over 14 days; in 1949 it was 872 over 20 days; in 1950 it was 733 over 17 days; in 1951 it was 542 over 9 days and in 1952 it was 36 calves over 4 days. He was paid 3s. 6d (17.5p) per calf. The scheme ended in 1952 and over the 42 months of its existence it brought in a total income of £452.20 (equivalent to £13,521 in 2013 - Bank of England Composite Price Index). Heywood bought a dark-blue Ford van and travelled all over Llanboidy Parish, which extended from the river Taf down to Whitland, and visited farms with exotic names like Blaensarngoch, Cilhengroes-isaf, Ffynnonfoida, Trebleiddied, Pistyllefrith, Pantygwenin, Pantyffynnon, Gellydogin, Llanlliwe, Llwyncroi, Blaenwernddu, Glynpebyll, Trwyn-y-graig, Dyffrynbroidyn, Blaencediw, Maencoch-yr-wyn, Blaenwauneirch, Wernoleufawr, Ffosddufach, Bryngwelltyn, Penrhiwgoch-isaf, Blaenwernddu, Ysguborwen, Llwyn-ty-gwyn.

Heywood improved Cefn as a farm by ploughing and re-seeding one field every year or so. He bought a second hand Ferguson tractor popularly known as *y Ffergi bach* (little Fergie). Harry Ferguson did farmers a great favour in designing and developing his tractor. Up to that time Allis Chalmers and Fordson tractors were simply mechanical versions of the horse in that they simply pulled the implements along. But the Ferguson tractor was based on hydraulics which enabled implements to be lifted off the ground and placed wherever they were needed. For example, it enabled ploughing to start right from the hedge. In the early 1950s it was the turn of the field-by-the-sand-pit (*parc pwll sand*) to be improved and after it had been ploughed it was necessary to run a disc over it and then a harrow (*oged*). It was either during school holidays or on a Saturday that I was left on the Ferguson tractor to go over the field with a harrow while the rest of the family went in the van to Whitland to do some shopping. I was severely warned to keep clear of *pwll sand*. But somehow or other during the afternoon I did drive too close to the sand pit and the wheels on one side slipped over the edge leaving the tractor balanced on the edge. I was terrified but soon regained control of myself and ran over to Cilhernin where, thankfully, Wyn and Dai were available and immediately started-up one of their Massey tractors, found a link chain and the three of us drove over to the site of near catastrophe. In no time at all the big Massey pulled the small Ferguson out of the sand pit much to my relief! When the shopping party returned I was busy finishing-off the *ogedu* as if nothing out-of-the-ordinary had happened!

It was a sign of Heywood and Lil's improved financial position that the *Western Mail* was delivered daily by post. In addition to the sports pages, the adventures of Twm Sion Cati in a strip of illustrations by Geoffrey Evans each described in two-line verses by Beryl M. Jones was a huge attraction. The *News of the World* was delivered on Sundays and introduced us to Football Pools. Littlewoods Pools were filled regularly at the start of one season but the match results announced in the Wireless' Sports Report at 5.00 pm on Saturday was invariably disappointing and after switching to Vernons Pools made no difference, the practice was abandoned. The daily *Western Mail* was particularly important in keeping us in touch with activities in the big wide world beyond the confines of the chapel-orientated community of the Taf Valley. It informed us about war in Korea, the ascent of Everest and the dog Laika's one-way-ticket into space. Once a week we raced home from the school bus to listen to the weekly *Awr y Plant,* the one-hour-a-week children's broadcast in Welsh on the so-called BBC Welsh Home Service whose output was almost entirely in English. Only a flat wet-battery stopped us listening to the *Galw Gari Tryfan* detective series as well as the science fiction series *Journey into Space* on BBC Light Programme; the start of both being announced by some haunting music. On a Sunday evening in winter we sometime fiddled with the wireless' tuning knob and came across stations such as Athlone before finding Radio Luxembourg with its mix of advertising, game shows and music. Someone called Horace Batchelor promoted his 'Infra Draw' system for winning the football pools but we ignored him; another announcer was called Bob Danvers-Walker who, also, was the anonymous off-screen commentator for the British Pathe newsreel shown in cinemas. And we had our first introduction to Hughie Green - or at least to his voice - as the host of 'Double your Money'.

Heywood's interest in Boxing led to an order for the monthly *Boxing News* which we studied eagerly. Boxing in those days was a genuinely competitive business with eliminators and final eliminators held at every weight to find a challenger to the champion. In sharp contrast to the farcical miss-matches that occur so often these days the vast majority of fights were between well-matched boxers. Of-course there was far greater poverty in the 1940s and 1950s compared to today and boxing offered a chance to escape a lifetime of drudgery. This was reflected in the high number of registered boxers and in the numerous tournaments enabling boxers to fight as often as possible to earn some money and attempt to progress towards the top. In 1948 a total of 200 British boxers had bouts during the year; in 1949 the number was 300 and in 1950 the records of 280 British boxers who had fought during the year were listed in the Boxing News Annual. Welsh boxers made up 10% of them; an indication that deprivation in Wales was about twice that expected on a population basis. Those were the days when there was only eight divisions: fly (8st), bantam (8st 6lb), feather (9st), light (9st 9lb), welter (10st 7lb), middle (11st 6lb), light-heavyweight (12st 7lb) and heavyweight and there was only one champion at each weight. Every champion was deserving of the accolade because he had to defend his title regularly against the best in his division. But the seed of discord and confusion in the heavyweight division was sown in 1949 when the Americans ignored the strong claims of the British and Empire and European champion, Bruce Woodcock, as a contender for the vacant world title and matched their own Ezzard Charles and Jersey Joe Walcot for the title; a fight won by Charles. The British Boxing Board of Control retaliated in June 1950 by matching Woodcock against another leading American, Lee Savold, for the British version of the world title. Woodcock was a knock-out specialist but his weak point was the ease with which his face cut and as we crouched around the wireless at Cefn straining to hear Raymond Glendenning's commentary and W. Barrington-

Dalby's inter-round summary we managed to make-out that by round three Bruce was badly cut and the fight was stopped giving Savold the British version of the world title and then the battery went dead. Ezzard Charles strengthened his case for being the undisputed champion by defeating the great Jo Louis, the former undefeated champion who had come out of retirement in September 1950. When Louis, in his next fight, knocked-out Savold the British Boxing Board of Control quietly forgot about its version of world order.

Eddie Thomas from Merthyr was another boxing hero in those days. He became British welterweight champion in 1949 and successfully defended his title against fellow Welshman Cliff Curvis of Swansea at the St Helens ground in September 1950. Eddie gained the Empire title in January 1951 and a month later he fought the Italian Michele Palermo for the European title at the Market Hall, Carmarthen where Heywood saw him outpoint Palermo over 15 rounds.

The outstanding boxing star of the early 1950s and everyone's hero was middleweight Randolph Turpin the Leamington Licker. In September 1950 Turpin set out on a fight-a-month programme which he carried on, remarkably, for 11 months taking on and beating the best in Europe and collecting the British and the European titles on the way and finishing with a world title fight at London's Earls Court Arena against the great Sugar Ray Robinson from the USA. Sugar Ray is still reckoned by many to be the greatest pound-for-pound fighter of all time. Turpin was brilliant against Sugar Ray but you would not have thought so from the wireless commentary! Amazingly, Raymond Glendenning and W Barrington-Dalby allowed the claimed invincibility of Robinson to cloud their judgements resulting in their pro-Robinson commentaries! We were glued to the wireless whose wet battery had been freshly charged for the occasion but we gathered from the commentary that Robinson was going to win. But lo! and behold! the referee gave it to Turpin! Biased referee? It was only after reading the *Western Mail* reports that we found out that Turpin had boxed brilliantly and had clearly outpointed Sugar Ray to whom the referee gave only 4 out of the 15 rounds! It was very disappointing that, with the batteries for once fully charged, the incompetent commentators spoilt what should for us have been a deliriously happy hour! Glendenning and Dalby were soon dropped by the BBC to be replaced by the golden-voiced Irishman Eamon Andrews.

Talking of commentators, the 1950s was the time when G. V. Wynne Jones ruled the roost as the Wireless rugby commentator. Photographs showed him to have a handlebar moustache and his posh accent made him the unlikeliest Welshman! But he got very excited when Wales scored. I remember him describing a Wales match on a very misty day when it was impossible for him to see the farthest corners of the pitch. When Wales surged towards their opponents line and players disappeared in the far corner mist, G V Wynne Jones had to wait for the referee to re-appear from the gloom signalling a try had been scored before gleefully announcing 'It's a <u>beautiful</u> try for Wales'!

3.2 Early 1950s – 1958

3.2.1 Rugby and soccer

I did not know that such a game as rugby existed until I went to Whitland Grammar School in September 1949. But my interest was immediately aroused and when Wales won the triple crown and grand slam in 1950 a photograph of the 'Triple Crown Winners' in the *Western Mail* was duly cut out and stuck on the *palish* above the door into the living room at Cefn and there it remained until it was stored away on moving to Glanrhyd in 1958. Wales had an outstanding captain in schoolmaster John Gwilliam the No. 8 forward born in Pontypridd and educated at Monmouth School and Cambridge University who played for Edinburgh Wanderers. Outstanding also was the full back, centre or wing, 18-year-old Lewis Jones, born in Gorseinon and educated at Gowerton Grammar School, who played for Neath, the Navy and Llanelli and, after helping Wales to a second grand slam in 1952, went north to play professional rugby for Leeds and Great Britain. They also had a brilliant flank forward in Ray Cale of Pontypool but he was the only one of the Welsh forwards not picked for the 1950 Lions tour to New Zealand and Australia; the reason given was that he was over robust! The triple crown match of 1950 was at Ravenhill Park, Belfast on 11 March when Wales scored two tries to Ireland's penalty goal to win by 6 points to 3. There was a ploughing match in Llanglydwen on that freezing and bitterly cold day but thankfully someone had a wireless in a van on the field and I remember crowding around the van listening to a very close game which remained stuck at 3 points all for ages. Wales was awarded a penalty a long way out and Gwilliam called up the acknowledged long-range specialist kicker, the Rosslyn Park prop, J D Robbins to attempt the goal kick. A 'knowledgeable' local remarked that Gwilliam should take the kick himself rather that give it to Robbins! The kick was missed and with the final whistle about to be blown the match was won when the Newport wing Malcolm Thomas crashed over for a try in the corner. The unsighted referee had to get confirmation from the Irish touch judge that Thomas was not in touch and the try was valid. The Welsh success was put in perspective when a plane-load of returning Welsh supporters crashed in a field near Llandow killing 80 passengers and crew. With only 3 survivors the tragic incident was the world's worst civil aircraft disaster up to that date.

Two seasons later Wales again led by John Gwilliam and with the mercurial Cliff Morgan at outside half repeated the triple crown and grand slam success. As a mater of interest it is worth noting the fallacy of the often-made-claim that Wales' forwards in those successful times were all hardened miners or steelworkers. In fact the 1950 Welsh pack consisted of one miner and none of the others, which included two policemen and two teachers, were even manual workers. The 1952 pack was made up of one steel worker and possibly one other manual worker. So it was their playing ability and fitness that mattered, and not their occupation. During the 1950s Wales had some success against the touring teams from the Southern Hemisphere when in 1951 they lost by only 6pts to 3 against South Africa and in 1953 they actually beat New Zealand by 13 points to 8; a win that is never to be repeated it seems.

The 1950s were also a golden age for Welsh soccer in terms of having outstanding players to choose from. The Welsh football team was mainly if not wholly made up of players from England's first division (equivalent to today's premier league). Jack Kelsey (goalkeeper), Walley Barnes (fullback) and Ray Daniel (centre half) were leading players with Arsenal, Ron Burgess (mid-field) was at Tottenham Hotspur, Roy Paul (mid-field) was with Manchester City, Trevor Ford (centre forward) played for Aston Villa and Sunderland, Ivor Allchurch was brilliant at Swansea Town and later with Newcastle United, and the outstanding player of the decade, John Charles (anywhere), played for Leeds United and Juventus. However, despite having a team full of outstanding talent, for some reason, Wales still found it difficult to win games. Their 1950s record against England was W1,D3,L6, against Scotland it was W1,D4,L5 and against Northern Ireland W4,D4,L2. The one bright spot was getting to the 1958 World Cup finals in Sweden where they were unlucky to lose their quarter final game 1-0 to the eventual champions Brazil. Europe-wide club competitions were unknown in those days and the highlight of the season – more so than today - was the F.A. Cup Final. Aunt Glenys and family had a television – a rare possession in the 1950s – and we travelled by the Carmarthen service bus to her home near Llanginin where in 1952 we saw and suffered the agony of Wales' captain, Wally Barnes, forced off the field after half-an-hour with a knee injury and ten-man Arsenal failed to stop Newcastle United winning the cup for the second year running. The following year Stanley Mathews' brilliance provided the chances for Stan Mortensen to score a hat-trick for Blackpool who beat Bolton 4-3 in a thrilling final.

3.2.2 The 1950s General Elections

At the 1950 General Election the Labour government's majority fell to five. The only change in representation in west Wales was in Pembrokeshire where the Liberal Gwilym Lloyd George lost to Labour's Desmond Donnelly who had a colourful career as Labour MP until he resigned the whip in 1968 to form his own Democratic Party. He lost Pembrokeshire to the Tories in 1970 and went into business but when his ventures ran into trouble he committed suicide in 1974. After the 1951 General Election the Tories replaced Labour in government where they remained for the next thirteen years. Churchill became Prime Minister for the second time at the age of 77 and one of his first decisions was to authorize Britain's first nuclear test at Monte Bello islands. The scientist who actually did the countdown to trigger the explosion was for ever after known as the 'Count of Monte Bello'. In 1954 Churchill gave the go ahead for the development of a British hydrogen bomb as 'the price we pay to sit at the top table'. The General Election in May 1955 was again won by the Tories under Anthony Eden who increased his majority over Clem Attlee's Labour party. But within two years Eden was brought down by his adventure to the Suez Canal. The Liberals won only six seats in total with three of those in Wales.

There was no doubting Heywood's and Lil's disappointment back in 1945 when their hoped-for Liberal revival failed to materialize and the party's continued decline probably contributed to their loss of interest in politics. No doubt they continued to vote Liberal because Heywood saw the Liberal party as middle-of-the-road and for the ordinary people. He was anti-gentry because he saw them-*y gwyr mowr*- as exploiters of the ordinary people and therefore he would never vote Tory. He had no time for shirkers living on benefits and this unfortunate spin-off from the welfare state he equated with Labour and therefore he would not support the party of the left either. The 1955 General Election in Wales' 36 seats resulted in a total of 27 wins for Labour, but we still had a Tory government!

3.2.3 Studies and sport change everything

As already mentioned the *Eagle* was launched in 1950. The following year *The Eagle Book of Records and Champions*' appeared. The book was full of facts, figures and photographs which greatly increased our knowledge of the sporting world and of Britain's engineering achievements – information that had not been readily available in the pre-war world of our parents. The first part of the book dealt with 'Aircraft', 'Railways', 'Racing Cars', 'Motor Boats' and 'Ships'. It was a time when Britain led the world in 'Aircraft' with the world's largest airliner, the propeller-driven 'Bristol Brabazon' launched in September 1949 and intended to fly a regular non-stop London-New York service with a maximum of 100 passengers and the world's fastest airliner the turbojet 'De Haviland Comet' which flew at an easy speed of 490 m.p.h. with a maximum of 48 passengers. London Airport was in the process of conversion from the old RAF triangular system of runways to one in which two parallel runways could be used at the same time. 'Racing Cars' referred to the 'Grand Prix of Europe' held at Silverstone on 13 May 1950 which, in fact, was the first ever Formula 1 race. Italian drivers, Farina and Fagioli took the first two places and a Briton, Reg Parnell was third. 'Ships' informed us that the 'Queen Elizabeth' was the biggest ocean-going liner in the world able to carry 2,265 passengers and 1,260 crew while her sister ship the 'Queen Mary' was the fastest, having crossed the Atlantic eastwards in 3 days 20 hours 42 minutes.

The second part of the Eagle book covered twelve sports. 'Football' included Association Football, Rugby Union and League. We learned that Wales' centre-forward (striker) Trevor Ford was the costliest transfer in history when Sunderland paid Aston Villa £29,000 for his services. Born in Swansea, he played for Swansea Town before signing for Aston Villa. The stars of the English Football League were overwhelmingly English (the only foreign players were Welsh, Scottish and Irish). England's team was full of outstanding players like Billy Wright, Stanley Mathews, Tom Finney, Alf Ramsey, Bert Williams, Stan Mortenson, Jackie Milburn and Wilf Mannion. But they still lost to the USA and also to Spain in the group matches for the 1950 World Cup and were on the early plane home. There were only four photos in the rugby section and they were of Welsh players and matches. 'Cricket' had pictures of past England greats but a statement that it was difficult to spot 'immortals' apart from Len Hutton and Denis Compton, was the only hint that during 1950 England had been thrashed by Australia away and by the West Indies at home! 'Athletics' had many photos from the 1948 London Olympics. The list of world record holders showed that middle-distance running was dominated by white European runners; the age of the Africans was a long way off. The women's list showed the remarkable ability of Fannie Blankers-Koen of Holland who held world records for the 100 and 220 yards sprints, the 80 metres hurdles, the high jump and the long jump! 'Speedway' was a popular sport and Welshman Freddy Williams was World Speedway Champion in 1950. 'Golf' revealed that the winners of the British Open from 1900 to 1921 were British together with a lone Frenchman in 1907. But then the Americans got hold of some clubs and dominated the tournament although South African Bobby Locke won in 1949 and 1950. In 'Cycling' Reg Harries (G.B.) was the World Professional Sprint Champion in 1949 and 1950. 'Tennis', 'Table Tennis', 'Horse Racing' and 'Swimming' were also briefly covered.

It was Doctor Bach who 'prescribed' a bottle of Mackeson every now and again as an aid to my recovery from hospitalization. The removal of my tonsils certainly changed life for me; a chill no longer triggered a fever and a few days in bed and although I was back in school before the end-of-term exams the form master N.M.M.(Neville) Thomas very kindly excused my rather ordinary performance as being 'A very creditable record in view of his long absences this term'. Bryan was much healthier than I was in those days (*crwt llawer cryfach*). To further help my recovery it was arranged for me to get my fill of the remedy-for-all-ills - sea air (*aer y mor*). Lil discovered that two boys from the locality Hywel Lewis, Llwynllwyd who was older than me and Owen Gibbin, Penrallt who had been in my class in Penygaer School were going for a week's holiday to *Tidrath* (*Trefdraeth*/ Newport Pembrokeshire) and it was arranged for me to accompany them. We stayed in full-board lodgings near the castle. I enjoyed the week more than I realized at the time because, not only did I go back for another holiday the following year with Bryan and Goronwy Phillips, Rosehill - again full-board but in a large house named Sunnymeade on the Parrog - but ever since I have found *Tidrath* irresistible and have stayed there on a regular basis. Paying for those holidays must have stretched Heywood and Lil's finances but it was simply characteristic of them that whatever they thought was good for the boys *(y bois)* would be done if at all possible. In the following years we went on summer camps organized by *Urdd Gobaith Cymru* which in English is called 'The Welsh League of Youth' although it is far from being an accurate translation. The *Urdd* holidays were booked through the school and in successive years in the early 1950s we went to three camps: a house in Criccieth, bell tents in Llangranog and a converted mansion Plas Glanllyn near Bala.

Looking back now I realize how much our every-day-life changed in the 1950s. Perhaps the biggest change was the increased mobility. No longer was the Sunday School trip and the bus journeys to the c*ymanfaoedd* our only major journeys out of our own patch as they were in the 1940s. From about 1948 the few that passed the 11+ were transported by bus to Whitland Grammar School but everyone else stayed on in the primary schools until they reached school-leaving-age. It was sometime in the early 1950s that every pupil over 11-years-of-age left their primary schools and travelled by bus to Whitland to attend either the Grammar School or the Senior Centre. There was a bus service to Carmarthen on Wednesdays and on Saturdays which changed shopping habits to the detriment of Taf Valley village shops. The bus-stop in Carmarthen was near the West End Cafe in Lammas Street and for half-an-hour or so prior to the evening departure the cafe resounded to orders of 'fish a chips, *tê a bara menyn* (bread and butter)' as the passengers fortified themselves for the homeward journey. By the 1950s we had our own Ford van in which, often on a Sunday evening after milking, we went for a 'run' to Mynachlogddu in the Preseli Hills and in particular to *Comin Rhosfach* (common), where Waldo's (1904-1971) memorial now stands, at the foot of Foel Cwm Cerwyn and not far from Carnabwth, home of Twm or Thomas Rees (1806-1876) the first Rebeca of the Rebeca Uprising. Eirwyn George's feelings about nearby *Patshyn Glas:* ' *Mae holl gyfaredd y Preselau i'w deimlo yn y llecyn hwn'* (The whole enchantment of the Preselau can be felt in this place) is just as true for *Comin Rhosfach*. Sometimes we went up to the *Trath Mowr* (Big Beach) and the Parrog at *Tidrath* (Newport).

When we started playing rugby for the school we caught the Saturday morning train from Llanglydwen Station to Whitland and for away games a bus took us as far a-field as Llandovery in the north, Tenby in the south-west and Fishguard in the west. After the game and a quick lunch we returned to Whitland to catch the 4.00p.m. train to Llanglydwen. After home matches we had an afternoon's wait for the train to leave its parking bay in the station. On one occasion about half a dozen of us fooled around and made a bit of a mess in a carriage. A passing GWR official looked in and startled by what he saw uttered the immortal bilingual comment ' look at the *annibendod* in there then!' In 1953 I went to Cardiff for the first time on a school trip to watch Wales play England at rugby.

A major change in our lives in the 1950s was the decreasing importance of chapel activities. We continued to attend Sunday School regularly but other activities such as the young people's society as well as the Sunday afternoon service (*cwrdd pregeth*) were often missed because of homework commitments. Bryan and myself were admitted as members of Cefnypant Chapel in 1954 and 1955 respectively. Thereafter we attended the grown-ups class in Sunday School and the teacher Mr Howells, Glyntaf did his best to in-still some class discussion into the proceedings but with little success as our in-born diffidence ruled the roost. The grown-ups' Sunday School was not very well attended. Heywood and Lil had given up attending although they often reminisced about the time in their youth when the large numbers present necessitated separation by sex and age into several classes. But by the mid 1950s those days were long gone. Unfortunately it had also become the practice for the young men (*bechgyn ifanc*), to avoid joining the chapel choir. I have to admit that I was looking forward to joining the choir but when the choir master called for all those interested to stay seated at the end of a service, the young men took no notice and trooped out and I, not wanting to be different, followed the flock. Tom Williams, the choir master, came after us and asked the group to return to at least increase the numbers if not improve the singing but true to form there was a lot of giggling and looking at the ground and if anyone had the desire to return to the fold, then like me, they did not have the guts to break the mould.

In August 1955, Mam Canerw (Martha Elizabeth Owen), Heywood's mother passed away at the age of 71 after a relatively brief illness. The funeral at Cefnypant Chapel was the first one for Bryan and myself to attend. (An account of Mam Canerw's life and ancestors is in "*Hynafiaid Mam Canerw*", 2006, unpublished)

As described in Part I both Heywood and Lil had grown up in a community where the influence of the chapel was paramount. They and their brothers and sisters became chapel members as soon as they left school. A measure of Heywood's and Lil's commitment to chapel affairs during and after the war can be gleaned from Cefnypant's yearly reports. In 1939 after one year of married life, each donated 10s. 6d to support the ministry; an amount which was 80% of the average donation. For 1944, the last year of the war, each gave 15s. towards the ministry or 75% of the average. Over the following ten years their individual donations increased progressively to 30s. by 1955. After 1958 their increased prosperity in Glanrhyd was reflected in their significantly higher donations at around 125% of the average and from 1985 to 1992 each gave £30 per annum to support the ministry. Although they contributed equally in monetary terms, Heywood was considerably less committed to chapel matters than was Lil. However, both of them allowed chapel activities to be displaced by school orientated tasks and also in common with the overwhelming majority of people in the community by new attractions unconnected with the chapel. At the same time Lil's commitment to social activities at Cefnypant never ceased. She continued with others to write material – light-hearted verses (*penillion*) - for Cefnypant's concert party (*parti noson lawen*) which entertained audiences in chapel vestries at such places as Cwmfelin Mynach and Login during the 1960s. As late as 1969 the occasion of the young Reverend Jeffrey Williams' acceptance of the pastorate of Glandwr and Cefnypant was a significant community event celebrated by the concert party in front of a capacity audience.

However, at the same time the younger generations were increasingly enabled to sample new activities outside of the chapels' sphere-of-influence which widened their horizons and eventually led to the break-up of the traditional chapel-orientated communities of the Taf Valley and other rural areas. The changed pattern of schooling meant that children left their local primary schools at eleven-years-of-age to spend at least four years at a secondary school in a totally new environment based on a concentration of pupils collected from a wide area by a fleet of buses. Young Farmers Clubs established in the 1940s and 1950s provided opportunities for young people to develop their talents in a whole range of fields from practical farming activities to public-speaking and the performing arts and to meet and learn from others through over-seas visits. Bus services started in the 1940s made it easy to access Saturday night recreation in Carmarthen where there was dancing in the barracks and films in the Lyric and the Capitol although if you insisted on seeing the final twenty minutes in the Capitol you missed the bus home! At the cinema, Pathé News, introduced by a wake-up call from a crowing cockerel, informed us about life in other parts of the world and a double-bill of B-movie and feature-film would invariably open our eyes to all-sorts of worldly activities unknown to most from the sheltered confines of the Taf Valley. The films that I remember from those days are *The Last Days of Dolwyn* with Richard Burton making his debut, *How Green was my Valley* about life in a Welsh mining valley but filmed in Hollywood without a single Welsh actor among the credits, *The Corn is Green* based on Emlyn Williams' play of the same name but again no Welsh actors appeared in the American film and *The Robe* with Richard Burton - another classic which 'everyone' went to see.

The rapid spread of motor transport enabled people to widen their recreational activities in accordance with their own wishes. Particularly popular were the Fun Fairs held during the autumn although the season kicked-off at the end of August with *Ffair* Crymych. There were fairs at Llanglydwen and at Llanboidy with swings and roundabouts and the usual side-stalls but the fairs at Whitland, St Clears and Carmarthen were much larger events. They had 'bumper cars' and a 'wall of death' demonstration where two motor bikes, after gaining enough speed, were ridden horizontally around the inside of a massive cylindrical wall. In another prefab enclosure a ghost train ride left some looking in need of a blood transfusion. The big attraction for many was Cardiff-born Ron Taylor's Boxing Booth where half a dozen of Ron's 'champions' challenged the local tough guys to stay three rounds with them for a certain purse. Tommy Farr and Randy Turpin had started their careers in Taylor's Booth. At

Whitland Fair some of the local rugby players took up the challenge and Owen Edwards and Frank Leggat always did well. Before he died age 95 in 2006, Ron Taylor reminisced that colliers and farmers provided the fiercest challenges and he reckoned some of the best fights he witnessed in Wales were at Llanybydder Fair.

Increased mobility brought about the beginning of in-migration and a few farms were bought by English people. Having no knowledge of Welsh and with no measures in place to assist them with learning the language, the incomers relied on the indigenous population making the effort to speak their language of English. The community in general was still overwhelmingly Welsh speaking and many people had very limited vocabulary in English. In those days farmers helped their neighbours during harvest time and one Englishman was puzzled when a local requested him to move a ladder with the words 'Move the school'! 'Ysgol' is the Welsh word for both 'school' and 'ladder'.

Motorised transport in the form of a two-stroke motorbike enabled men of Indian origin to bring their silken wares to the heart of rural west Wales. One or two reached the Llanglydwen area in the mid 1950s and when one called at Cefn, he opened his leather case on the door step to show his selection of tightly packed silk goods and explained that he was selling the stuff at bargain prices. But the culture gulf was too wide to draw much of a response at all from Lil and the man from India or perhaps Birmingham was soon on his way with all his goods again tucked into his portmanteau. Much more welcome and successful at selling their goods were the *Shoni Winwns* (Johnie Onions), the onion sellers from Brittany. They came in the autumn by boat from Roscoff to Plymouth. One group was based at Newcastle Emlyn although they said *Castell Newi* because, as Breton speakers, they quickly picked up Breton's sister language of Welsh. They did their selling in Welsh and were a feature of the autumn scene for years until 'market forces' put an end to their trade. But not before they had set up Brittany Ferries, which is still going strong. When Gwyn Griffiths' book '*Y Shonis Olaf*' appeared in 1981 I was amazed to see in it a photograph of our onion seller of the 1950s. His name was Joseph Olivier and he came from Mercheroux near Roscoff where his widow and Welsh-speaking son Michael still lived in the 1980s.

However all was not perfect by any means in that developing 'modern age'. The ease of travelling to Carmarthen on Saturday nights resulted in occasional violence on the streets as rival 'gangs' from surrounding villages settled their imagined differences. But that paled into insignificance compared to what happened in 1953 when Llangynin villagers and the wider population were faced with a mystery which quickly developed into a pit of fear. It all started when farmer John Harries and his wife Phoebe of Derlwyn Farm, Llangynin went missing although their nephew Ronnie Harries of Cadno Farm, Pendine claimed they had gone to London for a holiday leaving him in charge. But up to that time John and Phoebe's furthest trips had been the occasional reluctant journey to nearby Carmarthen. After months of meticulous detective work by Capstick of the Yard Ronnie's unlikely tale was shown to be just that when the couple were found buried in a shallow grave in a field of rape at Cadno Farm, having been bludgeoned to death with a hammer. What made the case even more shocking for pupils of Whitland Grammar School was to be told that Ronnie Harries was the driver of the Landrover which often collected one of the sixth-form girls after school. We remembered the Landrover even if most of us had not been particularly interested in the driver. Ronnie Harries was hanged in Swansea Prison. The community was well used to coping with the pain of natural deaths, accidental deaths and even suicides but murder was something else.

3.2.4 'Rupture' repair

Rupture (hernia) was a fairly common complaint among farmers and Heywood succumbed to the dreaded bulge in 1954. He was admitted to hospital at Carmarthen in August 1954 and the resulting exchange of letters between Lil and Heywood were full of interesting information. Lil's letter was sent soon after his admission:

'Cefn

Login   Monday

Dear Heywood

Well how are you, I hope you're not very homesick. Every thing is all right here so far though its very lonely here without you. Denley went over to Canerw to meet Gon coming home [from visiting Heywood] and he said most likely you shall have the operation Tuesday morning so we shall ring-up tomorrow morning to see how things shall be. Denley saw Ken Llwyncelyn at Cefnypant today …, he said he will come to see you Sat. Well Heywood I hope to see you Wed and hope that you shall be home again in a weeks time. Stanley Rhoshill said today that Lewis Sylvania was only in for a fortnight and he had something [hernia] to talk about . Denley had some fun at Canerw today. Garfield said that you would be given some Epsom salts today, shitting tomorrow and operated Wed. Your Mother had a good laugh but at the same time she told Garfield not to be so silly. Well I got no more to say now, hope to see you Wednesday with **everything** over, so this is all for now as we are busy doing the weekly wash and the big bundle that was in the wak.

So with all best love to you

Lil and Denley'

Bryan was away at one of the Urdd camps. Heywood in his first letter reassured us that he was 'Enjoying grand so far' as if he was on holiday rather than in hospital for an operation! He went on to say that there were four of them – himself, a man from Pencader and two boys - in the ward preparing for the same operation. He had spent most of one day in the bathroom shaving his private parts. The man from Pencader was preparing for the operation that particular day and had had 'the cleansing job done' [enema] but was very nervous and confused and after a nurse told him to go to the bathroom to shave he re-emerged after an hour to ask Heywood for a loan of his shaving mirror! He was rather shocked when Heywood told him that it was not his face that he was to shave! Off he went again and when he re-appeared 'he looked wild and … said he had done a mess, he had cut himself several times and was bleeding, his vest and pyjamas were all blood, and the porter had to finish the job'. Heywood's writing was interrupted by the arrival of Lil's letter and he responded immediately to her first sentence by declaring : 'I am not homesick, I enjoy myself good I think it will be Wednesday before I will get an operation. The doctor came round to examine us yesterday … he told me that we would be operated today, but this morning the sister told me that it was only the Pencader man was to be done today, he is far worse than I am … . Brought my dinner but before I started eating sister came and took it away, I'm going to have operation sometime tonight. What about the trailer Denley? Have you finished it? I think I'll better finish off now, so that I can have a chance to post it.

With best wishes, Heywood'

After the operation Heywood was quite seriously ill and was convinced that the failure to give him an enema – a failure which may well have resulted from the on/off/on/off confusion that preceded his operation - was the cause. His recovery was helped by the presence in the ward of two colliers who kept the patients laughing all day and Heywood had to go under the sheets to avoid hearing their side-splitting jokes and hurting himself. And then: 'I hope the trailer wont turn Denley's career and at the same time hope it will be ready when I come home'. Clearly I had the task of building a trailer and I have a vague recollection about it but have forgotten the details. The final letter was headed :

'Ward 3 Carmarthen Glangwili 16/8/54 11:0 A.M.

Dear Lil and children,

Coming on fine feel 5% better only just had a good bath. They have changed the injections now from every three hours to twice daily and that means a lot to me. The man from Pencader … is now in a side-ward … so I can not see him [but] I can hear him coughing from here. I just had a look over the Western Mail the senior results not in it. Rev Edgar Phillips came in to see me this morning, he looked very strange to me with his new teeth, they did look well with him and I am sure that it was last Saturday he told me he had them, and he said he did not feel them. He sat with me for about 15 minutes and as he went he said he might call again if he could have a chance, I told him not to make any special journey that I was all-right. Dinner is coming now. 1.30. Had a good dinner and the black doctor has been round to see us. "You right now" he told me and off he went. You've been here twice now and I forgot to ask about the Cockerels, what results had Gon from his big dealers? ... Well I must finish , the one that does the posting is ready to go so all the best, From Dat.'

Heywood's recovery rate improved from 5% and he was soon back to full health. The reference to 'cockerels' and 'Gon' (Heywood's brother Gordon) referred to Gordon's prediction earlier in the year that a small fortune could be made in meeting the expected high demand for chickens at Christmas-time in the Rhondda and that dealers were ready to collect from farms. Heywood and Lil went along with his idea and promptly bought some young cockerels and fattened them for market. But as hinted in the letter, the dealers were slow to appear and none had materialized as Christmas approached! Gon was embarrassed by what was turning out to be a bit of a cock-up so he hired a van, loaded it with the trussed cockerels, took me along as a sort of assistant and headed for the Rhondda Valleys in search of the fortune. We called at numerous butcher shops and eventually managed to get rid of the cockerels but not for a 'fortune'!

The above account of the exchange of letters and of the cycle trip to Canerw to hear Gordon's news from the hospital illustrate very clearly the problem of transferring personal information in those days. Very few homes had telephones which left letter-writing and word of mouth as the means to convey news. Telegrams were used in an emergency.

It is interesting to note that the letters were written in English even though the spoken language in the community was very definitely Welsh. On the other hand the daily and weekly newspapers read in most homes were English language ones. The only Welsh language reading material that people regularly came across after leaving school was the hymns on a Sunday. Even the posters advertising monolingual Welsh events such as penny readings, eisteddfodau, dramas, talks and so on were printed in English ! There existed a curious mentality which categorized the natural spoken language of the community as being somehow unsuitable for more 'official' communications through the printed word!

3.2.5 Running and winning with Davies Maths

Heywood's interest in sporting events and competitions was passed on to us and together with two other factors helped to make the second half of the 1950s a time of intense participation on our part in track and cross country running on a local, county and all-Wales levels – activities not previously associated with residents of the 'remote' Taf Valley. The first factor was the tremendous interest in track events created by European middle distance runners who led the world in the 1950s and inspired youngsters to emulate them. On 6 May 1954 Roger Bannister became the first to run a mile in under four minutes when he clocked 3m 59.4s at Oxford University's Iffley Road track assisted by Chris Brasher and Chris Chataway as pacemakers. The 1950s saw some terrific races over 1, 3 and 6 miles and their metric equivalents of 1,500, 5,000 and 10,000 metres involving world famous runners such as, Bannister; the Australian John Landy, the most consistent four-minute-miler of the time; Gordon Pirie of Thames Valley Harriers who broke five world records during his career and deserved to be an Olympic champion but never was; Chris Chataway who in 1954 beat the 'unbeatable' Russian Vladimir Kutts over 3 miles at London's White City in a race that was televised and made Chataway a sporting celebrity; Chris Brasher the outsider who shocked everyone in winning the steeplechase at the 1956 Melbourne Olympics leaving the favourite, Wales' John Disley without a medal; Emil Zatopek the fantastic Czeckoslovakian who won the 5,000m, 10,000m and the marathon at the 1952 Helsinki Olympics and the Hungarian wonder Sandor Iharos who in 1955 and 1956 broke the world record for 1,500m, 3,000m, 5,000m, 10,000 m, 2miles, 3miles and 6miles! The second and vital factor in developing our athletics abilities was the arrival at Whitland Grammar School of a new mathematics teacher, W D Hubert Davies from Clydach in the Swansea Valley. He was a keen runner himself but more importantly he had a thorough knowledge and understanding of the training regimes developed by coaches such as Franz Stampfl in Europe and Percy Cerutty in Australia. And he had the commitment to spend time with those pupils who wished to benefit from his knowledge.

Davies Maths soon had those of us interested in improving our running performance - about half-a-dozen - turning out every school-lunchtime to do tough interval running, based on Franz Stampfl's methods. A special third-relay was laid-on just before the start of afternoon lessons to cater for our eating needs. We followed carefully planned schedules of interval running. For example, he reckoned that I should aim to run a half mile (880 yards) in 2 minutes in 1956. So my training on a Monday might be to run 8 x 220 yards, each in 30 seconds with a couple of minutes recovery time in between. The next day it might be 4 x 440 yards, each in 1 minute with a few more minutes of recovery time in between. The following day it might be 2 or 3 x 660 yards in 1minute 30 seconds. On another day it might be a series of 110 yards, the first half dozen of which invariably were run too fast and to teach us a lesson in keeping to the correct pace Davies Maths made us run many more 110s than planned. He timed and recorded all our runs and at the end of every session gave us the records to keep so that we could follow, as the weeks went by, our own progress in terms of being able to increase the number of runs in a particular time or to run the same number but in a shorter time. Lil copied the data into a hard-cover notebook for safe keeping and easy reference – a task she enjoyed and in different circumstances she would have made an outstanding administrative officer. We also adapted the stamina-building-schedule of running repeatedly up sand dunes advocated by Australian coach, Percy Cerutty, by running up the steep slope of the furthest Fron field (*Fron nesa draw*) about 10 times every morning before breakfast. Heywood had an input into our training as well. He had some knowledge of how race horses' strength and stamina were improved by feeding them with raw eggs. And so it came to pass that after running up the Fron slope Bryan and I each swallowed a raw egg with a drop of vinegar on it. In my case I carried on with the practice every morning for two years from 1954 until I left school in 1956. Our performances over distances from 100 yards to 1 mile and also over 3 miles across country improved out of all recognition. By the summer of 1955 Davies Maths produced a team of sprinters and middle distance runners which enabled Whitland Grammmar School to win the Under 17 Middle Group cup in the Carmarthenshire Secondary Schools Championships for the first time ever. The smallest Grammar School in the county had overcome the might of Llanelli and of Dyffryn Aman. The following year the success was repeated at the Senior Group level.

Heywood and Lil's support of our athletics interests was of course total and just a mention of the magazine *Athletics Weekly* was enough for a regular order to be placed with a newsagent at Whitland. However, schools athletics meetings were few and far between being limited to the school sports day, two meetings at county level and the national championships; a poor return for the months of training. So we risked our amateur status by racing for money-prizes at the highly popular sports meetings held over about 6 weeks in the summer in rural villages in west and north Carmarthenshire and south Cardiganshire. The meetings were reported in local newspapers and to avoid detection by Amateur Athletics officials we gave false names to reporters but races won by H Elliot, V Kuts, G Pirie and J Landy did not exactly provide the anonymity we were looking for! Most of the village sports were evening events tailored to enable dairy farmers to attend and we travelled in the van after Heywood and Lil had done the milking. However, the August Bank Holiday meeting at Llandygwydd was an all-day event and we had to find a way of getting there in the early afternoon. In 1956 a neighbour, Ieu Griffiths, Taf, Llanglydwen took Bryan and myself to Llandygwydd after an early lunch and we had managed two or three wins before Heywood and Lil and Ieu's wife Phebe Mary arrived after milking. In the summer of 1958 Brian Isaac, a fellow Whitland Grammar School pupil with Bryan, a pole vaulter and sprinter who lived about 3 miles from Cefn at Rhydyparc joined us on the 'sports circuit' and we travelled to a number of venues in his car. In all we attended professional sports meetings at Llandygwydd, Capel Dewi, Spittal and Llanboidy during 1956, Synod Inn, Talgarreg, Trelech and Llandygwydd in 1957, Pontshan, Synod Inn, Aberarth, Llandygwydd, Mydroilyn and Capel Dewi in 1958, Pontshan, Llandygwydd, Talgarreg, Synod Inn, Cenarth, Ffostrasol, Maesymeillion and Gorsgoch in 1959, Pontshan, Llandygwydd and Maesymeillion in 1960 and Bryan went to Pontshan, Llanddewi, Llandygwydd, Talgarreg and Cenarth in 1961. Heywood and Lil were present at most of those meetings and needless to say they enjoyed themselves. As previously mentioned, Heywood had three consecutive wins in the over 40s sprint at Llandygwydd and over all the meetings Bryan and myself shared a total of 76 wins in 29 meetings.

In 1956, my final year at Whitland Grammar School, the Welsh Secondary Schools Amateur Athletics Championships was held at St Helens, Swansea and much as they wished to be there, milking had to take priority for Heywood and Lil. That evening they sat in the van in Whitland waiting to collect us off the team bus. When told of my win in the senior half-mile race their delight was obvious.

There is no doubt that Heywood and Lil derived satisfaction and pleasure from our comparative success in scholastic and in sporting activities during the 1950s. At the same time they must have wondered where the education track was leading and what the future held for us all. It was increasingly likely that studies and employment would take us far from the Taf Valley thereby limiting 'regular' contact between us to letter-writing – telephones were rare, rail-travel inconvenient and road transport still in its early development – in fact the working-class community of the Taf Valley was finding it difficult to free itself of 'remoteness'. The resurgence in popularity of village sports meetings was particularly timely in that it enabled us and them to enjoy a common interest which they had enjoyed before the war. No wonder Lil kept a detailed record of our winnings over those happy years in the 1950s.

During the Summer of 1956 another list arrived; this one detailed the essentials for admission to the University College of Swansea and we were soon in the van on a major expedition to Swansea to do some shopping. I think it was Heywood's first visit to the town (as it was then), the rest of us had been there on a Cefnypant trip some years previously. An acknowledgement receipt from D.L.Davies and Son Ltd Specialists in Men's Wear, YMCA Buildings, 3 and 4 The Kingsway, Swansea dated 1/10/1956 shows that a blazer costing £8.18.6 (£8.96) and a badge costing £1.16.6 (£1.82) were bought. I remember buying a scarf at the same shop but it may have been on a later date. Heywood and Lil's next trip to Swansea was later in October 1956 when I left home, Cefn, and they took me all the way to Neuadd Gilbertson, a student hostel built at Clyne Castle, Blackpill off the Mumbles Road. They would not allow me to travel by train from Whitland because I might have trouble in getting my case by bus to Neuadd Gilbertson. I did not argue. Sixteen years previously they had taken Heywood's sister, Morfydd's box to Ty-isaf and his brother, Gordon's box to Cilsant, both to be farm servants. All three of us travelling along the old A48 in the van were glad that the end of our road that day would not be a farm. A few weeks later the do-it-yourself world of the Taf Valley stood me in good stead when I discovered that there was no athletics track at the college. I borrowed a measuring tape from the college sports staff and, as I had done at Cefn, measured and marked with sticks a 330 yards running track on the college playing-field. A week later a track in white lines appeared - courtesy of the sports staff.

Many of Heywood's and Lil's generation wondered if a third-world-war was on the cards when on 5 November 1956 British and French paratroopers dropped on the Suez Canal in an attempt to retake it from the Egyptians whose President Gamal Abdel Nasser had nationalized it a few months earlier in response to the refusal by America and Britain to fund the Aswan Dam project. Humiliation followed for Britain and France as the 'world community' condemned the action and the troops were withdrawn. Prime Minister Anthony Eden resigned and by April, British ships were paying tolls to Egypt for use of the canal. Knock-on effects included rationing of petrol to 200 miles per month except for farmers, ministers of religion and essential local authority workers who were allowed 600 miles per month; doctors and vets were exempt. Petrol increased in price to 6 shillings a gallon (30 pence) equivalent to about £4.50 today. Rationing ended in May 1957. The Driving Test was suspended for one year and provisional licence holders were allowed to drive without an experienced driver. I took advantage of this to practice during the holidays and passed the Driving Test in Carmarthen during 1957.

In 1958 it was with deep regret that the Independents of the Taf Valley from Llanfyrnach to Login agreed to release the Rev. Edgar J Phillips from his ministry at Glandwr and Cefnypant to allow him to accept the ministry of Capel Sul, Cydweli. He was a popular minister who made every effort to make regular visits to members of the two chapels. However his recreational activities of fishing and shooting rabbits sometimes caused delay to some of his proposed visits and one upset lady told him in no uncertain terms that if she had been a rabbit he would have called to see her without delay … to which Edgar Phillips replied 'My dear lady, if you were a rabbit I'd have shot you long ago!'.

In the summer of 1958, Tom Davies of Glanrhyd, Llanboidy paid a visit to Cefn. His wife Mary Ann had died earlier in the year and he was retiring from farming and offered the tenancy of Glanrhyd to Heywood and Lil. Glanrhyd, about 2 miles from Llanglydwen, was a 100 acre farm which in those days provided for a good living. Furthermore increased mechanization and the use of contractors to do heavy work such as muck-spreading, ploughing and harvesting meant that a couple could manage the farm on their own. This was the chance that Heywood had been waiting for: a return to full-time farming, because he was first and foremost a farmer but at only 40 acres Cefn was not a viable unit and to make-ends-meet he had been forced to take on other jobs. But now Glanrhyd offered the chance to pick up where he left-off on leaving Canerw ten years earlier. When I went back to college at the beginning of October I guessed I was leaving Cefn for the last time and true enough when I returned for the Christmas holidays it was to Glanrhyd that I came where Heywood and Lil and Bryan had moved on 23 October 1958.

Cefn, was a 40-acre small-holding near Llanglydwen.

The house at Cefn.

M.M.B. milk supply contract for Cefn, dated 5 April 1948.

Our new address in 1948

Dydd Gwi — Plasybwsy

Anwil Oll
   wele fi in anfon gair in
fyr gan fawr bleithio eich bod in
iach yna i gyd fel ag ir ydim
nine ar i hanes yma wel wif wedy
bod in disgwil i boys draw ond
nid ydint wedy dod ag wif in
hala bobo necloth bach iddint
in gulenig yn nw fawr o beth
te nam o tro i stchys blat
i'r ysgol

Wel ie wif in mind draw ir Wern
dywedd ir withnos may Emlyn
a Jizzie in mind i Llunden i
weld Sibbie a Stan goleithio na
nw ddim ar goll yna may Llunden
in dipin o sels cofiwch chy
Ser finaf nawr gida dimuniade
gore a llwiddianis i chwy oll
am i flwyddyn newy 1949

O ie cofiwch ddod am dro
ar ol i fi ddod nol or Wern

Letter written by 83-year-old Phebe Jenkins (author's great-grandmother) in 1948.

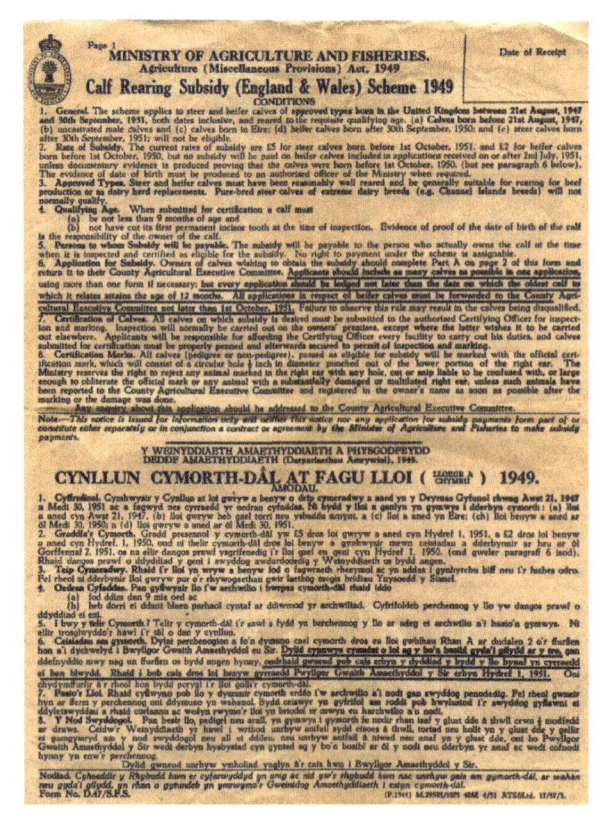

Bilingual information for farmers.

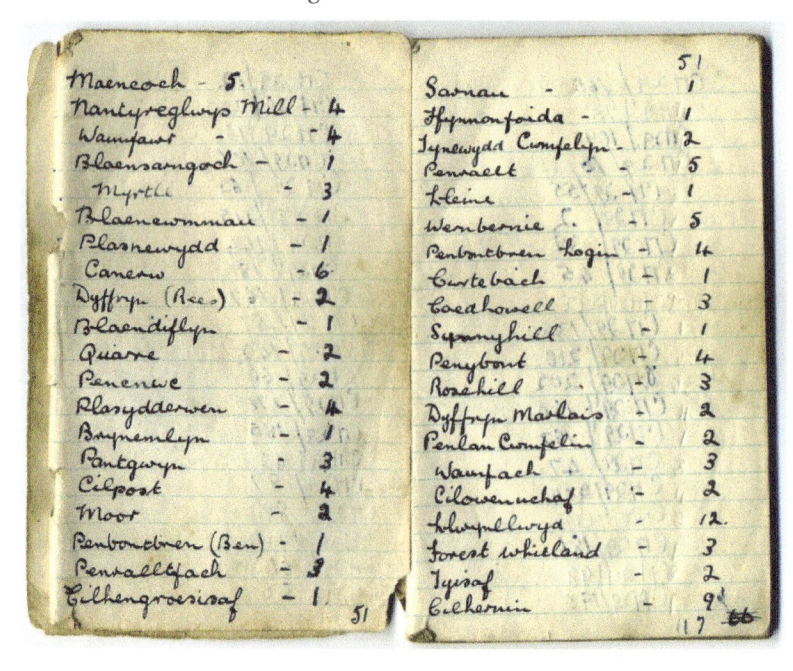

A few of the farms in Llanboidy Parish which benefited from the calf-rearing scheme.

Phone: Hebron 233.   "GLYNTAF," LOGIN, S.O.,
CARMARTHENSHIRE.

Dear Mr Owen,
I have another churning for you if you can let us know when it is convenient for you
T D. G. P

More pig-swill for delivery.
(Early 1950s)

To generate extra income to support his family of six, the Reverend Thomas Jones-Evans of Llysmyfyr, Login, minister at Calfaria Baptist Chapel, raised a dozen pigs annually and son Dafydd enjoyed a day off school in the late 1940s and early 1950s to help prepare the animals for market. He also kept hens, turkeys and goats.

Stên (metal pitcher) (1 ft high) used for carrying tea to workers in the field and for making butter.

Buddai (churn) (1 ft 6in high) used for making butter.

A hen-coop was easier to ride than a horse.

Feeding-time at Cefn in early 1950s.

Bryan on Rosehill's Fordson busy turning hay at Cefn in the early 1950s.

The next load can wait. L/R: Goronwy, Denley, Islwyn, Gwynfor, Leslie. In front: Bryan, Brython.

Haymaking was hard work: L/R: Leslie, Trevilla; Clodwyn, Trehir-isha; Glyn, Rhos; Gwynfor, Trehir-isha; Heywood, Cefn; Stanley, Rosehill; Ben Lewis Llwyncelyn; Ben James, Penbontbren. In front: Bryan; Brython; Denley.

Heywood and Ben Llwyncelyn take a break from the arduous task of plucking loose hay from the sides of the hay-rick at Cefn in the early 1950s. Careful with those matches!

On Gwilym Portland's all-weather bicycles

At the sea-side in fair-isle and 'shorts'

Cefnypant Sunday School trip to Tenby in the early 1950s. L/R: back row: Eifion Griffiths, Bryan Owen, Glenmary Griffiths, Brenda Owen. In front: Desmond Jones, Gary Griffiths, Roderick Reynolds, Desmond Griffiths, Glyn Jones.

Cefnypant Sunday School members at Tenby in early 1950s: L/R: Leslie Phillips, Trevilla; Stanley Phillips, Rosehill; Gwilym Lewis, Llwynllwyd.

Lon, Brian with mother Eppie and aunt Sarah in their Sunday-best on a visit to Tenby c1950.

Cefnypant Chapel trip to Hereford in early 1950s. L/R: Denley Owen, Lil Owen, Gwen Griffiths, Gareth Reynolds, Morfydd Owen, Bryan Owen, Marina Thomas, Gwenda Phillips.

Cefnypant Chapel trip to Porthcawl in the early 1950s: Olwen Reynolds, Glasfryn (Caretaker of Cefnypant for 28 years); Tegwen Phillips, Canerw Cottage; Meima Jenkins, Tower; Nansi Lewis, Cilhernin; Lil Owen, Cefn.

A class in the Taf Valley school of Glandwr, early 1950s: L/R back row: Dorothy Jones, Shirley Morris, Mer Bowen, Thelma Thomas, Huw Lewis. Third row: Megan Jones, Maisie Edwards, Margaret Griffiths, Jeni Davies, Carol Griffiths, Averil Griffiths, Kitty Thomas, Amy Hughes. Second row: Gerald Llewellyn, Hywel Mathias, Gerald (shop), Raymond Owen. In front: Gruffydd John Johns, Paul Thomas, Brian Owen, Mostyn Williams.

Another Glandwr School class, early 1950s: L/R back row: Esme Williams, Gwynedd James, Nelda Morris, Lon Isaac, John Green. Front row: Julia Morris, Marion Llewellyn, Mary Lewis, Hywel Evans, Meurig Johns, Tom Williams, Alan John.

In the 1940s the hamlet of Cwmrhyd, Blaenwaun had a shop in a cottage called Ffarmers. It was kept by Marged (right) assisted by her daughter Phebe (centre) who was a renowned dressmaker.

Taf Valley character, Walter Owen, Abertaf, Llanglydwen.

Keeping the Sabbath was taken very seriously by the older generation. 'No work and no play' was Arnold John's message to his trapped grand-children, Lon and Brian, at Rhydyparc, Blaenwaun c1950.

Baptising in the River Taf at Login was initiated by the Reverend Thomas Jones-Evans c1951.

Those with knowledge of the Taf Valley visited as often as possible. The Reverend William Evans (Wil Ifan) and Mrs Evans of Bridgend often stayed at Rhydyparc, Blaenwaun. Wil Ifan - Archdruid from 1947 to 1950 – was born in Cwmbach, Llanwinio and the inspiration for much of his poetry and prose came from the landscape and the characters he found in the Taf Valley. Lon acted as guide on some of their travels.

Members of the Sunday School at Ramoth Baptist Chapel, Cwmfelin Mynach c1950.

The EAGLE book
of Records and Champions

1951 EDITION

HULTON PRESS LIMITED 43-44 SHOE LANE LONDON E.C.4.

A wonderful source of information in the early 1950s.

The *Western Mail* catered for children daily and annually

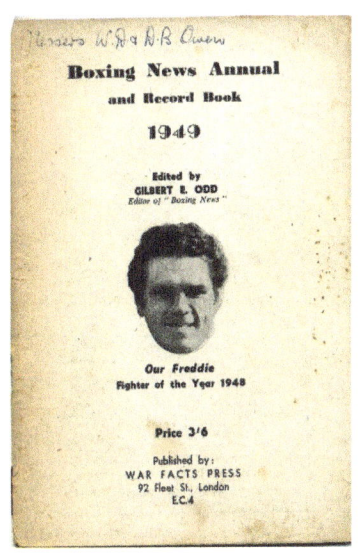

The Boxing 'Bible'.

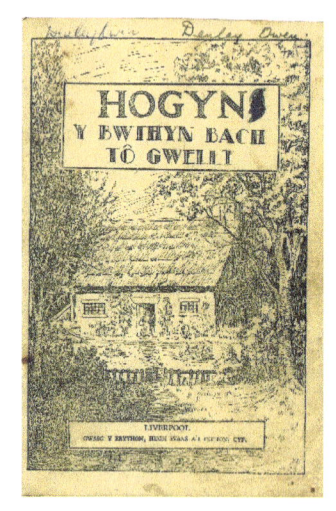

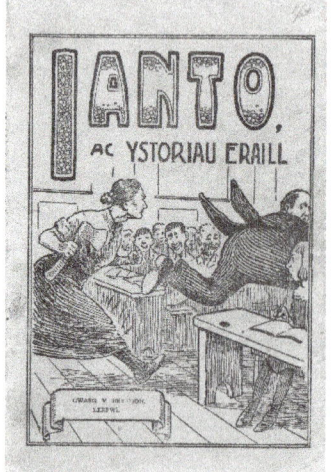

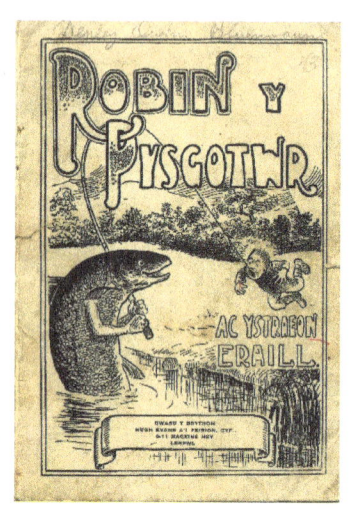

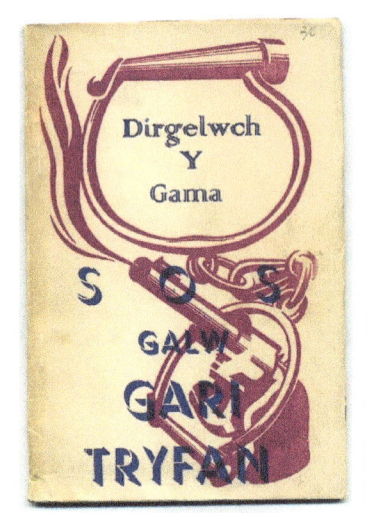

Some of the books we 'devoured' in the late 1940s and early 1950s.

'Isgol Whitlan' as it was in 1940s and 1950s.

Running rather than ferreting by the mid-1950s.

A golden era of athletics for Whitland Grammar School in the mid-1950s.

We made our own equipment at Cefn in the 1950s.

Another gruelling cross-country race is over at Whitland Grammar School.
L/R: Geoffrey Davies, Bryan Owen, Denley Owen, Ken Rees.

County Champions 1955: Whitland Grammar School Boys Middle Age-Group Athletics Team. L/R standing: Brynmor James, Brian Crowdie, Clem Evans. Seated: David Summers, W.D.H. Davies (Maths Master and running coach), Denley Owen, W.D. Coupland (P.T. Master and field-events coach), Charles Ormond.

County Champions 1956: Whitland Grammar School Boys Athletics Team. L/R standing: Brian Isaac, Edwin Phillips, Malcolm Howells, Brian Hursey, Clem Evans, Clifford Innes, Brynmor James, Michael Williams, Jeffrey Watts, Meurig Davies, John Rees. Seated: Keith Thomas, W.D.H. Davies, Meirion Jones, T. Trevor Thomas (Headmaster), Denley Owen, W.D. Coupland, Ken Rees, E.C. Davies. In front: Peter Phillips, John Mathias, Eifion Rees, Ian Griffiths, John O. Phillips, James Griffiths, Jeffrey Harries.

Whitland Grammar School Boys Athletics Team 1960. L/R back row: Robert Owen, Timothy Davies, Howard Wales, Barry Evans, David James, Brian Ross, Dennis Day, Meurig Davies, Gwynedd James, Clive Lewis. Third row: Leslie Crawford, John Clements, Ken Evans, Brian Williams, Peter Herbert, Michael Jones, Stephen Finch, John Mathias, David Howells, Keith Thomas. Seated: Roger Wyatt, John Lewis, John Phillips, T. Trevor Thomas (Headmaster), Bryan Owen, W.D. Coupland (Sports Master), James Griffiths, Eifion Rees, ----------. In front: -----------, Tony Toms, -----------, Jeffrey Rees, Philip Thomas, Billy -----, ------------, Keith M. Davies, Owen Bevan, Neil Howells.

ON THE BALL: The photograph shows Whitland Grammar School First XV in the 1949/50 season. This was the first year that the school changed from soccer to rugby. Pictured in the back row are Brian Morgan; Ieuan Thomas; Alan Bowkett; Richard Morgan; Peter Wills; David James; Morlais Richards and Kay Williams. Middle row is John Cook; Colin Griffiths; Mr EC Davies, sports master; Glyndwr Jenkins; Mr TT Thomas, headmaster; Alan Harries and Michael Jameson. And the front row is Roderick Richards, Cecil Davies and Harford Williams.

The first rugby team that the author ever set eyes on.

Deep in the Taf Valley: Llanglydwen Station from where we travelled to Whitland on Saturdays to play rugby.

TRIPLE CROWN WINNERS

The Welsh XV that beat Ireland by 6pts to 3 at Ravenhill, Belfast on 11 March 1950. L/R standing: Ifor Jones (W.R.U.) touch judge, J.D. Robbins (Birkenhead Park), D.J. Hayward (Newbridge), Roy John (Neath), R.T. Evans (Newport), W.R. Cale (Pontypool), W.B. Cleaver (Cardiff). Sitting: Ken Jones (Newport), Malcolm Thomas (Devonport Services and Newport), Lewis Jones (Devonport services and Llanelli), John Gwilliam (Edinburgh Wanderers) captain, Jack Mathews (Cardiff), Cliff Davies (Cardiff), Gerwyn Williams (London Welsh). In front: Rex Willis (Cardiff), D.M. Davies (Somerset Police).

Whitland Grammar School 1st XV players: L/R standing: Edmund Davies, Meirion Jones, David Summers, Brynmor James, Clifford Innes, David Constable, Geraint Roderick, Geraint Jones-Evans, Gareth Davies, Rees Thomas, Geoffrey Davies. Sitting: Clem Evans, Jeffrey Jones, T. Trevor Thomas (Headmaster), Denley Owen, W.D. Coupland (Sports master), Keith Thomas, John Phillips. In front: Gary Prothero, Idwal Williams.

Whitland Grammar School 1st XV players: L/R standing: James Griffiths, Clive Lewis, Michael Davies, Stephen Finch, David Jones, Barry Evans, Graham Jones, Graham Rees, John Phillips. Seated: T. Trevor Thomas (Headmaster), Gwyn Evans, Brian Williams, Robert Owen, Bryan Owen, David James, John Lewis, David Howells, W.D. Coupland (Sports master). In front: Barry John, Howard Wales.

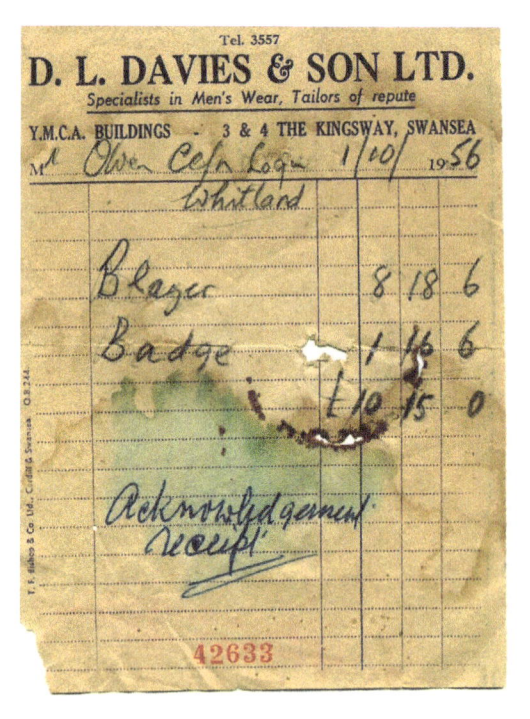

Preparing to leave the Taf Valley.

In London in 1958 for a race at the White City Stadium in the company of Ron Evans the wonderfully dedicated athletics supremo in Carmarthen.

Part IV

1958 – 1996: GLANRHYD – farming, travelling and arthritis

4.1 End of 'remoteness'

The farm house at Glanrhyd was much larger than the one at Cefn; it had a parlour (*parlwr*), living room, kitchen/dinning room, pantry and a lean-to for general use. Upstairs there were two double bedrooms, two single bedrooms, bathroom and toilet: luxuries experienced for the first time by Heywood and Lil. Glanrhyd was a dairy farm with stone-and-brick-built-buildings as opposed to the corrugated zinc-clad ones at Cefn. There was a cowshed (*glowty*) with an attached small building housing a mechanical milking unit (*mashîn godro*) and out-buildings (*tai mâs*) such as a calves pen (*catsh lloi*) and a barn ('*sgubor*). In the rickyard (*ydlan*) there was a three-bay hay shed at one end and at the other Heywood built a pig-sty (*twlc mochyn*) from concrete blocks and curved corrugated zinc sheets for the roof. At the farmyard entrance there was a milk-cooler-house conveniently sited by the milk-stand and a mature sycamore tree provided a welcome canopy on sunny days.

Mains electricity never reached Cefn while we were there and initially at Glanrhyd electricity was obtained from a generator driven by the milking-machine engine. Glanrhyd was soon connected to the mains electricity but there was no mains water and a dry summer proved troublesome when the 'spring' water dried-up. Why they delayed until 1973 before getting hold of a water diviner to try to locate a better 'spring' source I do not know. The diviner found water in a field further from the house and buildings of Glanrhyd than the existing spring and its higher altitude relative to the farm house and buildings provided for a gravity-controlled system. Heywood got help to dig a 'well' ('*winsh*' *yw'r gair Cymraeg a ddefnyddir yn Sir Benfro - '*ffynnon ddofn*' ym mhob man arall*) but he did most of the back-breaking work himself. He was an incredibly hard worker and no physical task however difficult was too much for him. He did indeed strike water which was then piped to the house, out-buildings and farmyard. This was a huge benefit for most of the time but during an exceptionally dry summer the water still dried-up and Heywood had to resort to carting water for the animals from the River Tigen, accessible at a ford (long since replaced by a bridge) 200 yards down-hill from Glanrhyd. A water-pump working off the tractor extracted water from the river into empty milk churns, mounted on the tractor and, when filled, these were taken to the farm and emptied into old baths sited appropriately for the cattle to quench their thirst. Even when mains-water eventually arrived, some dispute meant that only the house was supplied; the animals' needs in the driest spells was met by water carted from the river.

Farming improved in profitability during the 1950s and it was a timely move for Heywood and Lil from the 40-acre small-holding of Cefn to the 100-acre holding of Glanrhyd which was a very useful farm, easy to work since the land was reasonably level and it had been well farmed by Tom and Mary Ann Davies. Heywood and Lil were very happy to rent rather than buy Glanrhyd because renting suited their conservative thinking; a mortgage was seen as a stone around-a-neck for life. They did have a point because farm rents were comparatively low and increases were strictly controlled but years later when the value of land shot up, owners of farms found themselves in a position to make a small fortune. But who could have predicted such a development and anyway Tom Davies was not interested in selling his farm. The important point is that Heywood and Lil did well at Glanrhyd and became comfortably-off and thoroughly enjoyed themselves there. *'Netho ni'n dda in Lanrhyd'* (We did well at Glanrhyd) was Heywood's contented comment.

The motor car became affordable to ordinary people in the 1950s and was the main factor in changing the pattern of life in the Taf Valley and other rural areas. Up to that time local village shops provided for the community's basic needs but the motor car enabled easy access to shops in towns such as Whitland, St Clears and Carmarthen and the writing was on the wall for the local stores. Heywood and Lil changed the blue Ford van for a larger up-market green Vauxhall one and then changed to Ford Cortina cars. Although dairy-farming was a tied business because of the need to milk twice-a-day, seven-days-a-week, 52-weeks-a-year, Heywood and Lil were well organized and they found a way to be at every community or social event which they wished to attend. Lil kept diaries from 1972 till 1992 and it is revealing that top of the list of telephone numbers in the front page of the 1972 diary were those of 'relief milkers'. That was a clear statement that Heywood and Lil had no intention of allowing 'farming' to dominate their daily life as was usually the situation with most farming families in those days. They made maximum use of their new-found mobility and regularly went for 'runs' in the van/car to visit relatives and friends as well as to see some of the delightful sites in west Wales. When rain halted hay-making Heywood and Lil calmed their frustration by jumping in the car and going for a run! The ease with which they were able to hire extra manual labour when needed was testament to how well they paid their casual work force. Bryan had two years at Glanrhyd before entering the University College of South Wales and Monmouthshire, Cardiff in 1960 leaving Heywood and Lil on their own for the first time since 1938. They would have realised that their sons were unlikely ever to return as permanent residents to the 'remote' Taf Valley but rather were heading towards wherever the fruits of their education would lead them. However, marriage to Taf Valley girls ensured that contact with 'home' remained high in their sons and their families' priorities. And by that time the 'remoteness' of the valley was substantially overcome by improved roads and better cars and in the mid-60s Heywood and Lil thought nothing of travelling 200 miles to southern England to visit their family. The farm was left, for a few days, in the capable hands of neighbours. Very soon it was two-way traffic as grand children converged on Glanrhyd to spend holidays experiencing life in the Taf Valley.

The pleasure of the arrival of grand children is often accompanied by the pain of the passing of parents. Lil's parents needed care over the last many months of their lives and that was provided for Margaret Ann in Glanrhyd where she passed away in June 1969. William was cared for by his son Johnny and family in Eglwyswrw and he passed away in March 1971. A verse specially composed for William's funeral service recalled his passion for music and singing:

Yn ystod blynyddoedd ieuenctid
Cerddoriaeth a lanwodd ei fryd,
Yr oriel ar ddydd y Gymanfa
A'i cafodd ef yno o hyd.

Fe'i daliwyd yn gaeth gan afiechyd
Fe'i collwyd o'r oriel yn lân.
Ond para yn ddewr wnaeth ei ysbryd
A chollodd ei enaid mor gân

Change was everywhere in post-war Britain and in the world of politics the Taf Valley, as part of the Carmarthen Parliamentary Constituency, played its part in sounding a wake-up call for the Welsh nation. Throughout the 1950s economic growth in south-east England had allowed the Tories a good run in power but their Britain eventually failed. The Suez débâcle, signs of economic down-turn, spy scandals, the Profumo affair and the portrayal of government ministers as utterly inept in the television show 'That was the week that was' finally ended 13 years of Tory rule. Labour's victory in the October 1964 General Election resulted in Harold Wilson moving to Number 10 Downing Street. But, like his Tory predecessors, Wilson's government failed to address Wales' ailing economy and its over-dependence on coal and steel – both in decline – and in 1966 there was the first inkling that Wales or at least the Carmarthen Parliamentary Constituency was prepared to back Plaid Cymru's case for an Independent Wales. The Carmarthen by-election of 1966 was won by Plaid Cymru's Gwynfor Evans with 39% of the vote. But it would take another 31 years for the people of Wales to take the second step to Independence when they voted in a referendum in 1997 to establish the National Assembly for Wales. On the world stage the 1960s was a pretty murderous time. There was a wave of assassinations of American leaders committed to social change and equality. John F Kennedy, Robert Kennedy, Martin Luther King, Malcolm X and Medgar Evers were all gunned down.

However, at the same time advances in technology and mass production of goods brought increasing benefits to the general population and Wales' 'remote' rural communities benefited more than most as lives were transformed by farming mechanisation, Aga cookers, washing machines, televisions and motor cars. In the early 1970s Heywood and Lil took advantage of an opportunity to travel through France, Italy, Switzerland and Germany – something that persons in their situation would not have dreamt of doing a decade earlier! For the first-time-ever they spent a whole month outside the confines of the Taf Valley having entrusted the running of their farm to neighbours, Glyndwr and Nancy Phillips. And so it was that 29 years after Gwilym Penrhiw broke the news of her brother Clifford's death in action, Lil visited St Charles de Percy War Cemetry near Vire, Normandy and laid a wreath by the headstone recording Clifford's sacrifice and signed the visitors book. In later years they travelled extensively outside the Taf Valley, visiting many areas of Wales and occasionally venturing across Offa's Dyke as well as over Hadrian's Wall.

Statistics gleaned from the diary entries provide further evidence for the passing of the 'remoteness' of the Taf Valley under the influence of the motor car. Heywood and Lil went shopping to Carmarthen, Whitland, St Clears or Cardigan and visited those towns' cattle marts on average three times a fortnight up to 1985 when they stopped milking and started dealing in store cattle which meant more buying and selling of animals and more frequent visits to marts. The shopping and mart attendance rate went up to an average of five visits per fortnight from 1986 to 1991 although increasingly as the years went by after 1986, Lil's rheumatoid arthritis limited her presence on these trips. Owning a car enabled them to attend more concerts and Urdd Eisteddfodau than in the past and from 1972 to 1991 they went on average to eight concerts a year. They became keen followers of Whitland Rugby team and attended around a dozen matches per season during the 1970s. Occasionally they travelled the 40 miles or so to Parc y Stradey to see Llanelli play and Heywood witnessed the club's historic win: Llanelli 9, Seland Newydd 3 on 31 October 1972. The gradual change in role of inns from simple drinking dens to places for meeting and eating reduced community reliance on chapels as centres for socialising. Heywood and Lil averaged one visit a month to an inn compared to an average of two services per month at Cefnypant Chapel for the period 1972 to 1984 before the onset of rheumatoid arthritis curtailed Lil's ability to spend an hour sitting on the wooden pews. The diaries reveal an exceptionally high number of visits to local inns in the years 1972 to 1974: 24 visits in 1972, 18 in 1973 and 12 in 1974. The explanation is that the game of TIPIT (recorded as 'titbit' in the diaries!) enjoyed a surge of popularity in pubs during those years and Heywood was an enthusiastic member of a Bont team of three – farm worker Glyndwr Phillips and coal merchant Tomi Williams were the others. The trio won a major TIPIT tournament (prize £9) held in Llanboidy in October 1973. The influence of the church at Cefnypant on the community declined steadily from the 1960s and it was left to the older members to carry on the tradition. In 1975 it was deemed necessary to build a new toilet-block at Cefnypant and Heywood was one of the volunteer 'builders'. He returned home early one afternoon after his two co-volunteers offered weak excuses before abandoning the project for the day. Quite rightly Heywood was having none of it. Caring for family graves remained a priority and a diary entry in June 1974 read 'Had a go at the tombstones in Llanboidy, Login, Nebo – very cold'.

A remarkable revelation in the diaries is the list of names of acquaintances of theirs who had passed away in the local and wider community. On average 140 names were listed every year from 1973 to 1991 with a peak of 190 in 1983 and a minimum of 105 in 1990. The large numbers is an indication of the comparatively static nature of their generation with few venturing beyond the confines of the Taf Valley. They attended, together or singly, an average of 20 funerals a year from 1972 to 1991. The advantage of owning a motor car was nowhere so evident than in the ease with which friends and relatives were visited as compared to pre-war years and over the years 1972 to 1992 they made ten visits a month on average and over the same period they received visitors to Glanrhyd at an average of five per month. For two or three years after 1983 the almost doubling in the number of visits to Glanrhyd was mirrored by the decrease in visits undertaken by Heywood and Lil which reflected Lil's growing problems with arthritis. Treatment of the disease under the guidance of G.P., Dr George Penn of Whitland, was reasonably successful and their social life returned to near normal for the years 1986 to 1988.

During the early months of 1972 the miners' strike indirectly caused some disruption to work on the farm. In February, power cuts were introduced for a period starting at 6.00 a.m. to conserve the use of coal and when Heywood and Lil returned from a very successful Preseli Motor Club dinner at 4.00 a.m. they milked the cows before going to bed! A wick and paraffin were bought to bring some of the old lamps into operation.

Leisure opportunities in the form of evening classes found their way to the Taf Valley in the early 1970s and Lil attended sewing classes at Ffynnonwen near Login – more for the company, I would guess, than for learning because she was very accomplished in the art of sewing and knitting as evidenced by my brother's and myself's fair-isle pull-overs in the early

1950s. She also attended W.I. meetings at Llanboidy and was, as ever, a regular attender of all *Ysgol Gân* (rehearsals) in preparation for the annual *Gymanfa Ganu*. Heywood played his part in the community and was elected to the committee for the Llanboidy Market Hall – a magnificent stone structure with a slate roof built in 1882 by the then local squire, W. R. H.Powell M.P. of Maesgwynne Mansion. Heywood was also appointed to the committee of the Llanglydwen Village Hall – a large corrugated zinc shed which lent itself to drowning-out the sound of its stage-performers by the rain-generated-noise from its roof. With the Llanboidy Market Hall meeting the needs of the wider community including Llanglydwen, it was a sensible decision by the committee to dispose of the corrugated zinc hall to an entrepreneur and today it houses a flourishing farm-equipment manufacturing business.

Reorganisation of local government required elections in the spring of 1973 to elect members to the council of the new county of Dyfed. Five candidates hit the canvassing trail for the single-member ward of Llanboidy and Heywood's and Lil's natural reluctance to promise their votes persuaded one of them, Plaid Cymru nominee Aled Gwyn, to call at Glanrhyd three times to solicit their votes and his representative called once! Heywood was eventually persuaded to sign Aled Gwyn's nomination paper and he and Lil thoroughly enjoyed the celebrations of Aled's win. The result demonstrated a welcome change in attitude by the Taf Valley voters since the 1921 district council election in the Llanglydwen Ward when the local squire, Captain David Garrick Protheroe of Glyntaf was persuaded to oppose the radical candidate, farm labourer Edwin Davies, whose voice was not welcome to the short-sighted, conservative electorate. By 1973 the radical mantle had passed to Plaid Cymru and Aled Gwyn topped the poll showing that the spirit of Rebecca and her daughters and of Powell Maesgwynne was still alive in the Taf Valley.

The motor car enabled businesses such as farmers' co-operatives based in some of the rural villages to employ travelling salesmen to seek more sales and to collect customers' dues. Heywood's brother Gordon was employed as a salesman by Clunderwen Farmers' Co-operative Society and his Monday morning travails during the 1970s and early 1980s ended at Glanrhyd in time for lunch. He was the only un-married member of the family of William and Martha Owen, Canerw and his main interest was promoting activities associated with Cefnypant Independent Chapel. He was a deacon from 1962, treasurer 1963-1971, arolygydd yr Ysgol Sul (Sunday School superintendent) 1952-1954, athro Ysgol Sul (Sunday School teacher) 1953 and Trustee from 1963. He researched much of the history of Cefnypant Chapel which formed the basis of a booklet 'Canmlwyddiant Cefnypant' published in 1978 on the occasion of the hundredth anniversary of opening the chapel. 'Gon' died from heart disease in 1982 and arrangements for his funeral fell to Heywood. The diary entry on Thursday 8 July read: 'Nice day. Heywood running around for funeral. Turned hay. Had a very bad thunderstorm during night.' The following day it was: 'At Carmarthen – re. funeral'. Gon's cremated remains were buried in his parents' grave at Cefnypant. Sometime later an inscribed commemorative stone tablet was inserted in the outside wall of the chapel, high above the door, in recognition of his lifetime of service to the cause.

Heywood's advice and counsel was often sought by fellow travellers trying to chart their way along life's winding path. One of the least taxing request was for driving-lessons. Even though he never took a driving test himself - because he rode a motor bike prior to 1 April 1934 when testing became compulsory - Marion Frowenfach and Eleri Trevilla – both daughters of long-standing family friends - were guided to success in their tests in the early 1980s giving them the means to overcome the remoteness associated with the Taf Valley. I had a few driving lessons with Heywood in the mid- 1950s in the Ford Van. He was rather impatient with me - which is usually the case with father and son - and I was glad when the need for learner drivers to be accompanied was temporarily suspended following the Suez débâcle. However, I have always valued his advice never to look at the oncoming vehicle but rather to concentrate on the road. His view was, and I agree entirely with it, that looking at the oncoming vehicle draws you towards that vehicle and therefore increases the risk of the most unfortunate of consequences.

To meet their grand-children's wish to have ready access to a pony the motor car made a few journeys to Llanybydder pony sales. 'Marco' was bought and, perhaps recalling the failure of his sons to make much of trying to ride bare-back in the early 50s, Heywood also bought a saddle and bridle.

In the 1960s and early 1970s the availability and the cost of oil made it a competitive fuel for heating. Oil-tankers became an increasingly common sight on rural roads as more and more 'cookers' were converted from solid fuel to oil. But all-good-things come to an end and by 1980 the price of oil was 782% more than it was in 1969 – the major hike having taken place between 1974 and 1980. Rural areas were hit hard because in addition to heating-oil the rural economy depended on T.V.O.-burning tractors to work the land, petrol or diesel guzzling lorries to deliver and collect goods, and similarly demanding buses, land-rovers and cars to move-around. The Taf Valley was in peril once again of being labelled 'remote' – not because of distance but because of costs.

In 1975 Wales' district council areas were given the opportunity to vote on whether or not public houses should open on Sundays. Carmarthen District was one of five out of thirty seven districts who voted to stay 'dry'. Seven years later Carmarthen District joined the majority by voting in favour of Sunday opening although Heywood and Lil remained true to their non-conformist beliefs by voting 'no'. Another tradition that died out in the Taf Valley in the early 1970s was that of welcoming the new year in song. On new year's eve young people congregated in their chapel's vestry and on the stroke of midnight went out in groups to entertain the area's residents in song and collect *calenig* (money) thrown from bedroom windows. The occupants of some houses were known to give a bonus to the first group to greet them so there was always keen competition to be first off the mark from the vestry. The year 1976 was the last to be welcomed in song at Glanrhyd. The ending of the use of ten-gallon milk churns on 29 January 1976 and the introduction of stainless steel storage tanks from which milk was extracted and collected once a day by tanker lorries ended a practice that Heywood had been familiar with all his life. The European Common Market - which Britain had been allowed to join in 1973 - showed its teeth in October 1976 when the United Dairies milk accounts changed from gallons to litres.

Taf Valley's links with the outside world were strengthened in the mid-1970s by the successes of Llanboidy's tug-of-war team which reached a pinnacle in 1977 when the team won the 640 kilo World Championship. In July of the same year a European tug-of-war competition was held at Whitland and two Swedish competitors stayed two nights at Glanrhyd.

The first flight from London to Paris of the supersonic Concorde in January 1976 was evidence of considerable technological advancement in the British and French aeronautical industry but the British economy as a whole was heading for the 1978 'winter of discontent' which sealed the fate of the Wales devolution referendum in March 1979 by turning it into an opportunity to vote against the unpopular Labour government. A generation passed before another opportunity came along for the people of Wales to vote for a measure of home rule.

A surprising revelation in the diaries is that over the two decades 1972-92 snow fell during the early months of every year except for 1972. The Taf Valley was served by unclassified roads which did not feature high on the council's priority list when it came to clearing snow and making them passable to traffic. In January 1978 Lil walked the two miles through the snow to Cefnypant Chapel to attend the funeral of Phebe Davies, then of Clarbeston Road but who had lived at Bwt Cottage near to Cottage (*Y Ty Rownd*), both belonging to the Dolwilym estate in the valley of the Taf near Llanglydwen. They were neighbours in the 1930's and Heywood and Lil had kept in touch with Phebe and her husband Charles during the 1970's.

The year 1981 started with snow during January and February and finished with a heavy snow fall in December which disrupted traffic and made it difficult for their granddaughter Janet to return from college in Bangor for the Christmas holiday: eventually she travelled by rail down central Wales to Llandovery. Any hopes for better weather in the new year were soon dashed when January 1982 saw 'the worst snow in living memory in Wales'. Milk collection was disrupted during the first weeks of the year and to add to their woes Heywood and Lil spent a lot of time searching for sheep buried under drifting snow. They were taking sheep on tack over the winter months.

A funeral at Cefnypant had to be postponed over a weekend to allow snow-bound roads to be cleared. Huw Canerw bringing cattle feed by tractor got stuck in drifts half a mile from Glanrhyd and carried the feed to the farm. Nancy from Llanglydwen brought them bread. Lloyd of Fron Ganol farm walked through the snow to Glanrhyd for something to eat. The next day Heywood took some cawl over to Lloyd at Fron Ganol. Giving up on the council, Wyn of Fron Uchaf Farm cleared the roads using his own tractor and scoop. The big fall of snow occurred on Friday 8 January 1982 and on that day sheep at Glanrhyd were lost in the drifts. A week later it started thawing and two days later Heywood and Lil were able to go for a run in the car … at least for a few miles as far as Maesgwynne - to see the lie-of-the-land - but not down the hill to Llanboidy. On the tenth day since the first snow-fall the milk tanker reached Glanrhyd. During the snow-bound week they had searched for the buried sheep and with the help of neighbours had succeeded in rescuing 70 leaving 27 still missing. Amazingly on the eleventh day they found the missing 27 in neighbouring Lan Farm's fields. Before the snowfall a new minister, Revered D Ben Jones, had taken over at Cefnypant and Glandwr on 3 January 1982 but it was three weeks later before the roads were cleared to allow a service to go ahead at Cefnypant and Heywood and Lil were both at the postponed Communion Service held on 24 January. Later in the year things began to look up when Marks and Spencer opened a store in Carmarthen. When summer arrived, farm activity turned to hay-making and school holidays could not arrive soon enough for the grand-children who eagerly make their way to Glanrhyd to help during the late 70s and early 80s although grand-daughter Janet returned to Llandovery in time to be crowned Cilycwm Show Queen at the end of August 1980.

The motor car made it easy for Lil to seek treatment for her worsening arthritis and typically she tried everything possible to find a cure or at least some relief from the pain. In January 1983 she and others from Llanboidy travelled to Cardigan to meet a practitioner of divine healing the Reverend Peter Scothern. However the scepticism in the diary comments suggested that the encounter was not expected to lead to a miraculous outcome and unfortunately it did not. In 1984 accompanied by Lon she sought further unconventional treatment from a practitioner in the Aman Valley. They eventually found him in Cwmaman in an upstairs surgery reached by climbing 24 steps! Although no cure resulted from the consultation, the laughs about the adventure lasted for weeks and certainly provided a much needed tonic. For the rest of her life it was a matter of controlling the disease as best as possible by travelling to receive conventional treatment at hospitals and clinics in Haverfordwest, Brecon and Newport, Gwent. Heywood enjoyed remarkably good health apart from the occasional heavy cold but in 1983 his right shoulder was diagnosed as being 'frozen'. Forty years earlier in Canerw he had injured the shoulder when using a starting-handle to start the Allis Chalmers tractor … the engine back-fired, as they were prone to do at times … driving the handle viscously back against his hand and severely jarring his shoulder. It had bothered him ever-since but Heywood was not one to complain. A course of injections into the joint proved reasonably successful in restoring flexibility.

A sure sign that the 'old order' was breaking-up in the Taf Valley community occurred in 1984 when six persons with addresses in the villages of Llanboidy, Blaenwaun and Hebron were remanded on drug charges. According to the report in the *Carmarthen Journal* they were accused of the illegal importation of cannabinol ... hash oil extracted from cannabis resin. One of the six was born in Llanboidy but the others were incomers with 'foreign' surnames of Taylor, Michael, Denby and Potter. Some of them lived at Llwyncroi where in the more stable past a real character, Gwilym Lewis, farmed and worked as a mechanic.

4.2 Time takes its toll

The passing of time inevitably saw influential characters of the 1940s and 1950s become history, leaving those of us growing-up in those decades within the catchment areas of Cefnypant Independent Chapel and Penygaer County Primary School with memories without which we would be nothing. Lizzi Reynolds, the lady who fed us on the way home from school in the 1940s, passed away in 1960 at 79-years-of-age. She was followed by Sunday School teachers Albert Howells, Glyntaf (1962, 75) and Tom Williams, Frowenfach (1967, 84), choir conductors Ted Eynon, Penralltfach (1972, 67) and Owen Jenkins, Tower (1972, 69), retired collier Ben Lewis, Llwyncelyn (1972, 68) and the kindly mistress of Frowen Clarice Phillips (1974, 75). The rest of the 1970s claimed rabbit catcher William Williams, Coedfryn (1974), 'manager' of the vestry Phebe Williams, Frowenfach, (1976, 78), wonderful soprano Sarah Ann Phillips, Rosehill (1977, 74), our neighbour in the 40s Megan Davies, Penrhiw (1977, 63) and deacons Lewis Gibbin, Penrallt (1978, 83) and Percy Phillips, Cilhernin (1979, 79). Uncle Garfield succumbed to cancer at 59 years-of-age in 1978. The long-serving farm labourer at Frowen, David Reynolds, Cwm (1979, 94) was followed too soon by his son and sportsman Wil Glasfryn (1979, 71). The former Llanboidy Village Bobby P.C. Prytherch died in 1980 and the pain of loss and the pleasure of memory continued with the passing of our one-time neighbour the kindly and self educated Benja James, Penbontbren (1981, 85), Penygaer headteacher for almost four decades '*mishtir*' W Rhydderch Evans (1983, 80), the expert slaughterer of pigs Thomas John Thomas, Yetgoch (1983), the minister who held our attention at Cefnypant Reverend Edgar J Phillips BA (1986), neighbouring farmer and down-to-earth character Ifor Owens, Fron Ucha was only 63 years-of-age when he passed away in 1986. Only Heywood attended Ifor's funeral and this was the case for most of the 21 funerals attended in 1986. As one would expect Heywood was 'helping at Fron' once or twice a week for the following few weeks. Although Lil's health was better than it had been for the previous two years she was clearly not up to suffering an hour's 'torture' by chapel pews. The doctor who advised removal of my tonsils and an occasional bottle of Mackeson to aid recovery Doctor Gwyn Evans better known as doctor bach passed away in 1988. In a happier vein the motor car enabled Heywood and Lil to visit their grandchildren as, one-by-one, they moved away to pursue their studies in Bangor, Swansea, Plymouth and Southampton. Two or three letters were also sent during term-time.

Lil suffered particularly badly with rheumatoid arthritis in 1984 and 1985 and the number of visitors to Glanrhyd rose significantly to 90 visits in 1984 and 120 in 1985. She was admitted to the Royal Gwent Hospital in November 1984 for a course of injections administered by specialist Dr Peter Williams. A letter to Heywood revealed that she was in good spirits and she gave an account of conditions at the hospital and described a few of the patients. She reminded Heywood to attend a funeral and to check whether or not she had remembered to switch-off the electric fire in the parlour. In 1985 she was back in the Royal Gwent Hospital for more treatment after which she recuperated for a month in Cowbridge followed by a month at Llandovery. Lil was then dependent on full-time care which Heywood dedicated to providing himself for the rest of her life. He reduced his farm work-load by selling the herd of milking cows and switched to rearing beef cattle. At 68-years-of-age it was time they retired but farming for them was a way-of-life and giving-it-up was never going to be easy. However it was a timely switch out of milk-production because the European Economic Community's efforts to control milk production by the imposition of farm quotas in 1984 soon threw the milk industry into chaos. Ten years later the Milk Marketing Board – established in 1933 to stabilise prices – was scrapped and its farming clientele thrown to the wolves of the free-market. As a direct result the modern milk factory at Whitland – serving the largest area of milk producers in Wales and possibly in Britain - was closed with disastrous consequences for the economy of the town and the wider area. Heywood and Lil were thankful that their working lives had spanned the era of price stability guaranteed by the M.M.B.

As the 1980s progressed they went on their beloved 'run' in the car as much as possible and when Lil was unable to leave the house their enjoyment of television quiz programmes helped pass the time.

The last two lines of the following verse which she had written in her 1986 diary reveal a thought never admitted verbally.

> *I remember, I remember,*
> *The house where I was born,*
> *The little window where the sun*
> *Came peeping in at morn;*
> *He never came a wink too soon,*
> *Nor brought too long a day,*
> *But now, I often wish the night*
> *Had borne my breath away.*

In January 1989, a family friend, Nancy Phillips of Taf, Llanglydwen was privately engaged as a carer although the main reason for the arrangement was to provide company for Lil who was rarely able to leave the house. Chapel attendance ended and visits to friends and relatives were severely curtailed but visits to Glanrhyd correspondingly increased. Nancy and Heywood attended to the annual work of tending graves at Nebo.

The visits to the Royal Gwent Hospital scheduled for January and February 1990 were cancelled because of stormy weather which caused part of the roofs of the gegin fach, garage, garden shed and hay-shed at Glanrhyd to be ripped off and the electricity supply was off for a few days and the telephone for a week. Fallen trees disrupted movement throughout the countries of Britain and the Severn and the Cleddau Bridges were closed; the first by overturned lorries and the second by common sense. On the eleventh of February 1990 the diary entry recorded the event of the century: 'Watched Nelson Mandela being released from Victor Verster Prison after 27 years in prison … age 71 or 72'.

Lil passed away on 22 May 1992 and the funeral service took place at Cefnypant Chapel where she had first attended Sunday School as an eleven-year-old in 1928 and enrolled in the same class as Heywood. For the following 64 years she had been a faithful member and supporter of all chapel activities especially the *Gymanfa Ganu*. Her life in the pre-war years had followed the well-trod trail awaiting children of the working class, namely, school until 14 years-of-age followed by service on farms, marriage to a farm worker and raising a family – whose members could look forward to repeating the pattern. But Lil had inherited her father's faith in education as the way out of a life of labour for working-class children and when new opportunities for secondary schooling became possible from the 1940s onwards she left no stone unturned in ensuring that her sons passed the 11+ examination which opened the door to grammar school education and more … for which we shall for ever be in her debt. Her family was central to her life and the increased mobility provided by post-war motor transport was timely in that it enabled the family to remain in touch even if it meant travelling hundreds of miles. She showed great fortitude in her ten-year struggle with rheumatoid arthritis and her 'where there's a will there's a way' attitude prevailed to the end.

Glanrhyd, Llanboidy where Heywood and Lil farmed from 1958. In the fore-ground is the sycamore tree that provided shelter and shade for the cool-house and milk-stand situated underneath.

Calfaria Baptist Chapel, Login Cantata Choir 1959. L/R front row: Aneurin Evans, Peter Evans, Margaret Edwards, Pat Edwards, Bethan Thomas, Susan Vaughan, Carol Llewellyn, Mary Rees, Janet Lewis, Christine Batty, Gareth Griffiths, Tecwyn Ifan. Second row: Kenneth Davies, Tony Vaughan, Kenneth Phillips, Mrs Rhuana Evans, Nancy Rees, Albert Evans, Margaret Rees, Rev. Vincent Evans, Bryan Evans, Russell Davies, Steven Walters. Third row: Sally Evans, Betty Thomas, Iris Evans, Jaquelin Batty, Jocelyn Davies, Betty Phillips, Bronwen Thomas, Ann Lewis, Margaret Davies, Dorothy Evans, Yvonne Edwards, Veronica Evans, Leslie Owen, Alan Llewellyn, Tommy Evans. Fourth row: Aeres Jones, Brenda Davies, May Williams, Sarah Rees, Maggie Evans, Irene Saer, Alice Llewellyn, Eirianydd Lewis, Alvira Phillips, Nan Rees, Doris Davies, Mefin Lewis, Nancy Owen, Maggie Davies, Lizzie Evans. Back row: John Davies, Vivian Evans, Willie Jenkins, Ingli Owen, Denzil Llewellyn, Tom Lewis, Alun Jones, Howard Lewis, Vince Jones, Gwilym James, Alun Thomas, Myrddin Evans, Tyrel Griffiths.

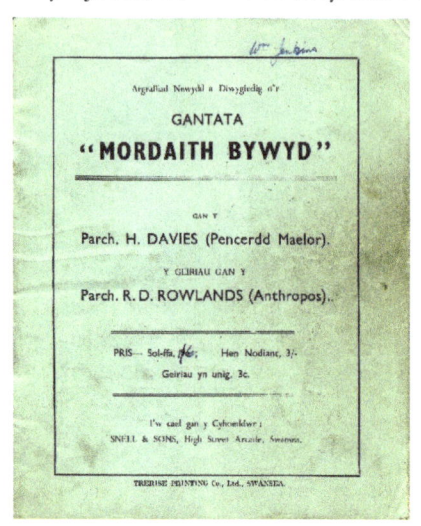

One of the compositions sung by the Login Choir in 1959.

After its renovation, Ramoth Baptist Chapel, Cwmfelin Mynach was re-opened in 1959. The impressive line-up of ten deacons is indicative of the chapel's continued influence in the community at that time. L/R standing: Tom Davies, John Edwards, John Saer, John Evans, James Howells, W.D. Richards, Cyril Evans, Reggie Phillips, Jack Griffiths, Arnold John. Sitting: Rev. D.J. Peregrine Davies, Rev. B.M. Davies, Rev. O.J. Hughes, Rev. James Nicholas, Rev. Garfield Eynon.

After its renovation, Cefnypant Independent Chapel was re-opened in 1963 by its oldest member Mr Ben Gibbin. L/R: Rev. Idris Morgan, Rev. Morgan Jones, Mr Ben Gibbin, Mr Tom Williams, Rev. Edgar Phillips.

Baptism by total immersion in the river at Cwmfelin Mynach was the choice of Rhydian Isaac in 1964. The Rev. O.J. Hughes performed the ceremony.

Invalided by multiple sclerosis, Catherine John of Rhydyparc, Blaenwaun lived her life within the confines of the Taf Valley.

In 1970 Rev. Idris Morgan retired after 37 years service to Moriah Independent Chapel, Blaenwaun. The deacons, lined-up to present him with a retirement gift, look a formidable force. However, chapel influence in society was now on the wane. L/R: Gwilym Williams (seated), David John James, Danny Thomas, Dafi Lewis, James Saer, Re. Idris Morgan, Cyril Isaac, Glan Harries, Alfred Martin, David Griffiths, David Thomas.

Tea-time in the Vestry at Moriah. L/R: Glan Harries, Alfred Martin, Cyril Isaac.

Membership of six Taf Valley Chapels

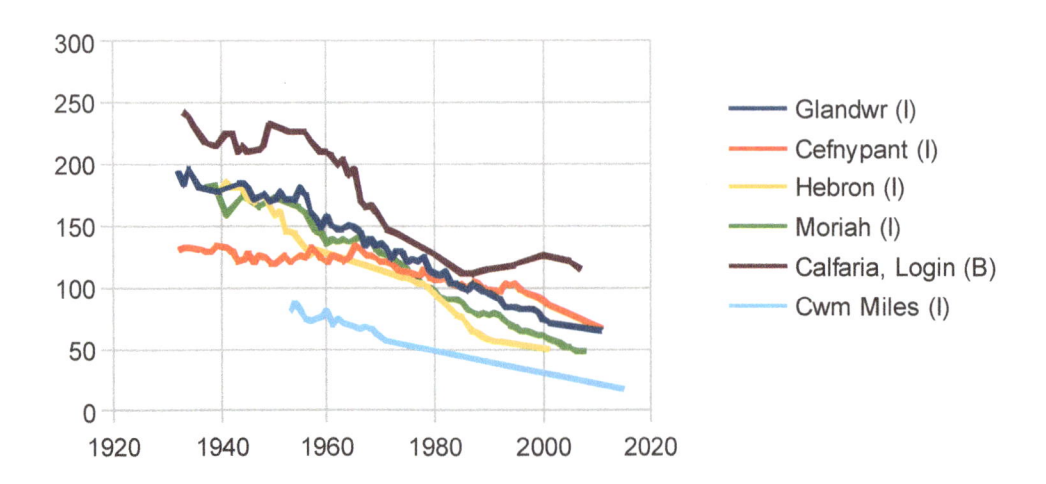

- Glandwr (I)
- Cefnypant (I)
- Hebron (I)
- Moriah (I)
- Calfaria, Login (B)
- Cwm Miles (I)

Declining chapel membership reflected the decreasing influence of chapels in society.

Llanboidy characters of the 1950s: L/R: Gwilym Davies, Penrhiw; Jerry Williams, Cloth Hall; Jack Jenkins, Greenhill (seated).

Penygaer County Primary School, Login in the Taf Valley was closed in 1959. L/R back row: Mrs Doreen Jones (Assistant teacher), W Rhydderch Evans (Mishtir), Gwilym Lewis, Joshua Phillips, Miss Elizabeth Morris (Cook). Middle row: Emrys Phillips, Iori Phillips, Elfair Owen, Rose Griffiths, Sheila Jones, Sheila Evans, Ieuan Griffiths. Front row: Susan Phillips, Iris Griffiths, Neville Rees, Mary Owen, Wendy Phillips, Geraint Phillips.

On the occasion of the closure of Penygaer School in 1959. L/R standing: Dafi Reynolds, Cwm; W. Rhydderch Evans (Mishtir). Seated: Miss Elizabeth Morris, Ffosargoed (Cook); Mrs Lizzie Reynolds, Cwm; Mrs Doreen Jones (Assistant teacher).

The horse-man Owen Jenkins, Tower Farm, Cefnypant celebrating the 'victory' of horse-travel over rail after Beeching's axe made Llanglydwen level-crossing redundant in 1963 (passenger trains stopped in 1962). Seated L/R: Benja Penbontbren, Dennis Llysmyrddin, Mrs Davies Trawstre, Lizzie Bont.

THEY'LL NEVER REPLACE THE HORSE

SUNDAY PICTORIAL, September 30, 1962 PAGE 7

THEY'RE back to the days of the horse and buggy in the little Welsh village of Llanglydwen, Carmarthenshire.

They're living in the past because Dr. Beeching took the railway away from their valley three weeks ago.

The Transport Commission said it had to go. They were losing about £25,000 a year on the line.

Before it closed, the villagers used to live it up in such places as Cardigan or Whitland by jumping aboard the local train —the Cardi Bach.

Not any more.

Even the buses can't help the people of villages like Llanglydwen. The roads are too steep and narrow.

So it's back to the quiet life ... back to the hymn-singing and card-playing.

But now and then, Owen Jenkins drives his pony trap (left) across the old railway lines ... and a few of the villagers go with him.

Those railways? They'll never replace the horse!

How one newspaper saw things.

CUP FINAL SIDE

Left to right. Standing: H. Lewis, D. John *(Chairman)*, D. Morgan, G. Richards, G. Jenkins, A. James, T. Bowen, B. Morgan, D. Jones, D. Howells,, G. Eynon, G. Davies, W. Lewis *(Team Secretary)*, D. Thomas *(President)*, B. H. R. Evans.
Sitting: B. Owen, G. Protheroe, B. Harries *(Captain)*, I. Williams, J. Bassett, G. Williams.

A number of rugby players from the Taf Valley enjoyed sweeping success with Whitland R.F.C. in 1967 when the first XV won all three competitions organised by the Pembrokeshire Rugby Union – league, cup and sevens.

Llanboidy tug-of-war team in the 1970s. L/R standing: Jim Swinson, Eifion Griffiths, Jeffrey Davies, Iori Morgan, Ken Davies, Elfyn Jones, Hywel Llewellyn, Harri Llewellyn, Rhyddid Davies.
In front: James Davies, Rowland Davies, Frank Storer, Cyril Phillips (Coach), Harry Harboard, Brian Edwards, Vivian Makepeace, Ian Plumb. Many in the photograph were members of the team which won the 640 kilo World Championship in 1977.

Ffynnonwen Sewing Class enjoying a night-out in the early 1970s. L/R back row: Ann Jones, Maureen Eynon, Mefin Lewis, Doris Davies, Nansi Phillips, Janet Harries. Middle row: Aeres Jones, Margaret Williams, Ena James, Lil Owen, Muriel Harries, Dilys Davies, Olive Jones. Front row: Mary Llewellyn, Alvira Phillips, Ceinwen John, Betty Evans, Ann Thomas, ------------, Margaret Llewellyn.

Reverend Jeffrey Williams took over as minister at Glandwr and Cefnypant in 1969 and his welcome concert contained a number of 'home-made' items which benefited from Lil's fluency in Tonic sol-fa and her gallant efforts in writing rhyming sentences.

Their first ever holiday required passports.

From the Taf Valley to the Swiss Alps in 1973

Twenty-nine years after 'that telegram', Lil visited St Charles de Percy Military Cemetry in Normandy in 1973 to see the headstone commemorating her brother Clifford's sacrifice. L/R: Lil, Lon, Heywood. In front: Janet, Richard.

Visiting 'young farmers' try-out the Fergie fach.

Haymaking adventure with Nansi Phillips looking after Richard.

Grandchildren Kevin and Carol assisting Heywood.

Grandchildren Janet and Richard at Glanrhyd c1975 making sure of their Christmas turkeys.

Touring in 1977.

On 'a run' to St Davids in 1983

The kitchen at Glanrhyd with the Rayburn cooker that served them well for thirty years.

Heywood and Lil celebrated their golden wedding in 1988 with a gathering of brothers and sisters and in-laws, none of whom resided far beyond the boundary of the Taf Valley. It was a different story for most of the gathering's children and grandchildren.

Heywood and Lil welcomed their first great-grandchild, Owain Rhys James, in 1989.

Part V
1996 – 2001: MINAFON – end of the road

Heywood remained on his own at Glanrhyd for four years before retiring to a bungalow, Minafon, in the village of Llanglydwen where he lived for a further five years with a number of friends, old and new, as neighbours. Caffi Beca in Efailwen became a favourite place to meet for lunch. He sometimes drove to Llandovery or to Cowbridge for Sunday lunch although usually he spent Sunday at Carmarthen with his sister Glenys. Heywood was in good health and in retirement enjoyed visits to Paris and to Dublin. In 1994 he travelled with others from the village to Wembley Stadium to support Swansea City in their 3-1 victory over Huddersfield Town in the final of the Autoglass Trophy. He would have enjoyed the Swansea victory but he was the most neutral of supporters and nothing seemed to upset him ... not even Wales losing at rugby ... least of all Wales losing at rugby! After all it was only a game.

Heywood and Lil kept themselves and their successive homes clean and tidy at all times and at Glanrhyd the walls of out-buildings were white-washed and the doors were painted regularly. During his last few weeks at Minafon Heywood arranged for the boundary wall between the bungalow and the road to be painted and also called-in the local part-time barber who was the manager of the local farmers' cooperative to trim his hair. Every morning he insisted on shaving and the Reverend Edgar Phillips – half a century earlier at Cefn – must have been the last person to see him with more than a day's growth! He retained his sense of humour to the end commenting one morning as he made the finishing touches with the shaver "*Dwi eitha reit, shwr o fod ... 'sa i'n mynd i un man heddi!*" (that should be all-right ... I'm not going anywhere today). Heywood passed away at Minafon on 22 April 2001 and his funeral service was held at Cefnypant on 27 April followed by cremation at Parcgwyn, Narberth. A memorial stone in Cefnypant Chapel burial ground reads:

Er Cof Annwyl Am
Daniel Heywood Owen
Glanrhyd, Llanboidy
1917 – 2001

Hefyd Ei Briod
Phoebe Lilian (Lil) Owen
1917 - 1992

Minafon, Heywood's retirement home in the heart of the Taf Valley in Llanglydwen

Memorial Stone at Cefnypant Independent Chapel.
In the background is the headstone commemorating Heywood's parents and brother Gordon.
On the left his brother Garfield is buried. Lil's parents are buried at Nebo Independent Chapel, Efailwen.

A GRANDSON REMEMBERS

Richard yn 2001 yn cofio'r 1970au: 'Bore Glanrhyd'.

Dihuno i'r un siom fowr bob bore ... cliwed injin y mashîn godro wedi tano a Dat mas wrth i waith. 'Dw i'n cliwed y swn 'nawr ac yn dal i allu pitsho'r nodyn ... mmmmmmmm. Injoio gwishgo dillad drewllyd dwê a rhedeg lawr y stâr ... cliwed Mam ... bob bore ... in canu neu in hymian emine... wêdd hi'n galled whibanu emine weth. Agor drws gwaelod y stâr yn ddishtaw, ddishtaw er mwyn gweiddi 'bw!' a Mam yn isgus cal sioc a rhedeg ar i'n hol. Gwynt tost a rhywbeth in i ffwrn i gino ... amser hyn o'r bore? Gwishgo cot a welis a mas i oerfel y bore ... edrych draw dros iet y clos a perci Trwyngraig a synhwyro bod na ffermydd a phobl draw yn y pellter na wyddwn i ddim o'u hanes ... a pellach byth wê Llanglydwen, Llanboidy, Whitland a'r byd mowr.

Wê gole'r glowty 'mlan a'r lladdfa gwaith godro wedi dechre ... lladdfa ddwy waith y dydd ... bob dydd o'r flwyddyn. Hen siwt ore wê 'da Dat a chot odro lwyd a cordyn beinder rownd i ganol a wastod cap ar i ben. Dyn bach cryf. Clêr a dom a cwmwle anal Dat a'r da ... swn gwair in cal i fita ... swn fflap, fflap, fflap y da in domi ... swn Dat in poeri neu in hwthu'i drwyn ac in siarad da'r da. 'How how, how how' wrth hôl da. 'Be sy'n bod a ti' wrth y fuwch wê'n cico. 'Wow fach, wow fach' wrth ir un nerfus. Wêdd amynedd Dat in cal i desto i'r eitha wrth odro. Wêdd e'n rhoi corden dros gefn y fuwch a lawr odani a thu ol i'w chader. Os bydde'r fuwch in cico bydde fe'n tynhau'r gorden ac fel arfer wê hyn in ddigon i stopo'r cico. Ambell waith wê pethe'n mynd in ornest a'r ddou bron in gwegian ... un wrth dreial cico a'r llall wrth dynhau'r gorden. Cofio Mam in cario peiled o lath i'r ty-cwler ac in cwmpo ar y clôs slip ... Dat in helpu mam i'r ty a dod 'n ol i ail-gydio in ir ornest ... cofio sane du a coese gwyn y fuwch in cico ac amynedd Dat in rhedeg mas ... y fuwch ar llawr a Dat yn fyddar i'w chwyno ... y gorden yn torri ... rhyddhad i'r ddou. Wê trefen 'da Dat wrth odro ... in hitrach na dechre un pen y glowty a gweitho'i ffordd o un fuwch i'r llall wêdd e'n godro buwch a lot o lath in ginta a llanw'r pail 'da llâth o fuwch wê biti fod in sych er mwyn neid in siwr bod peiled llawn i'w gario i'r ty cwler ... ffordd effeithlon o neud pethe, Wê Dat in whibanu emyne wrth gario'r peile ugen llath ar draws y clos. 'Dwy i ddim in cofio helpu rhyw lawer – a'i Dat wê ddim ishe gwas neu Mam wê ddim ishe ffarmwr yn ŵyr? Ar ol allwysh y cifan o'r llâth i'r churns a rhoi labeli ar rheini a'u dodi ar y 'stand' ... i'r ty i frecwast o facwn a wy ... Dat in bita ac ateb cwestiwne a wêdd e 'n gweud llawer 'da'i wmed ... na bod ishe stopo cnoi. Ambell waith wê Dat in bita bara-te i frecwast gida menyn ar y top a digon o swgir... wedd e'n leico bara-te ers in blentyn. Wê'r te in ffein a we'r tebot in llawn trw'r dydd ... pobl in galw ... fel y postman ôdd hefyd in adrodd y newyddion diweddara tra'n bita brecwast.

Wê tair cegin in Glanrhyd a wê Mam in canu in bob un o nhw. Y gegin fach 'ble wê sgidie a dillad mas, toiled, hen seld in dala hoelon a phowdwr golchi, ford, planhigyn a sgidie a welis ni'r plant. Y gegin ganol lle wê ford ar gifer stîlo dillad a bita bwyd, Rayburn oil gida fframyn uwchben i sichu dillad - crefft wê'n stiried ir amser wê ishe i sichu gwahanol ddillad a phwy we'n codi ginta a phwy wê'n debyg o drochi fwya y diwrnod wedyn. Y gegin fowr lle wê ford ar gifer cino Nadolig a the i rai fidde'n galw … a man hyn wêdd y teledu. Yn y laethdy wê Mam in cwcan a wê ffenest fach in edrych dros ir ardd … mas trw hon wê Janet a fi'n mind pan na wê Mam in 'drych.

Wedi brecwast … mas i garthu'r glowty … we Dat yn fishtir ar i waith … whilber, rhaw a poerad ar i law a dim gormod o lwyth fel na bo'r whilber in diwel ar y llwybr anwastad i'r ddomen. Am dros gwarter canrif bu Dat in whilo'r whilber dros y llwybr twllog … rhyfedd na wêdd e wedi neid gwell llwybr i girradd y ddomen … ond wedd i grifder a'i istwythder in cario'r dydd in hawdd. Unwaith y dydd wê carthu ond wê biti ugen whilbered i'w whilo in ddyddiol drw'r gaeaf. I fennu clau'r glowty dangosai Dat mor dda wedd i anelu e wrth iddo dowli peleidi o ddwr - o gasgen a gasglai ddwr-glaw – dros lawr y glowty a rhoi brwshad iddo i neid y siment i sheino.

Nesa … lan i ben shed wair i ryddhau bêls a'u cario ar i gefen i'r wâc o flân y da. Des i i gario gwair i helpu Dat er gwaetha gorfod cerdded heibo'r llygod wê'n bita cêc yn y glowty isha! Wê cliwed i swn nhw biti neid i fi rewi … ond wê rhaid cadw find ac er treial rhedeg we hini'n amhosib dan y llwyth gwair!

'Heywood 'achan' … wê gwaidd Mam in hedfan ar draws y clôs heibo'r glowty a catsh y lloi a'r hen drwc-lein lle cadwai Dat ffowls neu dwrcis neu loi - in dibynnu pwy amser o'r flwyddyn wêdd hi. Lawr i'r idlan, dros y shed wair a trwi parc-dan-'rydlan i'r afon ac i Ffynnonlas lle wê Dat yn ratlan i ddanedd-dodi wrth gloncan gida – nage, wrth wrando ar Gwyn Trwynygraig – er mwyn canolbwyntio ? Neu, fel 'r o'n i'n hoffi meddwl ar y pryd … achos bod e'n galler! Gweud bod cino'n barod wêdd y waidd a dim ond unwaith wêdd ishe Mam i weiddi.

Wê lloi mewn dou gatsh a rheini'n cal llâth o bail pan wê nhw'n fach a wedyn gwair a cêc trw'r geia. Yn y gwanwyn … pan fydde Dat yn gweud bod hi'n bryd i troi nhw mas … agor y drwse i'r da ifanc a rheini'n camu'n ofalus lawr y llathed o ddom a gwellt a mas i'r houl … snwffian yr awel … camu'n slow, slow bach … wedyn rhedeg in wyllt dros y borfa a ffarwelio a'u haelwyd bore oes … aelwyd na ddaw fyth in ol … ond na ellir fyth ei anghofio.

Richard remembers the 1970s: A morning in Glanrhyd.

He awoke to the noise of the milking machine … a noise he can still hear clearly … in no time he was downstairs, past hymn-huming Mam and out in the cowshed watching Dat – held together with a baler twine around his middle – among the flies and the dung relieving the cows of their milk and sometimes confronting a kicking cow and through-it- all whistling a hymn. Buckets-full of milk were carried across the yard … Mam helped with the carrying but she fell on the slippery surface … and emptied into churns in the cool-house adding to the previous evening's haul. Morning milking over, breakfast of bacon and egg was devoured; occasionally Dat had a basinful of tea, broken bread, a lump of butter and sugar for which he had acquired a taste as a child in the 1920s. Bombarded with questions, he answered mostly with facial gestures so as not to interrupt his eating. After breakfast it was back to the cowshed and the back-breaking job of mucking-out - twenty barrows-full wheeled thirty yards to the dung-heap. The finishing touch was to throw water from a bucket over the concrete floor followed by a good brushing to bring up the shine. The next job was carrying bales of hay to the walk in front of the cows' stalls ready for the evening milking (when he was older Richard carried bales past a shed where rats were helping themselves to cattle-feed; terrified he tried to run but was hampered by the heavy load). Mam's call-to-lunch resounded around the yard and nearby fields and heralded a welcome break for the workers … one call was enough. Richard reminisces about the release of young cattle from their winter pens into the spring air. They stepped gingerly out of their cosy home, feeling their way into the light before scampering away in their new found freedom, bellowing farewell to their early home … a home they had left for ever … but one they would never forget.

TIMELINE

1900
    1
    2
    3
    4   Much loved minister Rev. O.R.Owen left Taf Valley for Liverpool.
    5
    6
    7
    8   Lloyd George introduced the Old Age Pension. Martha Elizabeth Griffin became maid at Frowen (Lewis).
    9   William Owen arrived in Taf Valley as farm servant at Glandwr Isaf. W.O and M.E.G bought biography of Rev O.R.Owen.
1910   William Owen became ploughman at Frowen (Lewis).
   11
   12   William Owen m Martha Elizabeth Griffin - lived in Bush, Cefnbrafle. William Jenkins m Margaret Ann Griffiths - lived in Patmos. Hermon.
   13
   14   Start of First World War.
   15
   16   William Jenkins worked as miner in Gorseinon.
1917   **Lil born at Patmos, Hermon 22nd August.   Heywood born at Bush, Cefnbrafle 30th September.**
   18   End of First World War. School leaving age raised from 12 to 14.
   19
1920
1921   **Jenkins family moved from Patmos to Carreg Grwca, Pentregalar. Edwin Davies lost council election to Capt. Protheroe**
1922   **Lil attended Glandwr school and Glandwr Chapel..   Heywood attended Penygaer school and Cefnypant Chapel.**
   23   Rev. E.T. Owen, Llangeler increased Labour vote in Carmarthen constituency in General Election.
   24   Lone voice of Rev. E.T. Owen called for Christian principles to be acted upon to relieve the suffering of the poor.
1925   **Owen family moved from Bush to Canerw.**
   26
   27   Heywood presented with Bible for learning Salm 119 (176 verses).

1928		**Jenkins family moved to Cottage (Y Ty Rownd). Lil attended Llanglydwen (Pantycaws) school and Cefnypant Chapel.**
29		Heywood presented with a book for collecting £1-3-8d towards the London Missionary Society.
1930		
1931		**Heywood a Lil left school. H farm servant at Sarnau, Llanboidy. L maid at Yr Efail, Llanglydwen.**
32		Jack Petersen won British heavyweight championship.
33		Milk Marketing Board established.
1934		**Lil moved from Yr Efail to Blaiddbwll, Llanfyrnach. Heywood moved from Sarnau to Frowen(Phillips), Llanboidy**
35		
1936		**Lil moved from Blaiddbwll to Frowen(Phillips), Cefnypant, Llanboidy. Lil's 16 year old sister Nancy died of T.B.**
1937		**Heywood's father passed away age 57. Heywood went home to farm Canerw. Tommy Farr lost narrowly to Joe Louis.**
1938		**Heywood a Lil got married. Denley born in Y Ty Rownd. H,L, D moved to Blaenwaun Cottage.**
1939		Lil's parents moved from Cottage to Gilboa, Hebron. Start of Second World War.
1940		**Bryan born in Blaenwaun Cottage.**
1941		Lil's parents moved from Gilboa to Llety, Hebron. Cymanfa Ganu at Nebo on centenary of birth of Dr Joseph Parry.
42		Points required to buy food.
43		230 people killed in three nights of air raids on Swansea.
1944		Lil's brother Clifford killed in Normandy on 14 August. Education Act ensures free secondary education. 11+ exam. End of War.
45		BBC Wesh Region revived. Labour landslide at General Election.
46		Bread rationing introduced because Britain had no money to buy wheat from USA. Rev. P E Price passed away.
47		Rev. Edgar J Phillips became minister at Cefnypant and Glandwr.
1948		**H, Lil and boys moved from Blaenwaun Cottage to Cefn, Login. H appointed calf certifying officer. H bought Ford van.**
1949		Denley started at Whitland Grammar School. Eddie Thomas became British welterweight champion.
1950		**Wales won triple crown and grand slam. Llandow air disaster. Eagle comic launched.**
51		Denley had tonsils out and recuperated in Trefdraeth. Randolph Turpin beat Sugar Ray Robinson for World middleweight title..
1952		Bryan started at Whitland Grammar School. H won silver cup for shearing. D and B holiday in Trefdraeth.

53	Murder at Llangynnin. Davies Maths started an athletics revolution at Whitland Grammar School.
54	Heywood had hernia operation. D passed O level. Roger Bannister ran first 4 min. mile. End of food rationing.
1955	Heywood's mother passed away age 71. Wales elected 27 [out of 36] Labour MPs. Yet we got a Tory government!
1956	Denley went to University College Swansea.
57	H won the 40+ sprint race at Llandygwydd Bank holiday sports meet. Repeated in '58 and '59. B passed O level.
1958	**Heywood a Lil took-up tenancy of Glanrhyd, Llanboidy.**
59	General Election saw Wales vote Labour but again we got a Tory government!
1960	Bryan went to University College Cardiff.
61	
62	
1963	Denley a Lon got married. H and L grandaughter Janet born. U.S. President Jack Kennedy assassinated.
64	D a L moved to Tadley, Hampshire. H a L delivered Janet.
1965	Bryan a Mearl got married. U.S. Black leader Malcolm X assassinated. H and L grandson Richard born
66	Plaid Cymru's Gwynfor Evans won Carmarthen bye-election.
67	
68	U.S. Presidential hopeful Robert Kennedy assassinated. U.S. civil rights leader Martin Luther King assassinated.
1969	Lil's mother passed away age 76 at Glanrhyd.
1970	H and L grandson Kevin born.
1971	H and L grandaughter Carol born. Lil's father passed away age 82 . Lil's brother Johnny passed away age 48.
72	Heywood saw Llanelli beat All Blacks 9-3.
1973	Heywood a Lil visited Clifford's grave in Normandy. Britain joined the European Common Market.
1974	D, L, Janet and Richard moved to Llandovery.
75	Marco bought at Llanybydder. Carmarthen District voted NO to Sunday opening.
76	10 gallon milk churns replaced by bulk storage tank. Gallons replaced by litres. Supersonic Concord's first flight.
77	A tradition dies as no singers visit Glanrhyd to welcome the new year. H a L toured Scotland.
78	H's brother Garfield passed away age 60. Glanrhyd cut off for a week by snow.
79	
1980	
1981	Janet went to college in Bangor. Decimal coinage in Britain.

1982	H's brother Gordon passed away age 61. Carm. voted YES to Sunday opening. Worse snow in living memory.
83	Seat belts became compulsory. Death of Carwyn James. Mishtir passed away age 80. H and L holiday in Anglesey.
84	Lil suffering from rheumatoid arthritis, treated at Royal Gwent H, Newport. Richard went to college in Swansea.
85	Heywood began selling off his milking herd. Obtained top prices at Cardigan mart. Lil in Llandough Hospital.
1986	Glanrhyd milk quota leased. Heywood switched to beef cattle allowing him more free time. Ifor Fron passed away.
87	Janet a Leighton got married.
1988	Heywood and Lil celebrated their Golden Wedding. Kevin went to college in Plymouth.
89	Carol went to college in Southampton. H and L visited Kevin in Plymouth. H and L great grandchild Owain Rhys James born.
1990	Nelson Mandela released from prison.
91	H and L great grandchild Steffan Aaron James born.
1992	**Lil passed away 22nd May age 75. She had lived at Glanrhyd for 34 years.**
93	
94	Heywood visited Wembley to support Swansea City who beat Huddersfield Town 3-0 to win Autoglass Trophy.
95	
1996	**Heywood left Glanrhyd after 38 years and retired to Minafon, Llanglydwen.**
97	
98	Heywood's great grandchild Cai Elis Owen born.
99	Heywood's great grandchildren Llyr Daniel Owen and Megan Llywela Greenhalgh born.
2000	Heywood diagnosed with prostate cancer.
2001	**Heywood passed away 22nd April age 84.**